SAVING BABY

Center Point
Large Print

**This Large Print Book carries the
Seal of Approval of N.A.V.H.**

SAVING BABY

*How One Woman's Love for a
Racehorse Led to Her Redemption*

JO ANNE NORMILE
AND LAWRENCE LINDNER

CENTER POINT LARGE PRINT
THORNDIKE, MAINE

This is a true story.
Some of the names have been changed.

The text of this Large Print edition is unabridged.
In other aspects, this book may vary
from the original edition.
Printed in the United States of America
on permanent paper.
Set in 16-point Times New Roman type.

ISBN: 978-1-62899-408-7

Library of Congress Cataloging-in-Publication Data

Normile, Jo Anne.
 Saving Baby : how one woman's love for a racehorse led to her
redemption / Jo Anne Normile and Lawrence Lindner.
 pages cm
 ISBN 978-1-62899-408-7 (library binding : alk. paper)
 1. Race horses—United States. 2. Animal rescue—United States.
 3. Normile, Jo Anne. I. Lindner, Lawrence. II. Title.
SF338.N67 2015
798.4—dc23
                                                    2014037681

To my husband, John,
and my daughters, Jessica and Rebecca,
who gave up so much so I could do
what I had to do.

You are, quite simply, the loves of my life.

FOREWORD

Many people remember the summer of 1973 as the summer of the Watergate hearings on television that marked the beginning of the end of Richard Nixon's presidency. But horse lovers remember it as the summer a gorgeous chestnut stallion named Secretariat won the Kentucky Derby, the Preakness, and the Belmont Stakes to become the first Triple Crown winner in twenty-five years. Secretariat did for horse racing what Muhammad Ali did for boxing, what Nadia Comaneci did for gymnastics, and what Michael Jordan did for basketball. He recruited millions of new fans by an unprecedented combination of charisma and talent. And though she was completely unaware of it at the time, twenty-five years later, Secretariat's stunning win would set Jo Anne Normile on a trajectory that would establish her as one of the great heroes of the Thoroughbred world.

Saving Baby is a book about what happens when you fall in love—first with horses, then with horse racing, then with one racehorse in particular who by an unintended set of circumstances led Jo Anne deep into the heart of racing. Horse crazy since childhood, by her mid-forties Jo Anne's backyard boasted two extraordinary athletes: one, Scarlett, the granddaughter of Secretariat; the other, Baby, Jo Anne's equine soul mate and himself the descendant of a fine racing lineage.

Part of the great charm of this story is reading how Jo Anne hand reared these two superstars with unsurpassed tenderness and love. It is a joy to hang over the fence with her as we watch these two titans grow from fuzzy-furred babies frolicking in their pasture to self-possessed masters of their sport. But it was only as she gradually became an insider with an intimate knowledge of racing that Jo Anne began to see beneath the veneer of this seemingly glamorous sport, and when she did, it forced her to reexamine everything she thought she knew. In the process, Jo Anne embarked on the incredible journey that became her life's work.

Saving Baby might be a love story, but it's a love story in which the love gets redirected into something bigger and more powerful than anything Jo Anne or the horse racing industry itself had ever imagined.

It takes a lot of guts for a woman to make it in the horse racing world, but it takes a lot more for her to try to change it. *Saving Baby* is the story of how one woman's love for a Thoroughbred propels her to fight a David-and-Goliath battle to save *all* Thoroughbreds from the cruel practices of the industry, a battle so stacked against its heroine the reader wonders again and again why she ever took it on in the first place and later, why she didn't just quit. We would have understood if she had. It's hard to imagine where Jo Anne found enough hours in the day to do all she did and to face the opposition she faced. The only possible explanation for why she didn't drop dead from exhaustion is love. Only the deepest love could have kept someone going like that—an indomitable spirit fueled by the agony and beauty of her cause.

But Jo Anne Normile isn't like most of us. Instead of running away, she converted the knowledge she gained into action, becoming an ex-racehorse owner turned Angel of Mercy who gets down to what is surely her life's calling. If it isn't, one wonders what else this remarkable woman has up her sleeve. What would happen for instance, if she was turned loose on world hunger or the nuclear arms race?

Fortunately for equines, Jo Anne seems firmly rooted in their camp. In *Saving Baby*, the reader is privileged to witness how one extraordinary individual can make a profound impact on a multi-billion dollar industry that has proved both inflexible and inviolate. Despite the odds, Jo Anne has managed to positively impact the lives of literally thousands of horses, not just in Michigan where her work began, but across the country as her efforts grew beyond her wildest dreams.

Jo Anne Normile was introduced to me via

email by a third person who referred to her as one of the "great people of the world." I assumed this was polite hyperbole based on the desire of someone for two strangers to like each other in order to form a working alliance. But in reading *Saving Baby* I discovered that wasn't the case at all. It's not hyperbole. Jo Anne Normile is one of the great people of the world. And though not a single equine can ever voice his or her side of this remarkable love story, if they could, it would surely be a chorus to fill the heavens.

Susan Richards,
author of *Chosen by a Horse*

CHAPTER ONE

It's very quiet in the barn at night, but when a horse is about to have a baby, she'll get restless and start to pace, and I wanted to be able to hear the rustling of the straw as Pat walked back and forth. That's why I started sleeping with my head right next to the video monitor on the coffee table that streamed in the activity from Pat's stall, the volume turned all the way up.

To catch a mare foaling is rare. Horses almost always give birth in the predawn hours, preferring to have their babies away from people, and even other horses. Some will tell you they can time their labors for privacy. But once their contractions begin, they can't hold back. And I needed to be there, as a midwife for Pat as well as for myself.

The first couple of nights, Pat didn't settle in but kept walking and biting at her sides—a sign of pain. She also swished her tail, yet another sign of discomfort.

Then, one night, some time before sunrise, she went down on her side, nipping at her flank. Her pain had increased significantly. She rose, circled several times, then went down again. Her body gave a heave. "This is it, everybody!" I called out, jumping up from my perch on the family room couch and running to the bottom of the staircase. "Grab your stuff!"

We had very little time. A horse gives only three or four major pushes before birthing her foal. The four of us raced down to the barn. My husband, John, would be on duty with the video cam, while one daughter had a camera for still shots and the other would stand by the barn's wall phone in case there was an improper presentation at birth and the vet needed to be called. Normally a foal is delivered with the front feet coming first, one several inches ahead of the other so that the shoulders, emerging at an angle, can fit through the pelvis. You see the hooves, one before the other, and then the nose laid down on top of the legs. Any other presentation can prove a life-or-death emergency for mare, foal, or both.

We were whooping excitedly, all smiles and eager chatter as we ran from the house, pulling on our coats. We had already seen the baby kick when Pat drank cold water. We loved watching Pat's stomach sway like a pendulum in her last week before delivery. We had placed bets on whether the foal would look like its mother, with her dark coat, or whether it would have any markings. New life now just moments away, it was a giddy anticipation.

When we reached the barn I had to tell everyone to lower their voices to a whisper. "No running," I said. We needed to tiptoe, contain our excitement,

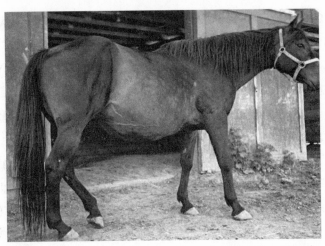

We had already seen the baby kick when Pat drank cold water.

so Pat wouldn't be alarmed or disturbed. The baby's front legs were already out. We could see its knees. We could see the bluish white sac, a filmy casing, enveloping the tiny foal.

By the book, you're not supposed to go into the stall. Birthing is something horses are meant to do by themselves. But Pat and I were already too bonded. The day we met, she had blown out through her nostrils to greet me, as horses do. She let me touch my face to her muzzle and blow directly into her nose so she could become familiar with my scent. And while some Thoroughbreds are very fine boned, Pat was a big, broad-chested mare with a look more like that of a Quarter Horse, which I preferred. More than that, she was such a people horse. Her eyes beamed empathy, intelligence. So of course I couldn't let her go through giving birth alone. I went in, knelt down, and stroked the side of her head as she lay there in labor, then moved closer to where the baby was emerging.

But Pat soon rose and started to walk around. The foal needed repositioning to be properly birthed, and Pat's movement would make it happen. "It's okay, Pat," I whispered soothingly while stroking her some more. "I'm here. Everything's okay."

Pat shortly went down again, gave a sigh followed by another heave, and out came the foal's knobby shoulders. They are the widest part of the birth, so we knew we were home free. One more heave, one more sigh, and whoosh, the baby was fully born. It took all of five or six minutes. Elated that we made it in time, we wanted to scream but just kept saying softly, "We have a baby. *A baby!*"

I was admiring the newborn foal in its sac, adoring its lashes, its tiny feet, when I suddenly realized that the water hadn't broken. I had been so absorbed in what lay before me that I forgot the hooves are supposed to tear open the sac upon delivery. The baby was in danger of suffocating. A foal needs air once it is out of its mother's body, just like a person.

"Oh my God!" I cried out, tearing at the sac with my fingernails. But the bluish-white shroud was like tough tire rubber. I was out of my mind with fright and desperation—and guilt. Not only had I wasted time looking at the baby through its sac, lost in awe over its beautifully closed eyes and its rounded forehead, like that of a human newborn. I had also forgotten to store a knife or other sharp instrument in the foaling kit even though I knew about the rare case in which parting the sac needs a human assist.

Finally, I did manage to break open the sac, and water gushed everywhere. I pulled out the foal's head, but it didn't start breathing. The newborn remained limp.

Frantic, I cleared the horse's nose and mouth of mucus, then fastened my mouth on its nostrils and exhaled deeply, expressing air into its lungs. Still nothing. The girls were crying. John and I were, too. You can hear me on the videotape saying, "I think it's dead."

The moment, gone disastrously awry, had been more than a decade and a half in the making.

Eighteen years earlier, almost to the day, the legendary Secretariat won the Kentucky Derby. The great Thoroughbreds who run in that race are magnificent beings—powerful yet graceful, and beautiful. I always looked forward to watching the Derby. But my fever spiked in 1973, when Secretariat won not only that run but also the other two races in what is known as the Triple Crown: the Preakness, held in Maryland, and the Belmont Stakes in New York. Two other horses won all three races in the Triple Crown after Secretariat, but it didn't matter. He was the superhorse; his record times still stand today.

I soon began collecting Secretariat memorabilia—Christmas ornaments, a program from the '73 Derby, numbered collector plates signed by his jockey. In 1988, we were even able to meet the great stallion. We were driving to Disney World, and our route from our home in Michigan went right through Kentucky, only twenty miles from the farm where Secretariat was living out his life as a stud horse. We took a detour in hopes of catching a glimpse of the magnificent steed.

But when we reached the farm, a groom actually led me right to him. He brought Secretariat out of the barn for me, and I lay my head on his strong shoulder. Surprised by how moved I was, I cried while John and the girls took pictures. I then scratched his mane, as horses will do for each other with their teeth. He was exceptionally well behaved—and massive. "Locomotive" was the word that came to mind, and I thought, "here is the most powerful horse I've ever seen."

Just one year later, Secretariat was euthanized at the relatively young age of nineteen. He suffered from a disease, laminitis, that causes swelling inside the wall of the hoof, increasing pressure on it and making it excruciatingly painful even to stand, let alone walk or run. I'll never forget the day I heard the news on the car radio.

It was around that time that Secretariat's owner,

My meet-and-greet with Secretariat. I was shocked that a groom led me right to him.

Penny Chenery, gave a speech at the Michigan Horse Council's Annual Stallion Expo, and I learned that one of Secretariat's sons, a stud horse, lived only a two-hour drive from us. I thought, what better memorabilia could I have than to look out every day and see a grandchild of Secretariat sired by that stallion? I'd have a piece of Secretariat in my own backyard.

By that point we had owned horses of our own for only five years. I had been one of those girls who grew up crazy about horses but never could have one. The feeling never dissipated, and when I turned thirty-six, I convinced my husband to move from our bustling suburb to a home in the country with a barn and pastures. We were not wealthy people—John worked for Michigan Bell and I was a freelance court reporter—but we sold our house at just the right time, for two and a half times what we paid for it, to be able to afford the new one, and then bought two lovely horses in short order. The first was a black Quarter Horse I renamed Black Beauty, giving into a childhood urge. The second we named Pumpkin because of the orange highlights in her coat.

It was an idyllic life, one that should have been enough. From almost every window, beautiful pastureland spread to the tree lines. I could work on my court transcripts, look outside, and take in a view of the horses. I could stop working at my computer at any time and go pet them, or hop on without a saddle and take a short ride to clear my mind. I could finish my work at midnight. It didn't matter, as long as I met my deadlines.

But the idea kept tugging at me to increase our "herd" with a grandchild of Secretariat. I couldn't get it out of my head.

Pumpkin was too old to bear a foal by that point, but not Beauty. So I sent her up to be bred to Secretariat's son. But Beauty miscarried—twice. And each time was an expensive try.

After the second failed attempt, someone at the breeding farm suggested, "Why don't you lease a mare? She'll go back to her owner once she delivers the foal, but the foal will be yours. You might as well lease a Thoroughbred. That way, the foal will have papers that will enable you to get it registered with the Jockey Club."

"I don't know anything about registering a Thoroughbred," I said. "I don't want to race a horse." It was true. While I loved to watch the Kentucky Derby, I had no ambition to race. I simply wanted to have a grandchild of Secretariat grazing behind my house, like a snow globe come to life.

"But a horse registered with the Jockey Club will always be more valuable," I was told. "It'll serve you well should you ever have to sell or trade it."

So I started making some phone calls to Thoroughbred racing farms. My vet ended up approving a Thoroughbred, Precocious Pat, a dark mare with some reddish hairs around her muzzle who was due to give birth very soon. Pat's owner, Don Shouse, was sick. He had had a heart attack, and he asked me to take his mare to our house to have the baby. The plan was that I would raise the baby for six months. At weaning time, by which point Don was expected to recover, I'd give it back to him. But I would be allowed to use Pat to breed a horse of my own with the sire of my choosing—Secretariat's son. I wouldn't have to pay to lease her since I would be taking care of her and her new baby for a while.

I said yes to the arrangement, and Pat and I took to each other right away. We immediately set up a large stall in the barn in which Pat could have her foal, making room by storing much less hay than we usually did—100 bales at a time instead of 400.

It was in that stall that before us now lay the baby horse's wet, lifeless body. Though I'd known from the start it wasn't going to be mine—this was the horse I'd have to return to Don before Pat could be bred to Secretariat's son—my heart had already laid claim to this baby and its mother. I thought of performing compressions on its chest, but I knew that wouldn't have been the proper procedure. Besides, a just-birthed foal is so tiny, so vulnerable. It weighs only about 100 pounds the moment it's born—all bone, with its body narrowly compressed. I was afraid I'd hurt it.

Miserable with my lack of options to pump life into the fragile newborn, I turned back to Pat to see how she was doing. She was trying to see around me, not aware yet that her baby was dead. Then, perhaps thirty seconds later, well after I had tried breathing into the horse's lungs via its nose, one of the girls cried out, "It's moving!"

The baby horse's head stirred ever so slightly. I leaned over for a better look at its sides and saw the in and out of the breathing. The baby was alive!

I went back down and blew into its nose a second time to assure continued respiration, and also as a sign of affection. I wanted the horse to know my scent. That's what the mare does, and I aimed to mimic her behavior so the foal would associate me with the beginning of time, or at least the beginning of *its* time.

It was kind of cold—the middle of the night in early May—and the foal was still wet and also shaking, so I hurriedly finished pulling the sac from around it and vigorously dried it with towels. I then waited for the placenta to come out and put it in a pail of water for the vet to inspect. If even a small part of the placenta isn't delivered, the mother can get an infection, just as with people.

Pat gave her maternal nicker, a soft, barely audible sound that all mares make to their newborns. The intimate message means "Come a little closer," and the foals respond to it immediately from birth, without any learning process. The bond between mare and foal is so strong, in fact, that animal behaviorist Desmond Morris once wrote about a case of a young horse who was taken from its mare and transported five miles to a place it had never been before, yet managed to find its way back to its mother in five days.

At the sound of the nicker, the baby lifted its head, its ears flopped to the side. It then let out a whinny, although it was more like the honk of a Canadian goose, and that, combined with our relief, I think, made all of us laugh hard.

I got out of the way so Pat could lick her foal's face and body, inspect her newborn, bond with it physically. About ten minutes later, I said, "We forgot to even look to see if it's a girl or a boy."

21

So, just before the baby attempted to stand, I spread its legs. It was still soaking wet underneath from being born, but I could see there were no "attachments."

"It's a girl! It's a girl!"

We watched the wonder of the newborn foal repeatedly trying to stand on its spindly legs until finally succeeding, only to fall again seconds later. It's no act of futility. It's an equine Pilates class. With each attempt, a foal's coordination increases, as does its strength.

Baby and me, a few minutes after the birth.

Proud, finally, to stand on all fours, the baby foal let out another honk, much louder than the first, and we laughed once more at our "Canadian goose."

Then she stumbled around searching for nourishment. She tried to nurse on everything her muzzle touched, from the front and back of Pat's legs to my own shoulders and face and even to the back wall of the stall. Patient mother that Pat was, she nudged the foal into proper position, and I assisted in helping the newborn locate its mother's udder, heavy with milk.

Soon the sun was rising, baby tucked up against mare, and it was clear to every one of us, exhausted and exhilarated, that at that moment all truly was right with the world.

CHAPTER TWO

When the vet arrived later that morning to examine both mother and baby, I told him we had in our barn the most beautiful little filly anyone had ever seen. He smiled, went down to the stables, checked out the foal, and said, "You've got a problem."

I could feel my heart rip apart. I had helped bring this foal back from the brink, its life having hung in the balance to begin with because of my own forgetfulness.

"You have a colt," he said, grinning mischievously, "not a filly."

The horse's maleness had been tucked in. By the time the vet came, he was broadened out and dried, and when you looked under him, you could see all his parts. I learned a lesson from the vet right there: when you're checking for the gender, you lift up the tail rather than spread the legs.

My feelings for the new foal grew stronger each day. I would take a plastic chair from our porch and sit in the field just to watch him, and he would come over and nuzzle against me. Like a puppy, he would run around and release bursts of energy exploring, then quickly fall asleep at my feet, and I'd pet his head as he napped. Sometimes we lay head to head in the pasture together while I put my arm around him. Or I'd sit cross-legged in the grass, and he'd put his head in my lap. I loved looking at his beautiful face and his little whiskers—the little beard of curly hairs all newborn foals have. I loved the smell of milk on his mouth.

He, in turn, expressed his feelings for me. He would hear me coming to the barn to say "hi" to him and let out his gooselike honk. Not all horses are vocal, but this one liked to talk.

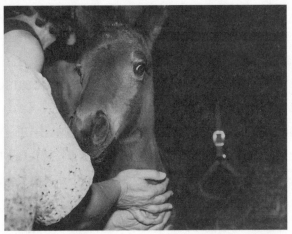

Baby not yet twenty-four hours old.

Sometimes he'd come over to me in the pasture and immediately turn around and present his rump. Usually, when a horse does that, he intends to kick you. But Baby, as we had taken to calling him after referring to him only as "the baby" for the first couple of weeks, was asking me to scratch around the dock of his tail. His head would tilt slightly to the side as if he was saying, "Ahh, that feels good."

All was bliss, and when Baby was about a

month old, we sent him with Pat to the breeding farm, as planned, so he could continue to nurse while she became pregnant by Secretariat's son with the foal that was to become ours. Pat was pregnant again within a month or so—in foal, as horse people say—and we brought her and Baby back home. A horse pregnancy lasts about eleven and a half months—anywhere from 320 to 360 days—so we knew we'd have Pat for that amount of time plus about six months more for our own foal to nurse before Pat went back to her owner. Baby, in the meanwhile, would be going to his owner in just a few more months. He was already a couple of months old and needed only a few more months of nursing.

I hated to think about it. It wasn't just I who had fallen head over heels for him—we all had—and I didn't know how we were going to give him up. We had watched him take his first wobbly steps in the moments right after his birth, then gallop across the pasture hours later, as horses do. It's why, in part, they're born in the middle of the night—to give them a few hours to learn to run with the herd come daylight.

Baby and our German shepherd, Cookie, liked to chase each other around the pasture. Baby would eat a carrot if you chewed it in your mouth first and then offered it to him. The girls did their homework in his stall while he lay sleeping with his head resting on their legs. We all fed him

Baby giving Pat a kiss.

apples and carrots when he came up to the sliding glass doors to the kitchen after walking up the patio steps. It wasn't unusual, in fact, to see Baby and Pat standing at the kitchen door waiting for a treat.

I taught him to walk up the patio steps to the kitchen not just because I loved him so much that it was a pleasure to be near him but also because I didn't want him to be afraid to step up into a horse trailer; of the bricks on the patio, which were a different kind of surface than he was used to; of the sliding glass doors as they squeaked open. Horses evolved as prey animals, flight animals rather than predators, and they bolt at the slightest sign of danger. Thoroughbreds, in particular, are skittish. I wanted to teach Baby not to react to every strange noise and sight so that he wouldn't flee unexpectedly and hurt either himself or his rider. I wanted to help him to like people so they would like him back, make his future safe for him, help him to feel calm and stable rather than prone to feeling spooked. Even though he wasn't mine, I was determined that Baby was going to grow to adulthood strong not just in body but also in mind so that nothing would ever hurt him.

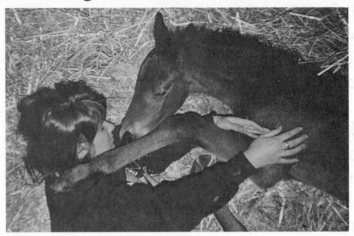

My elder daughter, Jessica, with Baby in his stall.

Sometimes I would take New Year's Eve noisemakers and blow them nearer and nearer to Baby in the barn, walking through so he wouldn't be surprised. I would go into the barn softly and slowly open and close an umbrella in front of him, letting him smell it.

When he was in the pasture, I would take a black garbage bag and wave it at him from a distance. He would stop what he was doing and stare, and I'd call out gently, "It's okay, Baby. It's just a bag." He'd walk over and sniff it, then I'd drop it and he'd paw at it. I'd touch his body with it. His owner planned on racing him. Who knew when a plastic bag was going to blow across the track?

Other times I'd put a piece of plywood in the pasture. I thought it might teach him not to be afraid of the wood's texture when he walked on it, or of the sound it made. Or I'd shake out a large white sheet while calling to him, then fold it up while walking toward him. After all, maybe somebody would shake a horse blanket in front of him, and his memory of my shaking the sheet would make it not so frightening.

Memory was key to Baby's learning. People use the phrase a "memory like an elephant," but they should really say "memory like a horse." When given scattered pairs of patterns to look at and identify for a reward of food—a circle versus a semicircle, for instance—not only can a horse often correctly identify the pairs with almost 100 percent accuracy (performing almost twice as well as zebras and donkeys), it will also retain the ability to distinguish the patterns and shapes a full year later, better than most people could. So of course I felt it was my job to teach Baby, especially while he was young and absorbing information like a sponge, how to get on with people, how to deal in a world away from our little farm.

One day all the connections I had built between

us helped save his life. Jessica, my elder daughter, took a look out the window and started to scream so loudly I couldn't understand what she was saying. Baby was running through the pasture in terror, a plastic patio chair stuck on his head. Sometimes, after bringing down a chair from the patio to the field outside the barn so I could sit and watch Pat and her baby, I left it out in the pasture—one more thing for Baby to smell, to get used to.

But he had apparently stuck his head in the space between the seat and the arm and now couldn't get it out. He tried to get near Pat, but she was terrified of the sight and kept running from Baby as he inadvertently jabbed her with the chair.

Oh my God, I said to myself. I was afraid he was going to trip and die from breaking his neck or suffer a fractured leg in a fall and have to be euthanized. I yelled at Jessica to stay out of the pasture, then walked out there as calmly as I could and started talking soothingly, all the while inching closer and closer. "It's okay, Baby," I called out. He was in an absolute panic, his sides heaving, but finally, he let me approach him. I tried to lift the chair off his head, but it wouldn't budge.

My mind was racing. What can I use to cut through the plastic? Do I need to call the fire department? As I deliberated, I continued to try to maneuver the chair, Baby trusting me sufficiently by that point to stand relatively still. Finally, I was able to turn the chair just enough, at just such an angle, that I was able to remove it. He immediately ran to his mother, and she to him, and he nursed, which provided solace for both of them. It had been a terrifying ordeal.

How, I wondered in the wake of that and other experiences, was I going to be able to part with him? How were John and the girls going to say good-bye? There was not one among us who hadn't fallen completely in love with him. "Remember," I kept telling the girls, "he's not ours. We can't keep him." My heart would sink with each reminder.

Don Shouse came once to see Baby soon after he was born, but he did not come or call after that. Beside the fact that he was still recovering from his heart attack, Baby was a racehorse to Don, not a family member, and it was simply expected that the horse would be picked up six months after his birth. I dreaded the phone call, alternately letting the idea overwhelm me and pushing it from my thoughts.

"You know," I said to John as we were having coffee one morning, watching the horses play together in the pasture, "the time is going to come when Don comes and gets him."

"I know you're not going to be able to part with that horse," John responded.

"No, I can't," I answered back and started crying.

Baby felt like ours. He was born here. He lived here. "Oh, come look at Baby!" I loved to cry out. "He's racing around the pasture with his mother." Or, "see how he's sleeping among the dandelions." I would run outside with the camera and take pictures. You just can't describe the beauty of a foal, those great big eyes with the huge eyelashes.

"I know what you're going to ask," John said, "and the answer is yes. See what the guy wants for Baby. And buy him."

In the unlikely event that Don was never going to claim Baby, I didn't dare call him ahead of time. But come fall, I did hear from him. By that point I wasn't too nervous because John and I had already agreed that we would pay for Baby whatever Don wanted. But I was surprised at what he had to say.

"I should be picking up my colt, but my health is really not good," he told me, "and I'm not well enough to care for the horse. I will offer him to you for sale before I offer him to anyone else. And I will offer him for no more than the price of the stud fee so I can recoup my initial investment— fifteen hundred dollars. But on one condition."

"What's that?" I asked. I didn't know at that point that a Thoroughbred of Baby's pedigree might have gone for as much as $5,000.

"You must race the horse," he said. As the breeder in the state of Michigan, he would get

$500 every time Baby won a race. And his hopes were high, because other racehorses sired by the same stallion were already doing well. Baby was expected to do a lot of winning.

My heart sank. I was going to have to go back to John and say there were strings attached. The girls had already been told we'd be keeping Baby.

"But I don't know anything about racing," I replied.

"There's nothing to know," Don answered. "Just find a trainer and get out the checkbook."

"What does all this mean?" John asked when I told him about the deal, that we could keep Baby as long as we raced him.

"I don't know," I said. "But it can't be that bad. The track is 13 minutes from our house down the expressway. It's close. I can go every single day and make sure he's okay."

Despite our misgivings, we allowed ourselves to get more and more excited about the idea of Baby racing. Jessica had been a competitive ice skater at a high enough level that she traveled out of state to participate in meets. Rebecca, our younger daughter, had competed in dance. But now the girls were nineteen and seventeen and Jessica, in particular, realized years earlier that she had hit her plateau and was not going to be able to take her skill to the next level. Thus, we were missing the rush of watching our daughters give everything they had for medals and trophies. With

Baby, our new child, we could indulge our family's competitive nature and experience the same kind of heady excitement—reverse time a little bit. What fun it would be to have our friends and family come to the track—and celebrate after the races!

Better still, we learned that a racehorse is considered an investment, with significant tax advantages. Our accountant explained to us that the minute Pat arrived at our house, the expense of taking care of her while she was pregnant with a Thoroughbred racer was a tax write-off, as was the cost of raising Baby. Thus, if we bought gravel for the road to the barn, we could deduct 50 percent of it, as two of our four horses were "business assets." A heater for the water trough—50 percent deductible. Hay, fencing, whatever—all partial write-offs. In that way, Beauty and Pumpkin could enjoy the material advantages afforded Pat and Baby. Once Pat's next foal arrived, our write-offs would shoot to 60 percent—three out of our five horses would be Thoroughbred "investments." And of course we were going to race that horse. There was no way we could keep a grandchild of Secretariat in the backyard and be racing another horse.

Not that Baby's grandfather was any low-level Thoroughbred. Nijinsky II, as he was known, was proving to be an even more productive sire of high-level racers than Secretariat.

Talk about dumb luck. Here we knew zip about horseracing, yet we were going to end up with two of the most promising Thoroughbreds you could imagine. I had never even thought about Secretariat's pedigree, and certainly not about Nijinsky II's. I had just wanted a piece of Secretariat in my backyard. In fact, while I watched the Kentucky Derby on TV every year, we had been to the track only once in our lives, giving each kid ten dollars to bet. I myself bet on a horse with the word "Scott" in his name because one of my nephews has that name. I knew nothing about looking at a horse's racing record.

On top of our beginner's luck, we felt like we were making money even before Baby entered a single race because of all those tax deductions. Incorporating at the accountant's recommendation, we called our new business Brookside Acres, for the huge brook right behind the barn.

It was going to be a full year before Baby started training, as he was still only an infant. Thorough-breds don't begin to get ready for racing until they are yearlings—somewhere between their first and second birthdays.

In the meantime, he needed a real name. All Thoroughbreds must have a name registered with the Jockey Club in order to be able to compete. Often, it has a piece of the horse's sire's name in it, or a piece of the broodmare's. Baby's father was Reel on Reel, so we settled on naming him "Reel

Surprise." His gender had been a surprise as was the fact that we were able to keep him, so it made perfect sense. We never referred to him by his official name, however. Once in a while people called him Surpriser, but he always remained Baby to us.

It was an idyllic time, that year between finding out we could keep Baby and his going off to train. Like a gigantic, energetic dog, he would play with empty cardboard boxes in the pasture, sticking his hoof into one, flinging it into the air with his leg, then chasing it.

He experienced his first snowfall, rolling in it out of glee and curiosity. To see such a huge animal go down on the ground and roll from side to side, then get up, shake, and buck and run off— nothing beats watching that playfulness. To this day, it's not an event that we take for granted. If John sees one of the horses rolling happily in the pasture he'll call out, "Sissy's rolling" or "One of them is at it." It's too adorable not to watch.

Of course, whenever a horse goes down on its side, there's reason for concern. While people have twenty-six feet of intestine, horses have eighty to ninety feet of gastrointestinal tubing that food must pass through, sometimes turning sharp corners that narrow to no more than an inch and a half wide. If everything doesn't go exactly right, a horse can end up with colic—a bowel obstruction or a toxic buildup of gas that unless

Baby making his own equine version of snow angels with Cookie, our German Shepherd, watching.

treated quickly enough can kill him. A horse with colic will drop to the earth and start to roll in an effort to get rid of the pain. So you need to watch closely. Is the horse nipping at its side to try to extinguish horrific cramping, then pawing the ground after it stands up and perhaps walking in a tight circle, or is it getting on its feet again and shaking from head to tail out of pure joy? Ninety percent of the time it's the latter, but the other 10 percent is real cause for worry.

Not only was Baby such a happy horse, out in the pasture making his own version of snow angels, he was also an unusually calm one, especially for a Thoroughbred. They tend to be high-strung, twitchy. But Baby was so relaxed that when we had the barn enlarged to be able to accommodate not just Baby but also Pat's next foal, workers would walk across the roof, tarp slapping against the wind, tools pounding above him, and he would lie down in the straw in his stall and take a nap. On a warm day, he would come over to me to swat a fly off his rump or neck, where a horse can't reach. I was even able to enjoy his calm company in the car, courtesy of Rebecca. She made a tape for me of Baby chewing on hay, and I would pop in the tape of that rhythmic, mesmerizing munching to soothe myself while driving home after an intense day of taking depositions.

Things got even better when, in late May of 1992, Pat gave birth again, just a year and a few weeks after Baby was born. We were all experienced midwives now. This time I was ready with a knife in my foaling kit in case the sac needed to be cut open—but this foal's delivery went perfectly. She was a beautiful reddish bay, and we named her Scarlett Secretary. (Her sire, Secretariat's son, was called Treasury Secretary.) On her head, right above her eyes, was a beautiful white star, and she had white "socks" with black polka dots on two of her feet.

Unlike Baby, who came out short and stocky with little ripples of fat along his rump, Scarlett had legs that went on forever—more typical of a Thoroughbred. I have hilarious video of her taking her first steps, looking down as if thinking, "Are these things supposed to work?"

Scarlett, Secretariat's granddaughter, just after her birth. I could hardly believe I was touching a piece of history.

As soon as the leggy foal found her source of nourishment on Pat, I took the big wooden board on which I originally painted "It's a filly" in pink for Baby on one side, then, when the mistake was found out, "It's a colt" in blue on the other. I brought the sign to the road with the pink side facing out, and almost immediately, friends and family started coming by—with pink helium balloons, with carrots for Pat. Here we all were, touching a piece of Secretariat, a piece of what was probably the most famous horse in the world.

Baby, across the way in his own stall, looked so lonely. I went over and kissed him, breathed into his nose, feeling guilty that all the attention was going to the new foal. "We're not neglecting you, Baby," I whispered gently. I asked neighbors who

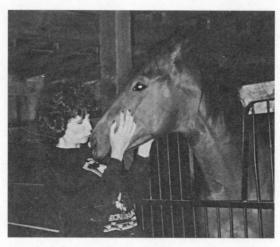

Baby looked so forlorn at all the attention newborn Scarlett was receiving in her stall that I had to go over and comfort him. "We're not neglecting you, Baby," I whispered.

brought carrots for Pat to please give some to Baby, to pet him.

Baby and Scarlett weren't allowed to play with each other until Scarlett was several months old. A playful kick from Baby, now a seven-hundred-pound yearling, could have killed the young filly. But from the beginning, I let them smell noses over the fence, and they took to each other immediately.

Once Scarlett turned about four months, I let them in the pasture together, keeping a line on Pat at their first introductions so she wouldn't become aggressive with Baby if she thought he was going to hurt her young foal. But she allowed her two children together without chasing Baby around, never doing more than perhaps pausing in her grazing and watching the two of them intently for a minute or two to gauge the intensity of their frolicking. After a while, you could tell that she enjoyed seeing her babies play well together. Her pride wasn't surprising. Even a decade after being separated, a mare put in with her progeny will recognize them.

Only a month or so later, in the fall of 1992, it was time for Baby to go to training. Despite my excitement at the prospect of his racing, I continued to have mixed feelings, not just because he wasn't going to be out my back window anymore but also because I was now going to have to lose Pat. Scarlett was essentially weaned, so it was time for Pat to go back to Don Shouse. This killed me. We had come to adore this gentle broodmare who had now been living with us for eighteen months. She loved to be groomed. She had particular spots where she enjoyed being scratched— under her mane, behind her ears, in the crevice under her chin between her two jaw bones. And she was such a proud mother. How was I going to be able to give her up? It had actually been nagging at me for a year, since I learned that we were going to get to keep Baby and Pat was pregnant with Scarlett. I was ready to plead for her, prepared to beg Don to let her stay with us while she went through any other pregnancies he decided on, even if we didn't get to keep the foals.

As with Baby, I didn't call Don, because I didn't want to risk speeding up the process of Pat leaving. When Don finally phoned me, he came right to the point. "I told my wife that we're not going to get that mare away from Jo Anne unless I hold a gun to her head," he said to me. "On top of that, my health isn't improving," he added. "I'll give Pat to you with her Jockey Club papers."

I was overjoyed. The mother of our children would be staying with us permanently, and now our family was complete.

I met with Don's wife to receive the papers as soon as possible because I didn't want to give him time to change his mind. She handed Pat's Jockey Club papers to me at an exit off the expressway, halfway between our two houses.

Now, with a little less trepidation as the business of Pat's future was settled, I could let Baby go to his trainer. The plan was for him to board at a training facility for two months, after which he would come home for the winter and then go to train at the track in the spring. The training facility was only a half-hour drive from my house. I would go to see Baby every single day, groom him, bring him treats, be with him. Still, it was hard, like letting your child go off to kindergarten. You want them to do well. You know they have to grow up. But it would never again be the same.

Baby and me shortly before he went off to train.

Baby was now going to be under someone else's influence. Except for the time Beauty went to be bred, none of our horses had ever left our little farm.

Baby, unlike me, was not at all nervous. He walked right out to the trainer's truck, took a look at it, and didn't freeze or try to bolt. He stood still for a moment, allowing me to rub his neck by his mane, after which he was led onto the trailer.

That night was a restless one, and the next day, when I went out to the training farm's stables, I was not happy with what I saw.

CHAPTER THREE

The barn in which the trainer housed Baby was fancier than mine, with sliding doors and cement walkways. But Baby couldn't hang his head out of his stall because the doors had bars on the top that went almost all the way to the ceiling, like a jail. So he wasn't able to see the comings and goings of the other horses or, literally, get much of a whiff of any of the action. He couldn't poke his head right or left over into the next stall, either. There were no distractions to buoy his spirits or keep his mind occupied in the absence of his family.

I understood the reason for the barn's set-up. This was a huge commercial facility, with horses making their way in and out all the time. And owners don't want their animals to pick up any communicable diseases. Horses do a lot of sniffing in each other's noses, so it's particularly easy for them to end up with another horse's respiratory condition.

The boarding facility also did not want to be responsible for any horse getting hurt. Sometimes horses who are strangers to each other can become dangerously aggressive if they don't get a good feeling. One might take a swipe at a horse in a stall as it is being led to its own.

It was so different from the situation at home. There, where we built the stalls ourselves with the horses' needs in mind, every wall in each stall except the one at the back went only half way up, about as high as a person's armpits. It was sufficient for keeping a more dominant horse from getting into another stall to bully one lower on the totem pole, yet it let each horse see all the others and communicate with them. Thus, at night, when Baby, Pat, Scarlett, Beauty, and Pumpkin were all in the barn, they were still a herd, taking comfort in each other's presence. But Pumpkin, for instance, wouldn't have to worry that Beauty would come and take her food. It made her feel safe rather than cooped up. Each horse could also walk over to the side of its stall and groom the neck of the horse next to it. Baby and Scarlett's stalls were together, and the two of them would groom each other shoulder to shoulder. They also liked to play, nipping at each other before bedtime in something reminiscent of a pillow fight.

I could feed each horse what it needed, too. At the boarding facility, a kind of institutionalized setting, all the horses were given the same amount of food. But just like people, horses are different. Some are easy keepers, needing much less food to maintain their weight, while some have high metabolisms, requiring more hay, more grain, even a supplement.

At home, my horses could graze to their hearts'

content out in the pasture all day, and then at night, I could give each one just the right amount of grain and hay to accommodate their body styles. Fortunately, while most Thoroughbreds have high metabolisms and require more food than the average horse, Baby's metabolism hovered around the middle ground, so the amount of food they gave him at the facility was enough.

But there was no grazing for him. It soon became clear that even though horses naturally graze for a good sixteen hours daily, Baby was being kept in that stall almost all day except for the hour or so when he was being trained to walk, trot, and canter in a dusty indoor arena. He was not allowed out in the pasture with the other horses, instead getting only a little free time outdoors in a tight round pen with dirt but no grass to munch. He couldn't even see the other horses from there, or let out a whinny to greet them.

"Why," I asked his trainer, a tall, thick man in his late twenties named Lyle Coburn, "can't he ever be turned out?"

"Because he's a stallion," Coburn answered me. The owners of the farm were afraid Baby would try to mount females.

I understood the rule that stallions couldn't be turned out with mares, but at the same time, I knew horses that haven't been gelded don't tend to start showing signs of testosterone until they're about two years old. Baby, at barely one and a half, certainly hadn't been showing any. He was still acting like a young weanling, not studdish. I never had concerns about his being together with Beauty in the pasture. Even with Scarlett, all he wanted to do was play. I thought at the very least, since this was such a large farm, he could be put into a pasture by himself or with other young horses not yet exhibiting signs of sexual maturity.

Baby looked so forlorn. I felt like I had taken my young child from his neighborhood, away from all his friends, and plopped him into a different neighborhood where all the other children were strangers and said, "Okay, you're not allowed out of the yard. You can't play with or even say 'Hi' to the other children."

"Baby!" I'd call out every day when I came to see him. I'd try to brighten his spirits and my own by bringing him treats—cut-up carrots and apples. Some trainers tell you not to feed horses treats, especially horses who have not been gelded, because it makes them nippy. But I've always fed my horses treats, and I've never had a nippy one. Yes, they always search my pockets for more, but when the treats are finished, all I ever have to do is hold up my palms and say, "All gone." And they quit searching. A horse can be taught by degrees to walk, trot, and canter solely by voice command. So why wouldn't a horse understand "All gone"?

Baby would return my "hello" with a hearty "Hooonkk!" But he always looked so pitiful as I walked down the barn aisle toward him and his nose showed through the bars. He couldn't get his nose out past his eyes, so he wasn't able to see me until I came close, although I'd glimpse his nostrils go in and his mouth open as he whinnied back to me. The sight of him like that made me miserable.

Sometimes I would take one of the brushes from home that I used to groom Pat or Scarlett and let him smell it before I used it on him. I was trying to let him know, you're not alone, Baby. Your mother and sister are waiting for you. Then I'd bring it home and let Pat and Scarlett sniff. The three of them had a communication this way; it was my system for letting them know they were still all together. And because the scent of Baby was always still fresh on the brush, it was like showing Pat and Scarlett a picture of Baby I had taken that very day.

Leaving Baby each morning before I headed for my court reporting duties was the hardest. The look on his face was so plainly puzzled. Normally his demeanor was alert and perky. I could see he expected me to take him away from there, back to the field where he could run with his herd. Sometimes I'd get three or four stalls from his, and he'd whinny or nicker. "You're not leaving, are you? I'm still here. You're walking out without me." I'd go back two or three times, brush him some more, talk to him some more. "Big things are going to come, Baby," I'd tell him.

"You're not going to be here very long." Finally I'd have to force myself all the way back down the aisle and out the barn door. I'd turn around, take one last look back and see that nose sticking out. He couldn't see me, but he was still trying to get that last sense of me.

Baby in his "prison" at his first training facility.

Often I thought I should press harder that Baby needed some pasture time, some fresh air and ability to cavort with other horses. But I didn't want to make waves—I was new to this—and I took comfort in the fact that it was only going to be for a couple of months before he came home for the winter.

And while I wasn't happy about what I thought of as Baby's prison, I did like that Coburn was soft-spoken and patient, teaching Baby very slowly. His manner was methodical, not quick and jerky.

Still, it bothered me that Baby bolted whenever he heard the whip behind him. I knew the long lunge whip was part of training and that he'd never be struck with it. And I comforted myself with the fact that he'd figure that out soon enough. But I was very much looking forward to December, when he'd be back with me.

The time couldn't have passed quickly enough. One night, around 10:30, a feeling grew in me that something was not right. I had left my horses in the barn at last check a half hour earlier, and I was ready to go to sleep with their rhythmic munch, munch, munching in my head. But I couldn't relax. Maybe one of the horses has colic, I thought, and I missed it. That's one of the reasons last check is so important. If there's colic at bedtime, it could become a surgery case by morning if you don't intervene.

I'm not a believer in psychic ability—it's completely out of character for me—but I climbed out of bed, ran down to the barn, and flipped on the lights. The horses all started blinking—what's going on?

I saw manure in all the stalls—nobody had a blockage. Everybody was still munching or just standing there peacefully. I thought, gee, this is really strange. What's got into me?

Then I had a flash. Oh my God, it's Baby. Maybe *he's* colicking. Maybe he scratched his eye on something rough. Maybe there's a fire in the barn. My mind was racing. I don't believe in premonitions, but how was I going to handle this? If I went out there and started poking around with a flashlight, the farm owners were going to call the police. It was a half hour away. Should I go? Shouldn't I go?

Because I never had that type of feeling before in my life, I went. It was about 11:30 by the time I arrived.

Baby was fine—surprised to see me, but fine. I gave him some treats, followed by an extra flake of hay just to make sure he had an appetite and no colic, and he broke right into it.

Then up and down the stalls the other horses started whinnying because they thought it must be feeding time. Of course I couldn't leave them like that, so I spent some time putting a flake of hay into each one's stall. I felt foolish that I had driven all that way—and glad no one woke, even though I had the flashlight shining—but what did it cost me to put my mind at rest? I would have done anything for Baby.

Finally, it was December and time for him to come home. It was part of the traditional route for a Thoroughbred. You take them for training in the fall after their first birthday, when they're still juveniles but no longer babies, then return them to your own pasture for three or four months, then bring them back to the trainer in the spring to start serious training at the track.

But Coburn said to me, "I have to keep him over the winter. He's really stubborn, the type of horse that will forget everything he's learned. We've come too far, and I don't want him to regress."

I felt suspicious. I was paying Coburn almost $1,000 a month. And Baby was his first and at that point only Thoroughbred—Coburn was trying to grow his business. And it was early December, so if Baby stayed, it was time to write another check.

At the same time, Baby did have a stubborn streak. He knew he was powerful. And he could be pushy, albeit in an adorable way. When you walk a horse on a lead line, he's supposed to respect your space, but Baby was always moving closer, brushing against us. It didn't bother me, but I knew it wasn't proper training, and I didn't want to be this person who knew nothing about racing telling the trainer what to do—that wouldn't allow for a good working relationship. And yet, all in all, Baby was such an agreeable horse. My doubt tugged at me.

Against my better judgment, I wrote Coburn another check. So we had Christmas without Baby. And January. And February. And March. And through all those dark months, I didn't see Baby do any progressing from the point he had reached. He had learned to walk, trot, and canter, and that's what he did every single day in that little training arena, never being allowed out into the pasture with the other horses.

At the end of March, Coburn told me he was going to be moving Baby to a training facility with a track on the grounds. Baby would be learning to gallop. My doubts had intensified, but I still thought perhaps Coburn knew something I didn't. And in certain ways I was more than happy for the switch. Baby would have fresh air, which horses need. They stay healthiest when most of their time is spent outside, whether in sunshine or rain. Baby would also be able to expend some real energy if he wanted rather than just go through a structured canter indoors.

The facility itself wasn't in the pristine condition of the previous one, but Baby could hang his head out of his stall if he felt like it. He could see up and down the aisle. He seemed much happier there, which left me feeling much more relaxed. I was also happy because this new facility was only twenty minutes away instead of thirty. Baby and I would be closer to each other.

While the place was a bit ramshackle, Coburn bedded Baby's stall well. He also always made sure Baby had clean water. There were a couple of little turn-out areas with grass in them, too, and while Coburn still didn't let Baby play with other horses, he did turn him out into these areas for an hour or so here and there when they were unoccupied.

At those times that Baby actually trained, it was exciting to watch. At first he would try to scoot toward the gap—a spot on the track with no railing that opened to a path leading back to the barn. Still a youngster, he wanted the comfort of his stall over the rigors of running, and his discomfort and uncertainty would pull at me. The newness of things sometimes unnerved him, too. One day he saw, for the first time, a white-colored horse—called grey among equestrians—and planted his feet squarely. You could see the "What do I do about this?" in his face. He had to be coaxed past the "apparition."

But before long, he was flying around the track in a gallop. Seeing him run, people would ask me about him, and when I'd say, "He's a Reel On Reel colt," it was plain to see that they were impressed. Baby's prospects looked good.

I couldn't completely shake an unsettled feeling, however. When I'd go to visit Baby each day, I'd pass a very muddy area where a mare was caring for her foal, born just that month. The foal would have nowhere to lie down but right in a mixture of straw and mud, which was never mucked of its manure. Worse, the newborn was often drenched in cold sleet mixed with the dirt, as April can be pretty wintery in Michigan. Furthermore, the drinking water wasn't changed regularly, and the two horses were surrounded by wire fencing, which could have hurt the foal if it kicked up in a frolic and became tangled in the metal.

Hay was thrown over the fence for the mother

and would mix in with the dirty straw and horse droppings. No one made sure to keep it separate.

The sight was stomach-turning. I couldn't bear to look, and didn't. But I wondered aloud who were the owners of this mare and foal living in filth.

"I don't know," Coburn told me. "Someone's boarding a horse here." It was a first glimpse of how Thoroughbreds could be treated that I worked hard to push from my mind.

Come the end of April, Coburn told me I needed to get Baby castrated in order to move him from this practice track to the real one, where spectators came. Baby was going to be two years old May 8th, so I was okay with gelding him. He would soon be showing interest in mating, and a stallion will break down a fence to get to a mare in heat.

I was also okay with gelding Baby at that point because I knew it wouldn't affect his height. Studies at the time suggested that if you castrated a horse before his second birthday, he would grow taller than he would have otherwise. You would have meddled with his genetic predisposition. But if you waited until the horse turned two, there would be very little difference in his final height versus what he would have achieved anyway. And I wanted for Baby what nature had intended.

Baby was just starting to nip at me in the week or two before his castration—a sign of his growing sexual urges. I'd go to pet him and he'd turn his neck and take a not-so-gentle bite. Coburn also said he was beginning not to concentrate on his training because he was looking around for mares. A stallion can smell a mare in heat a half mile away.

In May, shortly after Baby's gelding, Coburn moved him to the Detroit Race Course, as promised. Now he really was just thirteen minutes down the expressway.

John and I went to the State Racing Commission for our licenses within a day of his arriving there. We wouldn't have been allowed onto the backstretch of the track without them. Because racing is a gambling entity, access to where the horses are kept is highly restricted.

After fingerprinting, a background check for any criminal record, and our filling out the requisite forms, we had our pictures taken and were each handed back a laminated card, much like a driver's license.

It was a heady moment. The Detroit Race Course had once been hailed as one of the premier tracks in the country. Seabiscuit had raced there.

But I was in for a letdown. The backstretch was in a rather decrepit state. Things looked like they had not been painted since the track was built in 1950. The main roads, made of asphalt, were cracked, with potholes everywhere. Secondary roads, composed of gravel, also contained potholes, along with deep, trench-like ruts full of mud because of poor water drainage. The track kitchen was built out of cinderblock, with old-style grayish tile that hadn't been replaced in decades.

I could also see immediately that I didn't look like anybody there. The men outnumbered the women by perhaps four to one, and a number of them had a grizzled, even homeless, look. Indeed, some lived in makeshift apartments on the grounds, I later learned. These were clearly not the kind of people I hung around with.

As surprised as I was, the regulars were doing double, triple, takes at me. I could have been three-headed for the way they were staring. Whereas they were sweating, wearing mismatched, rumpled clothing, hosing down horses, maybe walking in mud to bring a horse from a stall to another area, I had on makeup and nail polish. I was dressed like I was going to take a deposition. Of course, taking care of the horses down at my own barn, I could present a sweaty, muddy sight myself. But this felt different.

Part of it was that the people staring at me knew quickly that I was new. On the backstretch of a track, everybody knows everything about every-body else. It's a small-town system of passing information. But also, while I didn't know it at the time, most horse owners rarely showed up, unless they were also their horses' trainers. Their horses were purely investments, like a stock certificate or a mutual fund, with someone else managing it. Why would you come to see your money in person? You could check in via phone now and then and come to watch the horse race, but that was it. That's why I was virtually the only one there not dressed for grooming, training, or riding.

Despite my discomfort and surprise at the state of the backstretch and the mien of those around me, a part of me still felt like I had arrived. Here I was, licensed, one of the select few fortunate enough to see behind the scenes. And so many horses! Some were all black and glistening, some sported a large blaze, others had all white legs. And the horses led the day. They always had the right of way, with cars and trucks virtually never allowed on the roads that led from their stalls to the track, at least not during training hours— from 6:30 to 10:30 A.M. When vehicles *were* waved through instead of being relegated to the parking lot adjacent to the backstretch, they had to yield if a horse was passing. The horses were in all stages of training, some fractious because they had been cooped up for hours before being let out to train. Even jockeys' agents and trainers in golf carts and workers on bicycles pedaling their way across the acres and acres of back-stretch, along with those walking, had to stop for the horses.

As I made my way to Baby, I passed aisle

after aisle of shedrows, long rows of stalls with overhangs to keep the horses protected from rain or snow. Although spectators are generally not aware of it, most Thoroughbred horses are stabled at the track for the entire racing season, which in some states lasts all year long; only relatively few horses are shipped in for races.

There were enough stalls for 1,200 horses, although perhaps only 1,000 to 1,100 horses were present. Racing had by that point begun a decline in Michigan. In the late 1970s, federal law began allowing for simulcasts—broadcasting of races in other states on television screens at the track to increase gambling revenues—but Michigan, in a conservative bent, allowed simulcasting only a few times a year, reducing funds for keeping racing going at full tilt.

When I finally reached Baby at the far end of the backstretch, he was not in a shedrow but one of the track's several barns, called annexes. This was not good. The annex barns were long, with no windows. The only natural light came from the exterior doors. You could barely see in there. At least in a shedrow, a horse could watch other horses coming and going and get a look at the trainers and exercise riders. Here, Baby was in a perpetual twilight.

He let out his happy Canadian goose whinny as soon as he knew I was there; a horse can recognize his guardian's footsteps. But while I stroked and nuzzled against him upon reaching his stall at the back end of the barn, I couldn't come up with anything to say in return.

Baby, I wondered to myself, what have I gotten you into?

CHAPTER FOUR

"Excuse me, Ma'am."

A trainer was apologizing to me for having just said within earshot, "That fuckin' horse—I never thought it was going to beat mine."

About eight or nine of us were standing at the rail that stretches all the way around the track, watching the horses go through their paces. Everyone out there except me was a trainer or assistant, or perhaps a jockey's agent.

"That's alright," I answered. "I'm familiar with the word."

I had been coming to the track to watch Baby train for only a couple of weeks, and the regulars were still tiptoeing around me. I wanted them to feel comfortable to talk in front of me because I knew that was the way I was going to learn things, get the lay of the land and keep Baby safe.

In my determination, I acted in as friendly a manner as I could. I smiled and said "hi" to people who stared at me coldly. I'd go into the track kitchen, see if anybody was sitting alone at a table, pick up an extra coffee, and offer it to him. "Would you like a cup?" I'd ask. "I'll get you cream and sugar if you'd like." They were only too glad, as many did not have the change to spare.

Before long I was making twelve dozen chocolate chip cookies at a time and handing them out to people in little baggies—the security guards, a groom in a shedrow hosing down a horse after a morning session, an assistant walking a horse slowly to cool it down; hot-walking, they call it. I'd "threaten" a group of guys sitting on metal chairs in the kitchen that I was going to join their poker game.

In this way I could ingratiate myself to the point of asking questions to which I wanted real answers. Often, the icebreaker with new people was that I had a Reel On Reel gelding. That piqued interest because Reel On Reel offspring born in the year before Baby were already racing well.

"Who's your trainer?" they would ask, but they had never heard of Coburn when I mentioned his name. Sometimes they'd shake their heads. I didn't get the sense that they thought I'd made a great choice for such a promising horse.

But the chitchat provided openings for me. "How come the place looks like this?" I would ask, pointing to chipping paint or a huge rut in the road. I assumed keeping the place up was everybody's collective responsibility, and they had let things go.

"Try getting the HBPA to move on it," they'd answer.

It turned out everybody at the track paid dues to

an organization called the Horsemen's Benevolent & Protective Association, which was supposed to look out for their interests by negotiating favorable contracts with the track owners. But I was told over and over, "Our board of directors doesn't do a thing." Or, "I didn't have water the first two weeks I was here."

I made a mental note to myself that *I* should be on the HBPA Board. I'd get things done. Why should a groom, who already worked hard, have to drag water in pails from another shedrow because his own pump wasn't working? Why should I have to use a woman's bathroom back near the stalls that had no sink, no toilet seat, mice running around, not even a stall door? In fact, I couldn't. I'd have to hold out for the bathroom in the kitchen. I would get things like that tended to.

I also learned of a second association called the Thoroughbred Owners and Breeders Association, or TOBA. It didn't have the power of the other group, which included trainers, but it still might be a place I could learn more about racing politics.

It wasn't long before it felt like I was on the same side of the fence as the people I was trying to ingratiate myself with; we all weren't being treated fairly. And it wasn't long before they appeared to have accepted me into their community. I knew I was "in" when they stopped apologizing to me for using curse words. I found,

Baby training at sunrise.

too, that for the most part, most truly were friendly. While our different styles seemed to separate us, it was easy to break through the barrier. I started to be able to tell people apart also. Jockeys were easy to spot—slight build, short, hovering around 100 pounds. Trainers tended to dress somewhat better than riders and grooms, but not always. Sometimes they were very hands-on and did the riding and cleaning themselves.

But for all the easy conviviality, I did get signals sometimes that left me feeling on the periphery of this little microcosm rather than in the thick of things, as I wanted to be. One morning, sitting around a table in the kitchen with a few trainers, one of them asked, "Doesn't your trainer object to your being here every day?"

"No," I answered. "Why should he?"

The guys laughed and said, "That'd be the day

that my horse's owner would be here every single day!"

"Why?" I asked. "Wouldn't you want them here?"

At that they all broke into peals of guffawing and one of them said, "Owners are like mushrooms. They're best kept in the dark."

I knew an owner could try to step in where he shouldn't, perhaps telling a trainer that a horse was ready for a race with a high purse that he clearly wasn't up to—so many owners think they have the next Secretariat in the making—or putting in his two cents about how hard a horse should be trained. But their response, vaguely sinister in nature, made it seem that trainers were wont to do things not in their horses' best interest, and it made me even more adamant that I was going to be there every day to protect Baby.

Other things made me uneasy, too, despite the overall friendliness. One morning, as I was walking through one of the annex barns on my way back to the car after seeing Baby, I came upon a trainer named Carl who was feeding a beautiful horse, nearly all black. He was putting a huge amount of hay into her stall and also filling a five-gallon bucket to the top with "sweet" feed—corn, oats, and molasses.

It was way too much food to be giving to a horse in one feeding. Horses are built to graze for their food sixteen to eighteen hours a day. Small amounts of food on an almost continuous basis rather than large amounts of rich feed all at once helps ensure that they don't get colic—there's much less chance of a blockage. For that very reason, back at home, I didn't just leave some feed for my horses in their stalls, but in winter with no grass growing, I also strewed the pasture with hay throughout the day. I wanted to simulate as much as possible what their eating habits would have been in their natural habitat.

"May I pet her?" I asked Carl. Just like with a dog, you have to be careful and seek the owner's permission, because you never know exactly how aggressive a horse might be, or whether the owner might not want the horse interacting at that moment.

"Oh, yes," Carl said.

I moved closer, and the horse, Simply Darling, nuzzled against me. She was so sweet, leaning her head out of her stall toward me.

Then Carl heaved up the bucket of grain, and I said, "You're not going to give her that heavy pail of grain all at once, are you?"

"I don't want to have to come back later," he answered.

"Why don't you give half and have somebody come by and feed the other half this evening?" I suggested. A lot of trainers would pay a groom a dollar to come by around 5 P.M. to feed a horse some hay and grain and top off its water to make sure it had enough through the night.

But Carl just waved his hand and said, "Oh, I'm not going to waste money on that."

"Carl," I implored, "she could colic with that much grain at once." Leaving the horse with that sweetened grain was like giving a four-year-old a whole tableful of candy and expecting her to go easy.

"If she can't figure out how to pace herself, that's her problem," he responded.

I was shocked. No one was going to come by later and check that horse for colic. And if she did get it, she was doomed. Part of the remedy for colic is getting a horse to move about to dislodge the toxic build-up of gas created when a horse's digestive process goes into overdrive. But Simply Darling was going to be standing still in her stall till the next morning. Even if someone had come by, there was no place to turn her out. I had already learned that despite the fact that the track owned acres and acres of grassland adjacent to the facility, it was never used. Horses always went from training right back to their stalls. It was another thing about the track that made me uncomfortable for Baby to be there—absolutely no free time to romp.

I also saw abuses beyond that improper feeding. One morning, when I came to say good-bye to Baby for the day after hanging out in the kitchen for a while, I heard a lot of loud noise and laughing as I approached the barn. A little filly was standing in the aisle, right opposite Baby's stall, a fine-boned, delicate horse who looked to be no more than eighteen months old. The exercise rider was in the process of dismounting her, and she was shaking from head to toe.

The rider was apologizing—I couldn't tell why. But as I came closer, I saw that the horse, a light-colored chestnut, was covered in welts from his whip. They were not three or four inches long, but eight inches, running on both sides of her body all the way from her flank to her backside. Some had actually broken through the skin and were bleeding.

"Oh, don't worry about it," the trainer responded to the rider, who felt bad about what he had done, realizing he had gone too far in trying to steer the horse on the track that morning. "This bitch will learn to run straight."

The man wasn't even an actual trainer. Lacking a trainer's license, he used the name of a trainer buddy to gain access to the back of the track. But everyone looked the other way; it was easier not to make waves.

In the meantime, it wasn't over for the horse. The so-called trainer put a lead line on her with a brass chain shank at the end that was a foot and a half long—the kind you might use on a horse needing strong control. The line hooked under the horse's chin, crossed over her nose, then through a loop on the other side of her halter until it came full circle. When you pull on a chain like that, the fine, sensitive bones in a horse's nose hurt, and it pays attention. It if doesn't, you jerk on the chain quickly. If you pull on it hard enough, it's possible the bones will break, causing the horse tremendous pain.

After the chain was put on the horse, who clearly didn't need it—she was scared to death and anything but fractious—the filly was brought into her stall, where the "trainer" applied a topical anti-inflammatory agent on the welts called DMSO.

You're never supposed to apply DMSO to an open wound. It burns. You're supposed to use it only for swelling, and even then, you're supposed to dilute it; you never use it straight. But this man forced the filly against her stall wall with the help of someone else and started applying full-strength DMSO all over her bleeding welts, and she couldn't move because if she did, the metal shank would hurt her nose. She was out of her mind with the pain, the burning sensation on top of it, and everybody stood around and just laughed. "Look at that bitch go," the man said.

I wanted to retch. Not a kind word was said to her. She was huffing and puffing, surrounded by loud screams and name-calling. She couldn't understand the words, but she certainly understood the tone.

Finally, they closed her stall door, and that was

it. The horse was given no cool down, no bath, no fresh bedding—all the routine things that are supposed to happen after training.

This really jolted me. I started to visit Baby not just once a day but often twice. I'd come by in the morning, before going off to work, and then later. If we went to a wedding on a Saturday night, I might have on an evening gown and high heels, but it didn't matter. I had to check in on Baby and make sure he was okay.

Most times he was. Each morning when I came to see him before training started, I would enter the barn aisle and call out "Hi, Baby!" and would either see his face pop out of his stall or hear his Canadian goose whinny—or both. That whinny was so distinctive, deep and loud, sort of like a foghorn.

Then I'd put my nostrils to one of his and breathe out, and he'd breathe into mine in return. As soon as I entered the stall, he'd start searching my pockets—nudging with his head for the carrots or apples I always brought. Once he had his treats, I'd groom him. He didn't need it—Coburn made sure he had a glistening coat—but who doesn't like having his back scratched? Besides, I needed to feel that I was still the one who took care of him, who had a routine with him that carried over from when he was a colt at home.

Once training was over, I would hurry from the rail to the barn to hot walk Baby, even though technically that was the trainer or groom's job. Besides just wanting to be with him, I wanted to make sure for myself he wasn't overheated. He never was. He was never blowing hard or even in a sweat. He always looked at me as if to say, "I just had a nice little run around the pasture."

Coburn would confirm my feeling that the training wasn't taxing Baby by saying, "He likes to go. I've got to hold him in. He's a lot of horse."

After Baby cooled down, I would hang around the rail for a while, watching other horses gallop around the track, or I'd have coffee and conversation in the kitchen. Then, when I'd walk back to Baby's stall to check on him once more and say good-bye before leaving, he'd generally be sleeping soundly, snoring, all stretched out on his side. I could see he was having a dream because his lids were moving. What is it about, I would wonder. Is he tearing through the pasture with his mother? Playing with Scarlett? Whatever it was, his slumber was restful.

Other times I'd go back to the barn, and Baby wasn't yet sleeping but was clearly relaxed, with his bottom lip hanging and his legs tucked under him. I'd go into his stall and sit next to him, talk to him, rub his neck under his mane, where he particularly liked it. I had noticed by that point that he had a good luck mark in the form of a Prophet's thumbprint—an indentation on his chest, like a dimple, that, according to legend, meant he was descended from one of the sacred broodmares belonging to the prophet Mohammed and should be treasured and treated with particular respect. I was more than happy to oblige. "Did you have a rough day today, Baby?" I would ask. "You did great. You *should* relax." Then I'd breathe into his nostrils—"See you tomorrow."

But there were days he had a questioning look on his face when it was time for me to leave. "Are you really going?" his eyes would say.

I'd turn the corner wondering if he was still looking in my direction. Those were the hardest days. As at his first training facility, I'd go back, seeing his eyes remained fixed on me. "Oh, Baby, it's okay. I'll bring you more carrots tomorrow." We'd breathe into each other's noses again, and I'd kiss the velvety part around his nostrils, then rub under his chin and out by his ears. If he tilted his head—"Mm, that's good"—I'd end up going back into his stall again so I could reach the part where his mane stopped and his withers, or shoulders, started, in order to scratch more. He'd move his tail from one side to the other so I could scratch by the dock, too. He was so beautiful, his body a rich mahogany, accented by four black stockings and a black mane and tail. He had a few white hairs, just a few, between his eyes.

A hundred times we'd repeat the scenario until he finally relaxed enough to get ready to fall asleep, or at least become distracted by the comings and goings of other horses. I'd leave the dark barn with my heart a little less heavy and head off to take depositions, having been at the track for three to four hours.

In hindsight, with the abuse to some of the horses that I saw and Baby's own intermittent sadness at my leaving, it's painfully easy for me to wonder why I didn't pull him out of there, my promise to breeder Don Shouse to race Baby be damned. But in many ways, Baby seemed perfectly comfortable. Had he been nervous and acting erratic, I probably would have removed him in short order. Yet he was the horse I had painstakingly taught him to be in those early days at home—fearless. He never spooked or shied at anything in his new surroundings, like many two-year-old horses do—jumping or planting their feet while staring at something intently, or rearing up and trying to throw their rider. He never tried to spin and bolt off the track in an effort to get back to his stall.

And all the huge pieces of equipment that Baby had never seen before—machines that compact the track, the gizmo that added water to the track if it was too dry—they hardly fazed him. It was like he was in our backyard. In fact, just before he went onto the track each day, he had a look on his face that said, "Hey, Mom, I'm going out. Come watch me!" He liked to go fast, faster even than Coburn wanted him to go in those early runs.

What also gave me comfort was my feeling that whatever went on with the other horses, Baby wouldn't get hurt because unlike other owners, I would always be there to protect him.

And while I felt bad that he was cooped up, I knew from my daughters' competitions that there are things you have to give up to accomplish wins. He wasn't allowed to make that choice for himself, true. But because he did seem to enjoy running so, I ran it through my mind in the same way I did with my daughters. If you want to be average, yes, you can take dance lessons and have fun at the recital once a year. But if you want to dance competitively, compete across the country, you're going to have to give up some of your freedom.

I was able to indulge that line of thinking by virtue of the fact that when Baby came out of his stall in the morning, he never seemed like he was breathing fire from having been confined. He appeared to adjust to the routine extremely well. Not all young horses do.

Some, in fact, display harmful displacement behaviors for the walking and grazing from which they are kept. They engage in stall walking, or walking the perimeter of the stall in a tight circle for hours on end, which can strain the joints and cause undue weight loss; or create big holes in the stall floor from repetitive pawing because of frustration about not being able to move forward;

or incessantly crib—hook their teeth onto the edge of the stall or stall door and suck air, which wears down the teeth in addition to causing digestive problems; or weave—repeatedly take a step to the right and then to the left, another strain on the joints.

Baby exhibited none of these stereotypical behaviors, which I was very relieved about, because they occur all too often in young horses confined to a single spot for hours on end. It made me all the more comfortable about having him there.

But the truth, too, to my discredit, was that I felt seduced by racing. I felt honored to be "in." The cold stares had faded, and I was now one of the regulars who could enjoy the easy camaraderie of the backstretch. I was also wrapped up in a certain euphoria. Here we were, engaged in what is often referred to as "the Sport of Kings," one of the privileged few who were licensed and allowed on the part of the track that the public never gets to see. When we told people we owned a racehorse, they would ask, "Oh, are you in harness racing?"

They thought we owned a Standardbred, a breed of horse that pulled a driver around the track in a cart called a sulky. There were more than half a dozen tracks for Standardbred horses across the state but only one devoted exclusively to Thoroughbreds, the fastest distance runner in the world. Cheetahs might be the fastest sprinters, but at a mile out, Thoroughbreds, sleek, graceful animals who sound like thunder coming closer as they gallop together around the track, would easily win the day.

When we told people that our horse was not a Standardbred but a Thoroughbred, it was as though we were saying, "no, not a cubic zirconia—a real diamond." It created an illusion that we were financially in a different echelon, like we had money to dabble in the most expensive of hobbies.

There was a certain amount of ego in that, and the aura intoxicated me. I couldn't wait for a jockey to wear our silks, for which we had chosen the colors maize and blue—the same colors as the University of Michigan, where our daughter Jessica attended college. I couldn't wait to be the one who handed out doughnuts the morning after Baby won his first race. It's tradition for the jockey's agent to buy a dozen doughnuts the day after a win and give them to the horse's trainer, who then sets them out for people to come around, take one, and offer congratulations. When would that be us, I wondered.

John and I started looking over racing programs with their glossy covers. It was fun reviewing the competition in that way, affording that same excited feeling we used to have when the girls worked toward winning in skating and dancing.

I had also figured out by that point that the

Detroit Race Course was a lower-level track. The abuses I saw couldn't possibly happen to horses who ran on tracks in Kentucky, in Florida, in New York and California, I told myself. Even here, I believed, there were only a few bad apples, that most trainers and others involved in the horses' lives treated the animals well. I comforted myself that only once in a while did I come across something untoward.

Furthermore, I was pleased that despite the fact that no one seemed confident Coburn was the right trainer for Baby, he treated Baby well, always talking patiently to him and going slowly as far as training so that Baby wouldn't ramp up too soon and sustain an injury.

And Baby appeared to be doing so well. His exercise rider, Mike, nicknamed him The Tank because he was so solid and broad-chested.

In September, when he had been at the track about four months, Baby did his first timed work. He was more than ready. At first, when he had been led out to the racecourse, he would whinny to the other horses—"Do I know you?" or "Is there somebody out here who can tell me what's going on? Does anyone recognize my voice?" But now he was taking it all in stride.

That wasn't true for the new horses in general. The number of two-year-olds at the track had dwindled to the point that the racing secretary was having trouble filling races meant for that age group. They either were simply not cut out for racing or had become injured.

One problem to which young Thoroughbreds were prone, I learned by degrees, was bucked shins, a very painful condition similar to shin splints in people, except that even a finger lightly touching the spot can cause a horse to cringe. The covering of the long bone in the front of the leg— from the knee to the ankle—becomes inflamed from the stress of galloping. If it gets bad enough, the damage can cause a fracture that leaves no choice other than humane euthanasia.

A second orthopedic condition of young Thoroughbreds was green osselets—an inflammatory arthritis on the front legs, at the joint that connects the lower leg to the ankle. When green osselets occur, experienced horse people can feel some swelling at that juncture. Like bucked shins, I found out, the osselets heal with rest and phenylbutazone, a kind of horse aspirin known as bute, and don't come back. A callous-like material forms that protects the area. But until then, galloping around the track causes agony. Turns, in particular, are painful, because in leaning, the horse has to put more pressure on the affected spot.

The potential for bucked shins and osselets tugged at my conscience, another reminder that all that was going on was a lot for two-year-old Baby to deal with. Even with his sweet, confident disposition, he had to accustom himself to the loud sounds of big dumpster trucks with large metal forks that would crash right in front of the stalls to clear manure. He had to learn to steer on the track—go around other horses and let other horses go around him without anyone getting hurt. He did fine in every way, but I worried more than once whether I was asking too much of a two-year-old mind—and body.

That racing could be a dangerous activity for horses was further brought home by the fact that I would always see veterinarians at the track. They were there not just to administer painkillers and other medications but also to perform ultrasounds or x-ray horses for injuries. These vets had received permission from the State Racing Commission to set up practices on the backstretch, like farm vets who make barn calls, except the "barn" consisted of the barns and shedrows where some one thousand horses were kept. It was a lucrative business.

It appeared that the vets sometimes worked in tandem with men involved in the administration of euthanasia. Early on, when I was standing at the rail with several trainers one day, a man came over and exchanged hellos with everyone. Somebody asked him, "What are you paying?"

I couldn't hear the man's response, but the trainer who had asked about payment responded, "Yeah, stall eight and stall fourteen."

Then another trainer piped up and said, "Stall three."

"Okay, we'll take care of it," the man said.

"Who was that?" I questioned the trainer standing next to me. I figured the man was buying used horse equipment.

"Oh, he's the meat buyer," the trainer answered.

"Huh?" I responded.

"He's buying horses for slaughter."

"Why?" I asked.

"Because that's what he does," came the reply.

I thought that meant the horses were being taken to be put down, that they had suffered injuries that were causing them incredible pain that couldn't be fixed. I assumed the man was going to be bringing them to the vet and that "slaughter" and "meat buyer" were just the lingo of the track. I was new enough at the point, and enamored enough with being around all these people who had by then started to take me in, that I couldn't consider any other possibility. Also, I was heartened that no debilitating injuries were going to compromise Baby. I felt confident that Coburn worked hard never to overdo it with him, accelerating him gradually precisely to avoid any orthopedic problems.

Still, I decided that Scarlett was not going to race as a two-year-old. The ball may have been rolling down the hill with Baby, and with him I may have felt sucked in to the point that it was too late to back out, but Scarlett would not train or race until she was three. A year old, she was supposed to begin training in the fall, around the time Baby would start racing, but it was now going to be more than a year before she left home. She would be fully protected from even the remote potential to suffer injuries that could befall racehorses younger than two.

Baby's speed, in the meantime, was going to be clocked for three furlongs, or three-eighths of a mile. He wasn't going to go as fast as he could. The highest speeds are saved for the race itself. But the pace with timed works is faster than with untimed training, and a rider can let the trainer know how much horse a Thoroughbred has left at the end of the run, setting the pace for further training.

The timed work informs bettors as well as trainers. The times are published, so serious bettors can get a sense of how well a horse might do during an actual race and base their wagers accordingly.

Of some forty horses who were timed for three furlongs that day, Baby ran the slowest, about fourteen seconds per furlong. I felt embarrassed, but at the same time, there was no heat or swelling on his legs. He had handled the increase in speed well. And some of the horses were seasoned athletes, having already been running for a few years. Baby was brand new to timed runs.

A week later, he repeated his three-furlong timed work and came in third to last out of twenty-four—better.

Two weeks after that, on October 3rd, Baby did a five-furlong timed work—five-eighths of a mile. Coburn had begun training him a little harder in the morning, having him go faster than he had been. That time, he came in the third fastest out of ten, about 12.5 seconds a furlong.

Based on those results, he could be entered in his first real race, a run of six furlongs to be held on October 10th. I could tell by Baby's demeanor that he felt ready to do well. I don't know if a horse can feel proud of himself, but I saw in him a swagger since his second timed run. And he was more anxious to get out there and run each morning, more excited as he would get saddled. After his third timed work, we actually had an exchange of looks, like a telepathy between us. It was as though he was telling me he knew what he was there for.

The night before the race, I hardly slept, then ran up the road to the mailbox 100 times once dawn broke to see if the *Detroit Free Press* had come yet. The sports column corroborated what Baby had been transmitting with his attitude, predicting that despite his slow start, he would come in first. "Reel Surprise well tuned for debut," it said. The *Daily Racing Form*—kind of like *The Wall Street Journal* for making predictions about money and investments when it came to Thoroughbreds—picked him to come in third, a "show" in the "Win, Place, or Show" lexicon.

Pleased as I was, a part of me was still gripped with fear. Horses get injured racing. I'd seen horses break from the gate, then turn around and run the wrong way.

I also knew horses didn't usually win their first time out, despite what the paper said about Baby, so my fear was mixed with a kind of competitive dread.

But Baby had become so focused out there on the track. And though trainers don't like to make predictions, even Coburn said, "I like to send horses out when they're ready to win."

A lot of the owners keep to the stands just before the race begins, but I stayed with Baby till the last minute, walking with the groom and the trainer from his stall over to the track, then shaking the jockey's hand and saying to him, "Just have a safe trip." I meant it. A jockey could endanger his life clipping other horses' heels as he wove in and out. Or a horse could stumble, throwing a jockey, or the jockey's feet could slip out of the stirrups. Some time after Secretariat won the Kentucky Derby, his jockey became paralyzed upon being thrown from a horse during a race.

After speaking to the jockey, I went right next to Baby, rubbed his neck, and kissed him. Be careful, I thought to myself. We love you. I felt bad for him. It was a maiden race for all the horses, meaning they had never won before. But it was Baby's first start—his first time racing for real. There are no pre-season "games." Even running furlongs in timed works, the horses go alone or with just one other horse. They are not running side by side with a field of horses while they are being clocked.

That's only one of many things that are brand new to a horse making his first start. When Thoroughbreds train, they go out in the morning, then generally like to take a little nap around 11:00 or 12:00. That's why, so many times when I would come back to Baby's stall after he finished training for the day, he'd be sleeping, stretched out and snoring adorably. While almost all horses sleep standing up some time after weaning, Baby always lay down in the straw, even at age two. I'd tiptoe away those days, not wanting to wake my sleeping child.

Races, in contrast to training, take place only in the afternoon, or at least they did in Michigan at that time. So already a horse, very much a creature of habit, knows something is different on race day. He hasn't been taken out in the morning for his usual training, and here he is being taken out later in the day. And when he gets out to the track, he sees not rows and rows of empty bleachers but a grandstand full of people moving around.

Horses have not only good distance vision but

also much better peripheral vision than we do, and are able to see almost in a full circle. It's easy to tell that what they see is making them feel unnerved. Many start to prance in agitation, wondering what is going on. Voices booming over the loudspeaker only add to their anxiety. Furthermore, the horses saddle up right in the grandstand area, whereas for training they are saddled in their stall and then ridden out to the track. It's like after years of putting on your clothes and then going out to your driveway, you now have to go out to your driveway and finish dressing there.

I could tell that Baby was very concerned with all the commotion in the stands, that it was making him feel disoriented. "Good boy, easy boy," I kept saying as my hand lingered on his neck, but I'm not sure how aware he was at that point that I was trying to soothe him, so distracted was he. I kept telling myself that it was not any different from a skater or dancer's nerves before a good performance, that Baby needed to get this experience under his belt and would feel less fearful the next time around, once he saw how well he could do.

I kept my hand on him as long as I could, until the jockey had to mount him. Then, like all the other horses, Baby was paraded back and forth in front of the grandstand with his jockey on his back, after which he was led into the starting gate, where the metal clanged shut behind him.

It is an extremely tight fit, which, because horses are prey animals, makes them very nervous. They want to be able to bolt. But they have to wait a few minutes for all the horses to load, adding to the tension. In fact, gate accidents are not uncommon. A horse might rear, catching his leg on the steel bars.

As soon as the last horse is loaded, the bell goes off. The deafening sound reverberates, piercing all other noise throughout the track. At the same time, the metal bars in front of the horse bang open while the jockey cries out as loud as he can to goad the animal into action. Then the horse is urged to run faster than it ever has, being whipped not only to make him go faster—animal behaviorist Desmond Morris likens it to trying to escape the sting of a biting predator—but also to keep him from bumping into other horses or from running through the gap back to the barn.

While Baby was being exposed to one new and unsettling sensation after another, I climbed the stands. We had invited more than twenty people to sit with us—my children, their friends, all our own friends, my parents, my sister and her husband, everybody in our inner circle. My heart was in my throat; I could almost feel the adrenalin rush through me as the bell rang. Here was the horse I had helped bring into the world, now ready to give it everything he had and show the world what he could do.

It felt like a frozen moment. Everything was shut off. It was as if I were waiting for someone to say, "Here's what happened." Then, in a flash packed with spikes of emotion that made me feel like I was going to explode, the minute was over and Baby had come in dead last, soundly beaten by fourteen lengths, a length being the length of a horse.

I felt so mortified that I almost wanted to give back to everybody the money I knew they had bet on him.

The horses continue to gallop for another half mile or so after the race is over. They can't stop immediately. But I was already running down the stands to reach Baby and comfort him. The poor thing was covered in sand and dirt from what was kicked up at him by all the horses running ahead of him. He was breathing heavily, never having run so fast in his life.

Though I tried to hide it, I cried on the way back to the barn. Coburn, uncharacteristically, was throwing things around, saying, "He did that purposely." It was so ridiculous I didn't even call him out on his nonsense but instead just whispered, "Oh, Baby, it's not your fault." Even at that stage I hesitated to contradict my trainer openly.

Baby had calmed down by the time he had been walked back to the barn, as if it were any other day. He was even hungry.

Afterward, people reassured me. "Don't worry. A horse rarely wins its first time out."

Baby's next race was eleven days later, October 21st, perfect in that horses do best with ten to fourteen days between races. They need that much time to build up their speed again before their next all-out run. For this race, the newspaper predicted that he would come in third rather than first.

Baby did come in third—he "showed"—and, better still, he missed first place by only three-quarters of a length. You'd think I was the jockey, the way I was shouting out. It was an excellent display, and we were paid $730 out of the $7,300 purse—very exciting. We could begin to recoup on the $10,000-plus we spent to train him.

The race itself was a thrill to watch. Baby had come from behind. Things didn't look so promising as he remained near the back of the pack at the last turn. But the jockey was saving him for the end, when he started "picking up" one horse after the other. Head after head after head, Baby edged forward, until finally coming out almost right at the front of the pack. One more furlong to the race, and he might very well have won.

The third race appropriate for Baby was slated to take place on November 5th—exactly two weeks away and also a perfect amount of time for him to rest up before giving it his all once again. "You're sitting on a win," people said to me. "Next time out!"

But when I spoke to Coburn about it, he seemed hesitant. "We'll see," he said.

"Why is it, 'we'll see,'" I answered. "Baby came out of this race fine. Is there something wrong, something I should know?"

"Oh, he's fine," Coburn countered. "But when he races is my decision."

I soon pulled it together. Coburn had taken on a second client in September, and that man had two horses in training and a third to start soon, meaning that Coburn stood to make two to three times the money off him as he made from training Baby. The man wanted one of his own horses entered into the race, and at that time in Michigan, one trainer couldn't race two horses at once. There was the chance he'd use one to create a traffic jam for others in the race while creating a clearer path to the finish line for the second horse. Coburn, I believed, no doubt wanted to accommodate the other owner's wish to race one of his own horses, since that man was paying Coburn more money.

Coburn's patient way with Baby notwithstanding, I had already become wary of him because I found out that he had been lying to me. Mike was supposed to ride Baby every day for training; 20 percent of the more than $1,000 I was paying Coburn each month once Baby arrived at the track was supposed to go to pay Mike to take him for a run, and on days I didn't see him go, Coburn assured me that he had been out before I arrived. But Mike gave some clues inadvertently that that wasn't always so. Now Coburn was refusing to race Baby when his chances for winning were so high. That was the tipping point.

After much back and forth, without letting on that I was aware of his subterfuge, I took matters into my own hands. Across the aisle from Baby's stall was Julian Belker, an older trainer in his sixties who had never asked me outright if he could train Baby instead of Coburn. I liked that. Others had made it clear that they were eager for the money to train such a promising horse. I liked the way Belker teased me, too. "I don't know about you, Girl," he'd say. "Don't you have anything else to do? You're here all the time."

"I've decided to fire Lyle Coburn," I said. "Would you take over?"

"Sure, I'd be glad to," Belker answered.

With the race two days away, the *Daily Racing Form* predicted that Baby would come in second.

Once again, however, he came in dead last, this time by 19 3/4 lengths. In the final drive for the finish line, he bolted straight for the bleachers rather than rounding the turn.

"What happened?" I asked Belker when I reached Baby's stall afterward.

"Let me show you something," Belker said, and he took his fingers to make an OK sign with his thumb and middle finger, getting ready to flick them against something. He then bent down on one knee and flicked the front of Baby's left ankle, and Baby pulled his leg right up. He did the same thing to the other leg, and Baby didn't move.

The leg that Baby had moved out of the way had a green osselet. He was in too much pain to put pressure on the ankle when turning curves, so he tried to run straight.

It was time to take Baby home. There were only three more weeks left to racing season, and his ankle wasn't going to heal in that time.

CHAPTER FIVE

I figured that Coburn knew about the osselet but didn't tell me because then I would have taken Baby home for the entire month of November, and he would have lost more than $1,000 in training fees. I was angry, but I felt much more guilty than angry. If I had insisted the previous year that Baby come home for the winter despite Coburn's talk about his stubborn streak, he would have had a chance to rest up, be a horse again, and not be prone to the osselet. I had known better than to let him stay at Coburn's training facility and not have any break whatsoever before he went to the track, and my remorse was only compounded by the fact that I now knew two-year-olds had no business racing in the first place because of the unique dangers to their legs, not to mention their minds. If I had only just let him come home and finish growing up first.

But Baby *was* finally home now after more than a year away, and what a terrific homecoming it was. As soon as his trailer pulled up to the house, Beauty, Pumpkin, Pat, and Scarlett started whinnying, and Baby recognized their calls and whinnied right back in his honking fashion. His mother and sister ran around joyously, and he was so excited that he was pulling to get down to the barn and smell everyone. The five of them together formed a herd, and now they were reunited, like a family unit. Baby and Scarlett, in particular, were wonderful to watch together. They were still young and mischievous enough to play halter tag, a game in which they pulled at each other's halters teasingly with their teeth in a tug of war that brought them off their front legs, literally standing. Then one would give up and run off, and the other was "it" and had to chase; it was hilarious, and wonderful to watch. They also loved to roll in snow, then walk up to the back door looking like white ghost horses coming around for tasty handouts.

The best news was that Baby's ankle was okay. I had my own vet check him out, and all Baby needed was some time to heal plus some bute to ease the pain and reduce swelling. He had no pain walking, only galloping, which flexes the ankle to a greater degree than walking.

Everything was as it should be again. Everybody was there, and their munching on their hay at night soothed me at last check, before I settled down for the night. I didn't have to worry.

It wasn't that I didn't feel Baby loved being out on the track. He did. He didn't know he was racing—a horse has no idea that there's a white post with the word "Finish" on it—but he clearly enjoyed running with other horses. And despite the fact that he hadn't won any races yet, he was good at it. And I was proud of that. I wanted him to win, the way I wanted my daughters to win the medal or the dance trophy.

As for the sinister things I had glimpsed—the overfeeding of one horse, the whipping of another—they were awful, of course, but they were aberrations. Even the so-called trainer who lacked a license seemed a rarity. Thus, by that point, most of what I had been seeing was peeling paint and pockmarked roads. I still believed the track was at its core an upstanding institution. After all, you could at any point have your purse or vehicle searched for drugs that were allowed to be prescribed only by the veterinarians on the grounds. You couldn't have a syringe in your possession unless you had, say, diabetes and had received clearance. All seemed pretty strictly regulated.

As for Baby's osselet, for which I blamed myself, I saw it as a compromise I needed to make for him in order to let him enjoy the freedom to just run. How many times had Jessica split open her chin learning to jump while ice skating? How nervous might Rebecca have been when I started to send her to ballet camps out of state at age twelve, and she had to fly by herself, hail her own cabs, figure out how much to tip the driver?

The bottom line was that I didn't at that point have major doubts about Baby's racing. Besides, I had made that promise to Don Shouse. And in those days, races were listed in the newspaper. It would have been very easy for him to check whether I was sticking to our bargain.

About two months after Baby arrived home, in January of 1994, I became installed as a director on the board of the Michigan branch of the Thoroughbred Owners and Breeders Association, M-TOBA. I had been voted in during the fall. It meant that even though Baby was home, I was still very much involved in racing, still going to the track for meetings. I liked the camaraderie and, just as important, it was a good way to meet other owners. I was in the unusual position of being an owner who knew the trainers, since I was at the track all the time, but I didn't know most of my fellow owners. And getting to know other owners was important because it was my aim to leverage my position on M-TOBA to get myself elected to the Horsemen's Benevolent & Protective Association, which had a lot more power to effect change. Owners, in addition to trainers, voted for the members of that board.

At home, Baby's ankle lost its soreness, and he and I would go for rides together. I was nervous to get on him at first. He was a lot of horse at the track. Only certain exercise riders and jockeys could handle him, in fact. He was powerful and stubborn, wanting to do what he wanted to do. And not all racehorses know the difference between being at the track and being at home.

They try to go as fast as they can no matter where they are, pulling the reins away as they run.

Before I mounted him, I talked to him a lot and breathed into his nose. "It's me. It's Mommy. This is different. We're going for a gentle ride." I got on with no small amount of trepidation, but Baby moved off just beautifully. He responded to "Whoa" for me. He turned when I prompted him to. He never pulled or tried to go any faster than I wanted. It was more like, "What do you want to do next, Mom? You want to go over here? Okay."

Having the horse I held in my arms carrying me, moving as one with him—how much closer a bond can you have? Over the trails we'd make our way, trees bare save the pines, all quiet except for the sound of Baby's hooves pressing onto snow lit by faint sunlight fading early from the winter sky. I've always said that if there aren't any horses in heaven, don't send me there. This was why.

Later that winter, in March, I received a phone call from Belker, asking if we wanted him to keep training Baby. Now I was nervous all over again. Why put Baby through the risk of more injuries? Despite all that was said at the track about what a good runner he was, maybe this was a Reel On Reel progeny that was simply meant to be with me in my backyard. He wasn't even three years old yet—still very young, still so playful. Pat loved watching him and Scarlett frolic. "Look at my little ones," her expression seemed to say.

Scarlett, too, was so happy because none of the other horses at home were young enough to play the way she enjoyed. Only Baby wanted to nip at her, to roughhouse.

Also, here, I didn't have to keep running back to Baby's stall at the far end of the track to make sure he was okay, to break up the monotony of being confined to that small space twenty-three hours a day. Here he could just be a horse. I was happiest when he was home with me. I felt very hesitant.

But Belker invited John and me out to his house to meet his wife, make us feel more comfortable with him, and we very much appreciated the gesture. Whereas Coburn had always been distant, cryptic even, Belker appeared warm and straightforward. He obviously had a warm, loving relationship with his wife. Pictures of his children and grandchildren were everywhere.

At least as important, he brought out loose-leaf binder after binder of win pictures—the official photos taken at the track when your horse comes in first. Belker had been a trainer for a lot of years, decades even, stretching back to the Kennedy administration, so there was a great deal of history. John and I were both impressed. Belker wasn't a leading trainer anymore—he was just doing it for fun. But we liked his experience combined with his hominess—his genuine friendliness. And he already knew that I was at the track all the time, which obviously didn't put him off. So we rehired him, leaving his house feeling pretty confident that maybe we'd have an album of win pictures ourselves someday.

We shipped Baby to the track a few days later, as spring training had already started, and races were going to begin that year in April. Again, those mixed feelings welled up. There were cries and whinnies from the other horses as the trailer left. "Where are you going? We thought you were home to stay."

Baby himself didn't appear nervous. "I'll be back," he whinnied confidently. "Just gone for a bit—have to make my mark." Of course, he would have rather stayed home with his herd. But I couldn't afford to read that into his calls.

For days after he left, Scarlett would look around for him. Pat was used to separation—she had had so many foals. But Scarlett wandered about, whinnying very loudly. "Where *are* you? *Hellloooo*—can you *hear* me?" It came from deep in her belly, then she'd grow very still waiting for a response. Finally, she gave up, and her ceasing to whinny was even sadder.

"It's okay, Scarlett," I'd tell her. "He's coming back."

As for me, despite my initial trepidation, I was now almost anxious for the season to start, my nurturing instinct giving way to my competitive nature. I was looking forward to Baby proving he was the horse everyone thought he was—a winner. Also, in certain ways, the track was the best place for someone who adored horses. Every single day I got to go where there were more than 1,000 horses of all colors and sizes. And everyone was always *talking* horses. At that level, I was really in my element.

Moreover, this time, going to the track felt like Old Home Week—big bear hugs and slaps on the back. I felt so much more at home than when I first arrived the previous spring. I felt like one of them.

Better still, I didn't have to worry about any of the orthopedic problems particular to two-year-old racehorses, or the fright that two-year-olds can feel in new situations. Baby was going to be three at the beginning of May.

Belker put Baby in his first race of the season— a six-furlong run—on May fourth. Baby wasn't at all disoriented. He knew the loudspeaker; he knew the whole routine. He knew that by being led to the track in the afternoon rather than the morning, he'd be allowed to run as fast as he could, as opposed to the measured runs of morning training. He was excited about running, even somewhat frenzied. Coming back to the track was Old Home Week for him, too.

He came in fifth out of ten horses. Of course I would have liked to see him win, but because it was his first race in six months, I knew he had to get reacclimated to the speeds required. I didn't see it as a major problem.

Eleven days later, Baby ran again. He had the same jockey from when he came in third the previous year, so my hopes were higher, not just because he had done well with that jockey and not just because that jockey had a reputation for bringing the best out of a horse but also because it meant the jockey's agent thought Baby was the right horse to ride. A good jockey's agent is better than any track handicapper, picking horses for his client that he expects to win. The jockey gets 10 percent of what the owner gets, and the agent gets 10 percent of what the jockey gets, so picking the right horse is key.

But Baby came in only fourth.

Fifteen days later, on May 30th, Belker decided to try Baby at a mile rather than six furlongs. Baby didn't have the build of a distance horse. Even Coburn had always told me he was meant for sprinting rather than distance. But a classic distance horse is an owner's dream, so I wasn't going to argue. Furthermore, someone in the *Daily Racing Form* picked Baby to come in second, so my hopes were high. The cherry on top was that he was going to be ridden by the top jockey at the Detroit Race Course, Terry Houghton. It was very difficult to get Terry. His agent, Frank Garoufalis, known universally as Frank the Greek, always had his pick. Frank also was keenly aware of which trainers had forty to sixty horses and therefore offered a lot of business and which had just a few, like Belker, and therefore didn't require special tending or relationship-building. So the fact that Frank chose Baby for his jockey was a promising sign. Maybe Baby would surprise everyone and turn out to be a miler after all.

As at every other race, I had all my friends and family there. I was feeling pretty confident that we'd all be going to a restaurant or bar to celebrate afterward. But Baby came in last—eighth out of eight, twelve lengths behind the winner.

I was more than disappointed. I was confused. Baby was extremely fit and muscled, to the point that he was hard to handle; I couldn't even walk him. And usually, that was a good signal. When a Thoroughbred takes on a "Don't mess with me" attitude, it means he's on his toes and ready to win.

Belker said Baby just needed to build up the stamina for a mile race and scheduled him for another one late in June. "When he goes back to sprints," Belker assured me, "it will be easier for him to win."

But Terry Houghton was not chosen as his jockey this time, and the newspaper picked him to come in fourth. If only. Baby came in dead last again.

On July 2nd, Baby entered his fifth race of the season, a six-furlong run. He lost that one, too, coming in sixth out of eleven.

I didn't doubt Baby's ability. I had had too many people tell me by that point, "That horse is a runner." They'd seen him in timed works. They'd seen the way he liked to gallop.

What I was beginning to doubt was Belker's ability. Baby was now running more slowly than he did with Coburn.

My suspicions were fueled by comments like, "Is Belker still your trainer? What are you with that old coot for?" It wasn't jibing with the fact that Belker had all those books of wins. What was Belker doing wrong, I wondered? Maybe he had a training style that worked way back when but that wasn't keeping up with whatever trainers were doing now.

On July 16th, he entered Baby in another six-furlong race, and while no one thought he would win, a handicapper in the *Daily Racing Form* did predict he would come in third. So even then, when Baby had already lost five races that season and three the season before, I was getting messages that he could race. But he finished seventh out of twelve, eight and a half lengths behind the winner.

Now I *knew* something wasn't right. In terms of soundness, Baby was perfectly fine. His legs were tight, he flexed just fine, and there was no swelling or heat after a race. But I did notice that when Belker cooled him down, he was thoroughly spent, exhausted. And I was able to start walking him again on my own; he had lost that tough-guy edge, as though there was no more fire in him. I saw, too, that he was losing weight. You should see no more than a hint of a horse's ribs when he walks, and nothing at all when he's standing still. But even when Baby was stationary, I could see rib outlines. Earlier in the season I saw that Baby was shedding some fat. But this had gone way beyond that.

I started looking around. Baby's grain looked good, and I knew he was getting vitamins. But I could see that the hay Belker was feeding was not high quality. Racehorses generally eat very good-quality hay, usually alfalfa. Baby's hay had no alfalfa, however, and it was yellow rather than having a greenish cast, meaning it had not been baled at the right time and had lost its nutrients.

I didn't want to say to Belker, "Your hay is lousy." I still felt deferential. I was loathe to interfere in a trainer's tactics. But I did point out the weight loss.

"Girl, he's looking good," Belker replied. "He's looking *racing* lean. You don't want a horse to carry around a bunch of extra weight."

"Racing lean" was a term used by some of the old timers. It wasn't in vogue anymore, and certainly not for a naturally stocky, broadly built horse like Baby.

"But his manner," I pressed. "I can even walk him again." He seemed dejected, too, keeping his head down and walking slowly. Baby's morning training sessions were becoming more lackluster as well.

But Belker blew me off. "Oh, it's all in your head," he said.

I let it go. Belker always bedded Baby's stall with deep straw, and he was always there, mucking away manure. He washed Baby himself, too, rather than leave that job to a groom. Also, as opposed to Coburn, Belker was such a truly nice man, almost fatherly at times, if a little condescending. One day, one of his sons, just a little younger than I was, dropped by at the track. "Hi ya, Dad," he had said, and Belker introduced me, making pleasant small talk. Their warm, relaxed style charmed me, so different was it from Coburn's weird, almost paranoid, way of interacting.

So when Belker wanted to enter Baby in yet another race at the end of July, I let him, although not without some resistance. It was another mile-long run, and I felt Baby had already shown a mile wasn't his kind of race.

But Belker came up with an excuse, saying, "a mile will be easier for him. It's harder for a sprinter to get to his top speed at a shorter distance. Besides, too much time will go by if we have to wait to pick up another six-furlong race."

So fifteen days later, Baby entered yet another mile race, albeit at a much lower level and with less impressive horses. I was okay with it because we really needed a win to start bringing in money and paying some of the bills, not just to Belker but also to the farrier and to the veterinarian, who injected Baby with his vitamins, with the bute he took the day before each race to guard against swelling, and with Lasix, which racehorses start taking at age three as a performance enhancer. "Need anything today?" the vet would call out as he came down the shedrow. Lasix was ten dollars a shot, bute, twelve dollars. At twenty-two dollars a horse and with more than 1,000 horses on the backstretch, a veterinary practice could pull in $150,000 to $200,000 a year, extremely good money for the mid-1990s. And that didn't include all the money earned from administering vaccinations, diagnostic tests, and every other type of veterinary care.

The newspaper predicted Baby would come in last, meaning that even in that cheap-purse race, the professional handicappers were giving up on him. He did not prove them wrong.

I was crushed. I'm not much of a crier in front of other people, but walking back with Baby from the grandstand to his stall that day, anybody who looked right at me would have seen that my eyes were wet.

"I'm going to get going, Girl," Belker said to me after he fed all his horses some grain and left each of them a few flakes of hay. "I've got a long ride home."

"I'm going to be leaving in a minute, too," I answered. "I'm just going to hang around for a little bit."

It was quiet in the barn, and I sat down on a bale of straw and just watched Baby for a while. For the first fifteen or twenty minutes, he ate his grain, which horses love, after which they switch to their hay. But Baby only pushed his hay around with his nose. He wasn't eating it. Then he did something I had never seen a horse do before. He started eating the straw with which his stall was bedded. A horse's muzzle is very tactilely attuned, and Baby was picking around for single blades that he would enjoy even with a whole pile of hay right beside him.

"You poor thing," I thought, kissing Baby's muzzle and rubbing my face between his nostrils, the spot on a horse where it feels like velvet. I had been right. There was something wrong with the hay. It may have even had mold. A horse will usually turn up his nose at moldy hay, which is a good thing because mold will make horses very sick. Whatever the problem with the hay, Baby was not getting the proper nutrition for all he was being asked to do—run as fast as a car, run so fast that his lungs could bleed.

When I saw Belker the next day, I said, "You know what happened when I lingered yesterday?"

"What?" Belker replied, going about his business.

"Well, he got done with his grain, and remember I was telling you he's getting too thin?"

"Yeah," Belker said, still not paying complete attention to me.

"Well, he didn't eat his hay when he finished his grain. He started eating his straw."

"That's your silly horse," Belker responded, pooh-poohing me, as he always did when I tried to disagree with him.

"No, I don't think so," I said, holding my ground. "He shouldn't be eating his straw. There's no nutrition in straw."

"Well, his hay is gone now, isn't it?" Belker asked, looking at the spot in which he had left the hay the day before.

"Yes," I answered, "but for him to first pick through his bedding and *then* only finally get around to eating his hay—"

"Girl, I can't believe the things you worry about," he replied, interrupting me. "You *look* for something to worry about."

"But this is why he's so thin," I said. "This is why his ribs are showing." By that point I was even starting to see Baby's hip bones.

"I'm telling you," Belker went on, not missing a beat, "he's racing lean. You make him carry a bunch of extra weight, and it's just going to put more stress on his joints." He then said quickly, "I have a race picked out. There's another one on August 12th. Not a mile. He really doesn't like a mile. Six furlongs. That's where he really belongs."

Belker was playing me. He knew I wanted so badly for Baby to win—I had now been at this too long—and he knew I and others didn't think Baby was a miler. I went for it.

"Okay, that makes sense," I said. I figured I'd try this one more time. But Baby came in sixth out of nine, nine lengths behind the winner. He had now run eleven races altogether—three with Coburn and eight with Belker—and had not won a single one.

After the race, the groom who had taken Baby to the track said to me, "I have always had horses dragging me to the post. I have never had one that I had to drag. He did not want to go."

The next day, the track vet, Larry Wales, came down the aisle of the barn with his usual "Need anything today?" and I said, "Yeah," which took both him and Belker by surprise. The vets never even make eye contact with the owners, even though the owners pay all the vet bills. They speak directly with the trainers.

"I just want your opinion on something," I continued. "Would you look at my horse and tell me if he needs to gain weight?"

The vet then looked at Baby—he, Belker, and I were standing right in front of his stall, and he said, "Yes."

"You see?" I said to Belker. "How *much* weight?" I then asked the vet.

"A hundred pounds," he answered. And then he left. Vets don't want to get into arguments with trainers, on whom they depend for their living at the track.

"You see that?" I said to Belker. "It's not racing lean. This is a big-boned, broad, stocky horse. He's *supposed* to carry all that weight. When he did, he did well. Now, the vet just said it. It's not me making something up. He's not that *style* of Thoroughbred, who races all tucked up, racing lean. He's just not that body style."

"Agh," Belker responded, waving his hand dismissively and turning back to his chores. "What does he know? He's a veterinarian. I'm a trainer."

"Julian," I said, "I can't do this anymore. He's got to come home."

There was a silence, followed by, "Do what you have to do, Girl."

No harsh words were exchanged. It was even kind of amicable. Yes, Belker had played me. Yes, he was a huckster. But he was more two-bit bumbler than huckster, giving all his horses bad hay, including a couple that he owned and raced at the track. This wasn't something personal about Baby or me. Perhaps he always fed horses cheap hay. Maybe that was the way it was done in the '60s and '70s.

In addition, this hadn't gone on as long as my relationship with Coburn. I had paid that man for thirteen months straight. With Belker, most of our association took place between March and August—just five months.

When the trailer with Baby drove up to the

house, all the horses started whinnying in relief. They began running around—"He's home again!" They were so excited that they started bumping into each other, jostling for position to get the first glimpse of him.

Baby, for his part, had begun whinnying from the trailer as soon as it began coming down our road. And with energy he hadn't managed in a while, he pulled to get down to the barn as soon as he was let out. I put him in his stall and then let Scarlett come into her stall right next to his. They immediately started grooming each other, and the other horses wanted to greet him, too, so I put everyone in their stalls where they could see him, all settle down and be happy.

Immediately, I started giving Baby better hay. I also let him out in the pasture to graze, but gradually. Horses don't do well with changes in diet. It upsets their delicate digestive systems, causing diarrhea and gas. And summer grass is rich food for a horse—a huge contrast from the bad hay and straw he had been consuming, so I had to be really careful, turning Baby out for only an hour a day at first and working up from there.

I called my farm vet, Allen Balay, right away, too. He would look at Baby very differently from the way a track vet would. Horses at the track are not pets. They're there to earn money for everybody involved, including the veterinarians who examine them. That is, they're vehicles for cash, like a deck of cards or a pair of dice at a casino, so the aim of the track vet is to keep them racing. A farm vet, on the other hand, is like the vet who treats a dog or cat. He understands that the animal is a companion, a member of the family.

Dr. Balay was immediately very angry. "Oh my God, what did they do to this horse?" he demanded.

"Well, he's sound," I said. "No torn ligaments or broken bones or joint problems. I kept saying he's a big, stocky horse, but my trainer insisted that he was racing lean."

"Well, he's more than racing lean," Dr. Balay responded, disgusted. "I'm getting some blood on this horse." And with that he went to his truck to pull out syringes and other supplies.

"How many pounds does he need to gain?" I asked, as he drew blood from Baby's jugular—a safe, easy vein to retrieve blood from a horse. "The track vet said one hundred."

"He needs to gain at least two hundred," he said. "Was he racing?" Dr. Balay asked, agitated.

"Yes, he raced just a couple of days ago," I told him.

"How was he doing?"

"He was coming in last a lot."

"Well, that's not surprising," came the curt reply.

"They tried him at six furlongs, and they tried him at a mile," I offered.

"They asked this horse to run a *mile?*" he questioned incredulously.

"Yes," I told him. "They said it was easier because the horse doesn't have to expend all his energy in one major spurt, like a sprinter."

Dr. Balay didn't reply. He just kept slamming things around.

"What do we do now?" I asked.

"You've got a decision to make," he said sternly. "His muscles have been damaged." Baby was so thin he had been breaking down muscle for energy, for fuel. "And he may be anemic. I want to make sure he's not. Either way, a horse in this condition, if you want to allow him to fully recover his body, it's going to take six months. The other option is that he could also gain back the weight and *appear* to be fine in sixty days. We could give him some additives."

But I knew before he reached the end of his sentence that I would not be sending Baby back to finish out the season. He couldn't just *look* right. He had to be truly healthy again, at the top of his game.

Dr. Balay called not long after to say that Baby was, in fact, anemic and needed an iron shot followed by supplements. He would also need as many flakes of hay as he would eat. The plan was to keep giving him more at night until there was some left the next morning. He would also be gradually going out more and grazing with his mother, Scarlett, Beauty, and Pumpkin.

Again, I was guilt-ridden, as I should have been. *I* chose this trainer. *I* let things go on for too long. Along with feeding Baby bad hay, Belker probably also bought cheap feed mixed up near his house rather than a name brand, like Purina.

I wondered if I should just retire Baby, let him stay home. I still had Scarlett to try out next year. But the option to retire Baby gnawed at me. I knew he was a runner. I had had too many people tell me that.

There's a TV in the track kitchen on which they run tapes of the previous day's races. One day, when the trainers started filing into the kitchen after morning training, one of them called out to me, "Your race from yesterday is coming up. Look. Your horse can *run*. Watch what he does." I looked up at the screen, and the horses were coming into the homestretch turn. Baby got caught up in traffic; a lot of horses became bunched up. His jockey had to pull him up, slow his stride, swing him out to the far right, then ask him to come forward again at high speed. And he did.

"Horses don't do that," the trainer said to me. "You pull them off stride, you ask them to come again, they don't. *That's* a runner."

Thinking of that only made me feel worse. I felt like I hadn't been fair to Baby on a level apart from compromising his health. He had been out there doing what I asked him to do. He was trying to show me, I *am* the horse you think I am, I *am* everything people are telling you I am, you *are* going to be proud of me. But I wasn't letting him do his best because I kept picking the wrong people to bring the best out of him.

I petted him and lay my head on his neck, apologizing. "I'm so sorry I didn't take you home the minute I noticed you were losing weight, Baby. Why didn't I pick a better trainer for you?" Baby, in response, turned his head and nuzzled me, rubbed his face against me. He was probably just enjoying the tenderness and looking for treats, but I anthropomorphized his actions, believing that perhaps he was apologizing for disappointing me.

"Oh, no, Baby, it wasn't you," I said back in this one-sided conversation. "It was me." Deep down, I knew I would bring him back. I needed to fix my own bad judgment.

CHAPTER SIX

As guilty as I felt that I let Baby become so pitifully underweight before I realized how bad things had gotten, and as angry as I felt not only at myself but also at Belker, I loved being able to nourish Baby. He was sound—there were no orthopedic problems—so there was no worrying about whether he was in pain or might not get over an injury. All I had to do was give him as much food as he could handle. And what mother doesn't like to feed her hungry child?

"Look what Mommy's *got* for you!" I would say as I came into the barn. I gave him his grain ration that I had sweetened with apples and carrots. The grain, very high-quality, pelleted feed by Purina, was easily digested, so there was no waste. It was totally absorbed in Baby's gastrointestinal tract, along with the iron supplements I was giving him so he could get past his anemia.

Between meals, I made sure Baby had the best hay. "There's a really nice snack here," I'd tell him in a rising voice, pointing it out. "Look at all this alfalfa!" When he finished, I'd say, "You ate it all up. You good boy, you! That's Momma's boy. I'll go get some more."

I'd groom him carefully, too, and for a long time. Baby was so relaxed, not having to go to train in the mornings. He grazed to his heart's content in the pasture. These were easy days for him, and I was so glad.

At first, it was difficult to see the weight gain. When you're looking at a 1,000- or 1,200-pound animal, you can't tell that twenty pounds have come on in a week. You can't rush the weight gain, either. When a horse is full, he'll stop eating his hay and stop grazing in the pasture (although he'll eat himself to death on grain, which is why it has to be rationed, even if the horse is under-weight). But gradually, after about four to six weeks, I was able to see that Baby was filling in. No longer were there hollows at the withers, at the dock of his tail.

He perked up, too, becoming more interested in playing with Scarlett again. By October, he was even ready to go for rides. I didn't want to ride him before that—why make him carry an extra 130 pounds when he was more than that many pounds underweight? But now, he felt like getting out a little.

Michigan autumns are just beautiful—the best times for riding. The tremendous palette of fall colors—crimsons next to bursting yellow-golds—arch against the backdrop of a sky whose blues couldn't be more brilliant. The daytime tempera-ture reaches sixty-five, seventy degrees, and there are no bugs. The first nighttime frost has already killed the flies, the gnats, the mosquitoes. You can ride to the woods, in the shade. You can ride in the sun.

Going along a wooded trail, all I could hear was the scrunch, scrunch, scrunch of Baby's feet. A leaf or two would drift slowly to the ground, swaying a bit before landing. I could feel how relaxed Baby was, how placid. His look let me know that he was aware this was down time. I wondered again, fleetingly, whether I should send him back to the track. But he did seem to like training. "I can run," I felt he was telling me. "Just find me the right trainer, and I'll show you. Don't let someone starve me. Don't let someone play games with me. Find the person who will bring out the best in me. Yes, it's great to come home. But when I'm at the track, I know why. And I want to prove it to you."

Once more, I was likening him to my daughters. Sure, they loved to come home and watch TV and do what kids do. But when Rebecca was competing, she'd wrap the blisters on her toes to be able to go out and dance *en pointe*. Jessica would be on the ice the morning after she tumbled during a jump and had to get stitches, attempting the very same move that caused her to fall the day before. I resolved to find a new trainer.

That fall, the elections for the Michigan chapter of the Horsemen's Benevolent & Protective Association were going to be held. That meant that not only did I have to keep going to the track to find someone to train Baby, I also needed to continue to have a presence there so I would get elected. Both owners and trainers voted, and while I had enhanced my standing among owners with my election to the Michigan TOBA board, I now needed to keep my face in front of the trainers whose trust and friendship I had spent so much time cultivating.

In the meantime, I wondered, how was I going to secure a serious trainer who had a good track record but who would be kind to my horse, understand that he was a pet; would not be so big that he had dozens of horses to train and not pay close enough attention to Baby, yet at the same time not be a Coburn or Belker, with just a few horses; and, at least as important, would not mind that I was going to be there every single day, talking to the vet, coming to the stall, feeling Baby's legs for heat or swelling, watching at the rail? For Baby's safety, I also found it more imperative than ever to find a trainer who would be able to keep him at the front of the pack.

One day, while I was idling at the rail watching morning training, a big van, like one you'd see at a furniture dealer's, drove onto the backstretch. I had not remembered seeing a vehicle like that at the track before. When I asked someone about it, I was told the truck was sent by a company called Darling International.

"What's that?" I asked.

"Well, they're going to pick up horses," the guy standing next to me said.

"Pick up horses?" I replied. "But that's not a horse van."

"No," I was told. They're going to the back of the track to pick up horses that have broken down—broken a leg or torn a ligament or fractured a bone—suffered an injury so bad that they needed to be put down.

I had heard the term "breakdown," but I always thought it meant a horse had overdone it and needed to rest. I didn't know it meant that there had been a catastrophic event, and that if it didn't cause death, it caused the need to euthanize a horse to put it out of unfixable pain.

I had not seen breakdowns, or at least I did not remember seeing them. It was one of those tricks the mind plays. John worked for Michigan Bell, but before he joined the company, I never saw a Michigan Bell truck. After, every tenth vehicle in my field of vision was a Michigan Bell truck. Now, breakdowns were going to go from some place outside the periphery of my vision to the center.

"Where on the back of the track are they taken?" I wanted to know.

"On those tons of acres back there. When they get enough dead horses, they call Darling International to pick them up and send them to a renderer."

I knew from the way the guy was talking that this was not about picking up two or three horses, certainly not with that giant rig.

No way was Baby going to end up on those acres of death, I said to myself, all the more determined to find a trainer who could keep him at the front of the pack. I knew Baby was going to remain sound because I took such special care of him, but I started getting scared that someone else's horse was going to break down in front of mine and that Baby would trip over it and go tumbling.

When a Thoroughbred gallops, he is going as fast as thirty-five miles an hour, sometimes thirty-eight. His heart is pumping at its limit. His tendons and ligaments are strained to their utmost. Bones might break. If he stops right in the middle of a race, it can create an impact as significant as that of a car wreck on a main road.

Learning about breakdowns wasn't the only unsettling education I received that season. One day in the track kitchen, someone casually asked, "Did you hear what happened at the track yesterday?"

"What?" I said.

"Word got up to the stewards that one of the jockeys had a buzzer."

"What's a buzzer?" I questioned.

"The jockey keeps it in his hand, and when they come out of the gate, he gives the horse an electric shock with it to goad it on. He also might use it in the middle of the race."

"They can use those?" I wondered aloud, surprised.

"No, of course not," I was told. "They're completely illegal. A jockey can be suspended for using one. But to try to stop it without punishment or embarrassment, the stewards told the gate crew to say to all the jockeys that they knew one of them had it, and that if it was left in the dirt inside the gate, before the race started, no action would be taken."

"What happened?" I asked.

"The bell went off, the horses left the gate, and the gate crew went looking in all eight gate sections for a dropped buzzer. They found one in each loading section."

I was astonished, but as with so much else, I let it go. I was too far in. And I felt my Baby was in a bubble, as would be Scarlett. I would keep looking after them; I would choose a trainer who wouldn't physically abuse them. Others, too, knew nothing was going to happen to any horse of Jo Anne's. She was too much on top of things, they'd say.

To choose a trainer judiciously rather than just by a feeling or by circumstance, I decided to do a survey of everybody I could talk to on the backstretch except trainers, who had a vested interest and often said to me that they'd like to train Baby. I would speak to jockeys, jockey's agents, the veterinarians, exercise riders, and maybe some grooms. Whatever name came up most often would be the person I'd interview.

I said the same thing to everyone I pulled aside. "I need some help. I want your opinion, and it's going to stay between you and me." Insuring privacy was important so no one would worry that they were hurting their relationship with a particular trainer if they named another trainer.

"You know I have a Reel On Reel horse," I continued with each person I interviewed. "And you know that I can't pick a trainer for shit. I need your advice," and then I'd list the attributes of the trainer I sought, throwing in that I also had a granddaughter of Secretariat who would be coming to the track the next year.

The name that came up most often was that of a trainer with whom I was not familiar, close community as the track was. It was a woman, Pam Thibodeau, who, it turned out, kept to herself. She wasn't one of the ones who hung out in the kitchen. She didn't become involved in track gossip. She didn't chitchat at the rail.

She had about ten horses in training, not too many, not too few. I went over to the shedrow in which she kept them, and it was immaculate— stall doors painted with a checkerboard pattern, all the floors raked well.

Pam had actually been an exercise rider in the

past, which I saw as a huge advantage over a trainer who had never galloped a horse around the track. She knew firsthand what it meant to feel how much horse a Thoroughbred had left in him after a run. She could watch an exercise rider and know whether he was following her instructions properly. Having ridden, she also had more knowledge than other trainers of the different types of bits, of subtleties in the way the reins were held—all of which meant that she knew about communication between the rider and the horse that went beyond voice commands.

I went over and introduced myself. Pam was blonde, petite, maybe eight years younger than I was, in her late thirties. Like me, she dressed very neatly, had her nails done and makeup on. I told her our situation—that we had a Reel On Reel gelding who had raced eleven times but never won and would be turning four next year—and that she had been recommended. When I said the part about Baby's never having won a race, she kind of tilted her head, waiting for an explanation. "Well," I explained, "he's still a maiden"—the term for a horse who has yet to win his first race—"because I didn't know how to pick a trainer. The first didn't have enough experience, and the second was Julian Belker."

I didn't have to say anything more on that score.

"Is there anything wrong with him?" Pam asked.

"Not other than that he needs to gain weight

because he wasn't fed properly. He's sound." I also had to tell her that Baby had developed a habit of not wanting to come out of the gate. He'd linger after the bell went off. It hadn't happened with Coburn, but it started, and became entrenched, with Belker.

Pam didn't like that he was what she called "gate sour," but she didn't rule him out because of that. She just knew it would require some retraining.

Then I told her about Scarlett, and she said that before she committed, she wanted to come to the house with her assistant trainer and see the horses. Her assistant was Jerry Bennett. Jerry's father, Gerald, was pretty much the leading trainer at the track, with a huge stable of some forty to sixty horses in training. His shedrow was right across from Pam's.

When Pam and Jerry visited the house, she noticed the osselet right away, and I assured her it was "cold." She didn't seem overly excited, like other trainers who wanted to pick up an extra horse. Instead, it was really she who was interviewing me, not drooling over the extra money she might make. She was more concerned about her win percentage. She wanted to take on horses who represented quality because their wins would reflect on her.

I liked that Pam had a lot of questions, that she wasn't hungry for a couple of extra horses, and I liked that while she seemed a little hesitant when I told her I'd be at the track everyday, it wasn't a showstopper for her.

Baby and Scarlett, for their parts, turned their heads to whoever was speaking, literally listening to the conversation. They were relaxed, but clearly showing interest with their ears pricked forward. They seemed to know that Pam and Jerry were there for a purpose, and that the purpose was them and decisions were being made.

"Here's the deal," Pam said, finally. "Racing is going to open at the track in March next year. That means the horses have to start training in January. How are you supposed to get a horse fit *here* in the winter so it can run in March? There's three days in a row of snow and ice, they can't get out on the track, they backslide. What we do is go down to Florida after the first of the year—Ocala, about an hour north of Orlando. We get the horses conditioned down there in beautiful weather, and just before they're ready to race here, we ship them back up. It gives them an edge. So if you want us to train your horses, they'll have to come to Florida."

After talking it over with John, who also met Pam and liked her, I said yes. It was scary, because now Baby—and Scarlett, who would be turning three—wouldn't be within driving distance. I'd have to check in by phone. It made me feel a little paranoid, but Pam told me the place was terrific, with training in the morning and pasture turnout for the rest of the day, where the Thoroughbreds could frolic and just be horses.

It was still only mid-fall at that point, so we were months away from shipping off Baby and Scarlett. In the meantime, I kept seeing other things at the track that took some of the shine off the "Sport of Kings." One day at the rail, somebody was talking about a trainer who got suspended because he got caught with an overage of drugs; one of his horses tested over the allowed threshold level.

"What's going to happen?" I asked. "He has at least forty horses that he trains. Does that mean they don't get to run?"

Everybody started laughing. "Look, he's right there," one of the guys said to me. And there he was, on the other side of the chain link fence separating the track from the parking area. His assistant trainer kept running back and forth to get instructions about what to tell the exercise riders to do.

In other words, suspension meant the trainer was not allowed on the grounds for a certain period of time, but it was business as usual. If cell phones had been in use by that point, the assistant wouldn't even have had to keep going back over to the fence.

I was glad to find out around that time that I had, in fact, been elected to the HBPA board. I'd be able to look into complaints better, learn more, improve things. I took office immediately after the election was over. The president of the board chose me to be chair of the communications committee; chair of the PAC, or political action committee; and a member of the purse committee, which looks at how the purses are structured for each race. I was going to be able to effect change from within.

While things were moving along on the ground, emotionally it was a difficult time. Before, feeding Baby when he first came home, riding him in the quiet, I was able to be a horse. That is, I allowed myself to live in the moment, which horses do naturally. They don't anticipate the future or mull over the past. Like someone in a deep meditative state, they have only "now," and so did I, and I relished its centeredness. But once Pam was chosen, I was anticipating again, anxious about time. I knew I'd have to see Baby and Scarlett go off.

The weeks of fall went by until Thanksgiving came and, with it, growing apprehension. I was glad to be able to excuse myself from a dinner table filled with twenty people that day and put on my barn clothes so I could check on the horses. I have always appreciated that about having horses. No matter how many people you're entertaining, you get to have that time away from them and just be with your animals and in that way reinvigorate yourself. You plan your day around going to the stalls, in fact, and no one can take that from you because, after all, you have to take care of them, of Baby, of Scarlett, of the others. But I was ticking off the last days of November on a calendar, and Baby and Scarlett's departure was now only six weeks away.

Throughout the Christmas season, their leaving made me more and more nervous. I couldn't just lay my face on Baby's shoulder and breathe into his body, recognize him by his scent and push all else from my thoughts, like I could in late summer and early fall. Whereas before that left me calm, renewed, like the way a special scented candle might for a non-horse person, now it left me longing for him before he was even gone.

And Scarlett, who was the whole reason all of this started—she had been with me in the backyard for the better part of three years. How was I going to let her go? I wouldn't be able to check on either one's eating or on the quality of their hay.

Then Christmas did come and go, and I filled the holiday stockings I had hung not just on Baby and Scarlett's stall doors but also on Pat's, Beauty's, and Pumpkin's—with special treats like apples and carrots, and, just this once, sugar cubes. After all, it was a big moment for everyone. The herd was going to be separated in a new way, and we all had to say our good-byes. Then New

Year's arrived, and apprehension evolved into a kind of dull, ever-present dread until finally, on January 5th, 1995, the huge trailer that would take Baby and Scarlett away came down our little road. It was so enormous it could not turn around in our driveway, so the driver had to back down our entire road from the main street.

I watched as Baby and Scarlett stepped inside for a two-day ride to Florida. Both loaded easily, unlike many other Thoroughbreds, with whom you have to fight for an hour before they walk on, and I was glad. Horses who have a reputation for being rank, or hard to handle, get treated more roughly. They don't receive the same kindnesses.

I gave them both a last kiss, worried that I wouldn't be able to check their legs for heat or swelling, that I couldn't assess ahead of time the conditions they'd be living in. I had just had two pretty bad years with poor trainers, and now my horses were going to a place I had never seen with someone I barely knew.

Still, I reminded myself that I did have a good feeling about Pam, and that she came recommended. Picking her didn't feel like such a crapshoot. I was relieved to some degree, too, about the trailer. It was an air-ride, specially made for animals to give them a smooth trip during which their slender legs wouldn't have to feel the constant rumble of vibrations and thereby make it difficult for them to keep their balance. And it was brand new. The man who drove the rig was very warm, friendly even, and had asked about Baby and Scarlett's personalities, saying he put them in the spot that would give them the most comfortable ride. With that, my never-ending roller-coaster ride of emotions took another turn and dip, a bit slower and easier than I had expected. Off the horses went, with me watching the huge trailer grow smaller and smaller until it was out of sight.

I had made a decision a few weeks earlier that I would check out the Florida facility for myself before training got underway in earnest and pull Baby and Scarlett out of there if I did not like what I found. So two days later I flew down, and I was overjoyed to see the place. It was immaculate, with a well-maintained track and hardly anyone there. It was as if Baby and Scarlett had been enrolled in private school. They were turned out when I arrived, and when I clapped, the two of them came running, first breathing into my nose over the fence, then letting me breathe into theirs. Baby out-jostled Scarlett to be nearer to me, pushing her out of the way with his shoulder. "No, she's *my* mother."

Of course I had treats with me that I had bought at a farm stand on the way from the airport. It helped me immensely that my coming so soon might help them to think I was only thirteen minutes away from them by car, as if they were no farther than the Detroit Race Course.

Baby (left) and Scarlett came running as soon as I clapped.

Both Pam and Jerry showed me around without any defensiveness, and Jerry said the two horses had traveled very well. "We saw 'Surpriser' come down the ramp," he told me, "and I thought, Boy, he's lookin' *good*. Then Scarlett came down—"

"I grabbed Jerry's arm," Pam said, interrupting him, "and told him, 'Jerry, there's our Sire Stakes horse.'"

The Sire Stakes is the most important race in Michigan, with the largest purse—$200,000.

"She is just incredibly put together," Pam went on. "She is a champion. You can see it in the way she walks, the way she moves. He's a good horse, but she's a classic distance horse. That's her conformation."

I was caught off guard. I don't know that I loved Scarlett any less than Baby, but with Baby the bond was so strong. There was just something between us—he truly acted like my little boy, my rough-and-tumble boy with his shirttails untucked—so I was surprised to see anybody passing him by to lavish more attention on another horse.

"We're going to keep the two of them in their own pasture for now," Pam said, pointing to a spot close by. The pasture was beautiful and even had automatic waterers. A horse could push on a lever when it was thirsty, and the water would come out into a big dish. That way, the water was always fresh. No standing water in dirty troughs.

The upkeep in the shedrows was immaculate, too. And the stalls themselves were huge, and very deeply bedded.

During the short time I was there, I could tell Baby and Scarlett were relaxed—and proud to show me what they could do. They were anxious to get out on the track. There was no dragging them.

Outside of practice times, I lavished as much attention on them as possible, even picking grass for them. They could chew grass of their own choosing in the pasture, but I would pull up grass right outside the fence, and they would eat it from my hands. They preferred it that way, standing there and waiting for me to pick more handfuls when they could have gone anywhere they wanted and eaten as much as they felt like.

I loved watching them get their baths, proud of

them that they stood so quietly, and happy for them that they would stretch their heads forward just so as the water sprayed onto them in the warm Florida sun—"Ahhh."

I flew home two days later, hugging Baby and Scarlett in their stalls before leaving and exchanging breaths with them through our noses, comfortable that they were in good hands. Letting go with Scarlett wasn't as hard as it had been with Baby, and not only because of my bond with him. It was like sending my second child off to school. I was more familiar. Also, they had each other. And Scarlett wasn't going to get green osselets or bucked shins, or any other problems of two-year-olds. She was closer to three now than two.

The plan was to stay in touch with Pam by phone, but it was actually she who called first, about four or five days after I arrived home. I hadn't wanted to appear overly intrusive.

"I've got to talk to you about these horses," she said.

Uh-oh, I thought. Maybe she was going to tell me it wasn't worth pursuing with Baby. He had run eleven races, and nothing. And maybe Scarlett was going to be a pretty show horse rather than a racehorse.

"Are you sure Reel Surprise never won a race?" Pam continued.

"Most definitely," I answered. "I can guarantee

you that I have never stood in the winner's circle with that horse."

"Well, this horse can run," she responded. "Now tell, me, what is this problem with the gate?"

"He's reluctant," I said. "They'd always announce it over the loudspeaker: 'Reel Surprise is reluctant to load.' It wasn't that he was nervous," I explained. "One of the jockeys had even told me that once he goes inside, he completely relaxes. Sometimes he even falls asleep. But he breaks from the gate really slowly, spotting the other horses ten to fifteen lengths before he takes off."

"Okay," Pam said after I finished my explanation, "but I have to tell you, when Jerry gallops him, he says, 'there's a lot of horse there.'"

"I'm glad to hear it," I responded.

"Now I want to talk to you about our star," Pam said, referring to Scarlett. "You told me this horse is not broke to ride, right?"

That was correct. But Pam then explained that Jerry just basically got on her after leaning over her back a couple of times, and they rode together. She had no problem with a man on her, no problem with the saddle. Jerry just took her to the track, and she galloped beautifully.

It was, no exaggeration, astounding. It usually takes a couple of weeks to break a Thoroughbred. The process starts out in the horse's stall, with the rider simply laying his chest and arms over her back and someone at the horse's head watching for a reaction—holding a lead line in case the horse tries to buck the rider off and inadvertently steps on him. All the while, the rider is talking soothingly, trying to inch forward a little further without having the horse "erupt." The goal is to eventually go from leaning over the horse to hanging over it with the rider's feet off the ground. From there, the aim is for the rider to be able to sit on the horse's back, first without a saddle, then with one. It's all two steps forward, one step backward, each short session infused with a lot of encouragement in a soft voice and ending on a positive note, just like with dog training, until the day the rider can actually ride the horse out to the track.

"If you hadn't told me," Pam said, "I would have thought Scarlett had been in training before. She's not a typical Thoroughbred—not the least bit flighty or nervous, just interested. She is so smart, we can't get over it.

"*Both* horses will do anything Jerry asks them to do," she continued. "They stand quietly while being hosed for their baths. They listen. They are just perfect to work with.

"I don't usually tell people too much about what I expect from a horse," Pam said, "because you never really know, certainly not after just a few days. But I have to tell you, Jerry is very high on Scarlett. Not just him. When she came off that trailer, there were other people waiting around for their own horses, and you could tell, they were looking at her. And now she's showing us that she is that horse."

I could feel my heart swell. I was bursting.

A month later, in the middle of February, John and I went down to check things out for ourselves. Even though the place was beautiful, and even though Pam said to call anytime and showed no reluctance to talk with me, we figured that in a month's time, things could change quickly. Once they really start training in earnest, they burn a lot more calories. Maybe Baby would lose weight again. And Scarlett was brand new to galloping. Maybe they were pushing her toward an injury.

But both horses looked fantastic. Each was gleaming. They were standing side by side in the pasture when I first came upon them, just like at home, grazing. I was so glad they had each other.

Because it had been a while, when I clapped this time, at first they looked up and stood still for a moment. Then, when it clicked, they came at a gallop to greet us. Baby beat Scarlett to the fence, but since John was with me, they both could get attention at the same time.

On our first day there, Jerry said, "I just have to show you about your horse. I don't know what the problem was with Surpriser at the gate. But he has no problem coming out of it. He breaks sharply." And indeed Baby did.

"He's really on the muscle," Jerry said. "He *wants* to run."

Then Jerry explained about Scarlett. He said it can take a long time for a horse to feel familiar with the gate. "But I gotta tell you," he went on, "she went through the whole process in a day. Nothing fazes her. Watch this!" he said, leading Scarlett through the gate. "She's just looking around, all relaxed. That's the sign of a class horse."

It was clear that Scarlett was Jerry's favorite. He didn't just ride her. He sweet talked her, patted her on the neck. His grin with her was ear to ear. "Did you see that?" he would ask excitedly when he showed me something else she could do.

I truly felt like a proud mom, and proud of myself for working so carefully with Baby and Scarlett at home—teaching them not to be afraid of things, treating them like the intelligent creatures they were, even tying beach towels around them within weeks of birth so they would have some memory of that feel, that pressure around their middles, when it came time to put on a saddle.

I felt that we had found the right trainers, too. My making friends at the track had paid off in the most important way.

John and I returned home after five days in Florida, brimming with excitement. I was only sorry that Baby had had to be the guinea pig, bearing the brunt of my mistakes in choosing the two previous trainers. Scarlett was going to get the benefit of all the mistakes I had made with him.

The two horses arrived home a month later, in the middle of March. While we waited with Pam for the trailer to arrive, she told me she had picked out a race for Baby on the twenty-sixth. It was a $5,000 claiming race. "Pam," I said, "we can't risk losing our horse."

In Thoroughbred racing, there are basically three types of races: stakes races, allowance races, and claiming races. The fastest horses run in stakes races, and those races are graded—levels I, II, and III, with I being the best. The races people see on television are level I stakes races. After stakes races come allowance races, also meant for very fast runners. At the bottom are claiming races. If a horse is entered into a claiming race, it means someone can claim him for the price set, so that as soon as the race starts, the horse belongs to the new owner. The point is to keep racing fair. An owner is not going to enter a stakes horse or an allowance-worthy horse into a low-level claiming race for an easy win because it would mean the risk of losing him to someone who claimed him.

Baby had been in $50,000 claiming races, in which the quality of the horses overlapped with allowance level horses. He had even been in a couple of $10,000 claiming races, which I wasn't too worried about because at the Detroit Race Course, people didn't have that kind of money to shell out. But $5,000—that was getting into territory that could possibly take Baby away from me.

"We have to talk this out," Pam said in reply to my alarm. "You need to understand something. The point is to place your horse where it can win. Because that's what racing is all about. If you want to sit in the stands and enter your horse and watch it come in last or in the middle of the pack, don't pay me. Take your horse out of racing."

Then she said, "Scarlett's not going to start there. But nobody knows anything about Scarlett. Everybody already knows this horse has raced eleven times—three times his first season and eight times his second—and has not won once. No one is going to claim him in the hope that he can deliver for them when he hasn't yet delivered at all. The Detroit Race Course rarely has horses claimed, anyway. Some other tracks, there's a lot of claiming that goes on. But not here.

"The next thing you need to consider," Pam said, "is your horse and what's best for him. His first race of the year should feel like a morning romp to him. It should take nothing out of him physically. We'll move him up—he's not going to stay there—but let him have this easy, relaxing ride that's going to take nothing out of him.

"I have never told an owner that they're going to

win a race," Pam continued. "But I'm telling you, this horse is probably going to win this race, and it's going to be easy for him."

I let Pam convince me and calmed down, but it looked like it might be a moot point.

The trailer arrived at the track late, well after dark, and as soon as the driver opened it and Pam saw where Baby and Scarlett had been standing, she became angry. I could hear her murmur to Jerry, "Let's get them *out* of there." They were positioned very close to a half dozen other horses, with their heads tied in such a way that they could barely move them. That significantly increased their risk of catching an infection from any of the others.

Sure enough, both had runny noses and had to be put on antibiotics. Pam was livid. Baby had been fit and ready to go, and here he was coughing and dripping with mucus. He felt so bad he wouldn't even eat. He was completely off his feed.

"He might not be racing on the twenty-sixth, like we planned," Pam said. "We'll just have to see how they do."

A week later, Scarlett's infection had worsened—she was coughing, dripping, and now had a gutteral pouch infection in addition to her respiratory infection, and it needed to be flushed out. But Baby, he was okay. He had responded to the antibiotics almost immediately. Maybe he had built up more immunity because he had been around other horses before.

I worried over whether I should bring Scarlett home, but by that point Pam felt responsible for her. Also, my farm vet said Scarlett would get better treatment at the track because track vets flush out gutteral pouch infections all the time, whereas he did it only rarely. His was a general practice.

As for Baby, Pam got top jockey Terry Houghton to ride him—a great sign. But the handicappers knew nothing other than that Baby was undergoing yet another big drop in class—from $10,000 claiming to $5,000. His odds to win were placed at twelve to one.

By the time we had gotten from the stall to the track, however, things had changed. A groom came toward me and said, "Ma'am, they made your horse the favorite."

I figured he just didn't know who our horse was. "Our horse is Reel Surprise," I told him. "He's not the favorite."

"No, ma'am, they made your horse the favorite," he repeated.

I went a little further and passed a security guard, who said to me, "Hey, bet the ninth horse in the sixth race. It's going to win."

That was Baby. "Who told you that?" I asked.

"My boss."

What had happened was that so many people at

the Florida training facility sent up money to be bet on Baby after seeing him run down there that his odds of winning went way up. Devices at the track called pari-mutuel machines automatically change the odds depending on how much is bet on a particular horse, up until the bell goes off.

Had John and I been bettors, we would have been angry that word had gotten out, because originally, for every dollar we bet, we would have gotten twelve back if Baby won. Now it was much less on the dollar, closer to one to one. But we never bet more than twenty dollars, so we didn't care. We were just so excited about Baby's chances.

Finally, there we were sitting in the stands after I shook hands with the jockey and murmured to Baby, waiting for the race to begin. There was no announcement over the loudspeaker that "Reel Surprise is reluctant to load." Then *bam,* out they came, and Baby led from that first second, winning by five full lengths.

Talk about screaming and jumping up and down. I cannot adequately describe the feeling I had right then, the feeling of having a foal born into your arms, breathing into his nose to try to help him live, then four years later, watching him come out first, never falter, and fly across the finish line. The win picture was incredible. Baby was so far ahead there was not another horse in the frame. He won $1,920—not significant money but everything to us at that moment.

If I was hooked before, even with the sinister goings-on that I had seen at the track, I was addicted now. I didn't wear a big hat, but all the glamour of racing, of the Sport of Kings—it was something I was now truly part of. It felt like a drug that at first gave a buzz but had now fully kicked in. It was a sensation, more than a feeling. It was as if I had been lifted off the ground.

CHAPTER SEVEN

We went rushing down to the winner's circle—a huge semicircle area between the track and the grandstand, decorated with flowers and surrounded by low hedges. You can see me beaming in a photo taken with Baby, thumb up, while Baby, jockey astride him, looks right at me.

He seemed pleased with himself, pumped. Normally, Thoroughbreds are completely spent after a race. They make a big, loopy turn and kind of jog slowly back, although some horses are so exhausted, they can't even jog and have to lumber along. You can see their sides heaving. But not Baby. He projected an attitude of, "Does anybody want to go again?" He wasn't even breathing hard.

I was so proud of him. He had done what we both knew all along he could do. He was showing me—you do your part by making the right decisions on my behalf, and I'll do mine. We're a team. I knew I'd hold his win picture from that race dearest to me. There'd be a lot more wins to come, but this was the first we accomplished together.

There were more than twenty people with us—our daughters, their friends, our own friends and relatives—and John and I told them all to go on to Steak 'N Ale, where we'd be treating them to a

Baby's win photo. Pam is between me and the groom, and John is to my left. I couldn't have been more excited.

victory dinner, and start without us. I wanted to spend as much time with Baby as I could.

Pam and I rode back to Baby's stall in her golf cart, and he was doing great, completely unstressed and with a lot of race still in him. There was no heat or swelling, either. It was exactly as Pam had promised—a walk in the park for Baby. I felt justified in having him there, completely confident that I was doing the right thing.

It was hard to tear myself away from him. I kept rubbing his mane and breathing into his nose. He remained alert the whole time, aware of all the comings and goings in his shedrow, where he had been moved from the dark barn annex once we had switched from Belker to Pam.

It was all so different from the year before, when

he had been losing too much weight. I had seen him drooping with exhaustion after finishing races the previous season, not even wanting to pick up his head. This race, by contrast, had been so easy for him that the jockey did not even use the whip in the final stretch run. Baby won by running at the speed that felt comfortable.

Finally, we went to join everybody else for drinks and dinner. But after they all went home, we went back to Baby's shedrow to see him one more time, even though the restaurant was closer to home than to the track. I had to say good night and tell him again how proud I was. After all, it was his effort we had been celebrating.

He was totally relaxed when we arrived, having had his bath and ready to settle in for the night. "Oh, hi, I didn't expect to see you again today," his eyes said. His nose went right back to his hay. "Oh, a little extra scratching from Mom— great!"

"I can't wait to show you the win picture," I whispered to him, hugging and kissing him until we finally left for the night. I had to smile to myself on the way out; the following morning, Frank the Greek would be bringing doughnuts to Baby's stall.

Baby's next race was scheduled for April 7th. Now it was no longer a maiden race. It was going to be a nonwinner of two—all the horses would have already won their first race and were now going for their second win. That meant it would be more of a challenge.

I wasn't worried. At the top of his game, Baby now had a cocky confidence about him, an aggressiveness, which was a good thing, because to race well, a horse can't be timid. He has to feel himself at the top of the pecking order so he won't be shy to overtake another horse on the track. Horses recognize body language; in a herd, they know who eats first, who drinks first. In the artificial herd a race creates, a horse has to feel okay about going in front of another, about splitting two horses and running through the middle of them. He has to not give a damn—the jockey wants me to go, we're going.

Baby had never been a shrinking violet—there was always something pushy, even bullish, about him. He was almost the dominant horse in our small herd at home, even though he was one of the youngest. But now he had no kindness for horses at the track other than Scarlett, to whom he always gave a nod when he walked by. He would stand off to the side in his stall where he couldn't be easily seen, and then, when someone would come by walking a horse, he would charge toward the stall door. People he was fine with, always, but if they were leading a horse, they now made a wide berth around his stall.

It wasn't just his great physical shape that made Baby so aggressive. Pam had him on a medicine called Equipoise. She said it kept a horse on his toes, kept him wanting to compete, and gave back some of the fire that's lost when a horse is gelded. I didn't know it was an anabolic steroid, and even if I did, I don't know that it would have registered. This was well before baseball players began getting caught with anabolic steroids in their systems, before the public knew anything about their effects. Everybody at the track gave them to their horses. But in retrospect, it explains why Baby was so feisty with other horses that Pam had to restrain him from attacking them.

I would see her hold him back rather frequently, as I would go with her when she hot-walked Baby after training. We had developed a comfort level with each other. She saw that I wasn't just this crazy person who was always kissing my horse but that I also knew a lot about horses, their physiology and temperament.

One day, after we had grown more friendly and were in her shedrow taking care of Baby and Scarlett, a man came by with a clipboard. "Who do we have, Pam?" he said, and she named Baby's stall. He looked in, made a quick notation, and said, "Okay, see you."

"Who was that?" I asked.

"That's the Racing Commission vet," Pam told me. I knew he was employed by the state of Michigan and that his purpose was to make sure the horses were sound and that there was integrity and fairness in racing. I had read it in a guide-book.

"What does he want?" I said.

"Oh, he was doing the prerace lameness exam," Pam replied. I knew what a lameness exam was. We had had plenty done at home. The vet flexes various joints on the horse's legs. He makes the horse go from a standstill to a jog. He feels the horse's legs for swelling, heat, or pain.

"But he didn't do anything," I replied.

"Yeah, how 'bout that," Pam said.

"But shouldn't he do something?" I pressed.

"Well, you saw what he did," Pam answered. Which was nothing. He hadn't even flipped Baby's lip and looked at his tattoo. The tattoo number, a Thoroughbred's Jockey Club registration number, assures that the horse racing is the horse thought to be racing. For all the veterinarian knew, he wasn't even checking off his clipboard for Baby.

It was at that moment that it clicked for me that horses were out there running lame even though it was the responsibility of someone hired by the state, someone whose salary was paid by taxes, to keep lame horses off the track—not only for their safety and that of the jockeys riding them but also to insure that bettors were wagering on an even playing field. If some horses were lame and some were not, it meant people were wagering on races that were in essence fixed, even if unintentionally. It could not be a fair wager if some horses were running on unsound joints, tendons, and bones but nobody knew which horses were affected and which were not.

I was very glad at that moment that Pam was not the kind of trainer who wanted a horse to save himself for the end of a race, to be forced by the jockey to hang back. If a horse liked to come out in front from the start, which was Baby's style, that was fine with her. It meant Baby wouldn't trip over a lame horse who broke down in the middle of a race while he was going thirty-five miles an hour just behind it.

I also liked that Pam had advised me to take Baby home once he ran through all his conditions— nonwinner of two, nonwinner of three, and nonwinner of four. Just three more, in other words. "It gets too hard for a horse after that," Pam advised. "The way to make money in racing and keep your horse sound is to run him through his conditions and then retire him."

I appreciated that Pam wasn't money hungry, that she wasn't interested in running a horse to death. I appreciated her knowledge, too. I enjoyed discussing with her the fact that there were four main entities in racing in the state of Michigan, all with potentially competing interests: the breeders, who wanted more of the money wagered set aside for them should a horse they bred win a race; the horse owners and trainers, who wanted purse money for themselves as well as a track maintained in top condition; the State Racing Commission, which wanted to run as many races with as many horses as possible, because it was paid a percentage of the money people wagered; and the owners of the track, who wanted as much money as they could get off the top of each wager while spending the least amount of money possible on maintaining the barn area and race track itself.

April 7th, the date of Baby's second race, came quickly. It, too, was a claiming race, but for $10,000 instead of $5,000. Baby was moving back up in the ranks. Unfortunately, jockey Terry Houghton was riding a different horse that day, but our hopes still remained high.

Baby came in second, however, beaten by only a nose. Having now had the taste of winning, I felt terribly disappointed, maybe more than at the end of any other race Baby had run. It was a race he should have won, and had Terry been available, we all believed, he would have. Terry had what it took to bring out the best in him.

Baby's third race of '95, scheduled for May 5th, was to be an allowance race—a huge move up from the relatively cheap claiming races he had been running. He had a full month for Pam and Jerry to get more training into him, and they felt he was ready for the next class. That kept my hopes high. When your horse is slated for an

So close, but not close enough. Baby lost his second race of 1995 by no more than a nose.

allowance race, he's in top company. Few horses ever reach that level.

The bell rang, and Baby flew out of the gate, just as we all wanted. But then a horse started coming between him and the rail. Baby moved over and, in his forceful, aggressive fashion, bumped it, throwing the other horse off stride. The horse came up on Baby again, once more attempting to pass, and he repeated the action.

"We're in trouble," Jerry remarked. Bumping was not allowed.

But Baby won, and Jerry, along with the rest of us, rejoiced, although he did slip in soberly, "I hope there's not an inquiry, because I think we could have a problem."

As we walked toward the winner's circle, people in the stands were yelling horrible epithets: "You cheaters! Get that nag out of there! You won't be in there very long." It was awful. Imagine an adult calling your child names. Of course, they simply wanted the horse on whom they had bet money to win instead of Baby. But if I could have picked out whoever called Baby a nag, I would have run into the stands to engage them—in what way I don't know. I was so angry that someone would refer to him that way.

Then the "Inquiry" sign came up and Jerry said, "Yup, we're in trouble."

It was humiliating to have to leave the winner's circle in front of the huge crowd. We went inside to watch the replay, a bird's-eye view from above, and if the first bump Baby gave the other horse wasn't bad enough, in the second, he really rammed his competition. I felt I had a sense of what he had been thinking, and although I had a sinking feeling we were going to be disqualified, I couldn't help but let out a laugh. The move was vintage Baby, who couldn't have cared less about the rules. "What do you think you're doing?" he must have been saying to the other horse. "Hey, if you missed it the first time, here it is again. I'm *winning* this race. Didn't you get the message?"

"That's it," Jerry said upon seeing the second bump. "We lost it." Baby then *was* officially disqualified, dropping from first place to fourth in a penalty.

Scarlett, in the meantime, wasn't running any

races at all. She was still having constant problems with her cold, going off antibiotics as soon as she seemed better but then, three days back into training, dripping with copious mucus from her nose again and back on antibiotics, running another fever. Pam, at a loss, suggested I take her home and have my farm vet check her out, which at that point I was more than glad to do. In a stall, a horse can only stand and look out. But the best thing for a horse when she has a cold is to have her head down grazing. That lets the mucus drain rather than keep re-collecting in her respiratory tract.

We were out a lot of money—we had been paying Pam thirty-five dollars a day for months to condition Scarlett to win a race—but her health came first.

When it came time to load Scarlett into the trailer, Baby thought at first that it was going to be both of them. "Okay, where are we going?" But then he saw that it was just she who leaving, and I could see he was wondering why I was taking Scarlett away from him; his expression became questioning. Till that point in the season, he could always just look out of his stall and see her right next door.

They whinnied to each other as Scarlett's trailer drove away, and then Baby became quiet once it was out of sight. His resignation hung in the silence.

It turned out Scarlett had been on the wrong antibiotic all that time—a very expensive one prescribed by the track vet, who apparently had never taken a culture yet made a healthy profit from the costly medicine he sold us. Our vet at home did take a culture and in short order put Scarlett on a much cheaper antibiotic, identifying it as the one that would clear her up. She began improving right away. Poor Scarlett had gone suffering unnecessarily for months.

I was glad to have her home, my piece of Secretariat, my curio cabinet valuable, away from the stress of the track. I was glad for her to be able to relax and graze, to settle in and let the medication do what it needed to do. I was also happy to be the one dispensing it and watching the discharge lessen.

And Scarlett was glad to *be* home. I let her get close to Pat right away. I figured that Pat's immune system wasn't under stress—she wasn't being ridden or asked to do anything—and that even if she did become infected, we knew which antibiotic to give her and she'd get better right away. But Pat didn't get sick. She just got close to her daughter, and the two of them, along with Beauty and Pumpkin, enjoyed herding together.

In the meantime, feeling thrown by Baby's disqualification but still having great hopes for him, we waited eagerly for his next race, which was going to occur on May 29th. It, too, was an allowance race, and the newspaper picked Baby to win. Again, however, we didn't get Terry—his agent was obligated to put him on a horse named I'll Run for Terry—and Baby ended up coming in second by two lengths. The jockey allowed him to drift out a bit on the turn, losing ground.

On June 18th, Baby entered his fourth race of the season, which was his third allowance race for nonwinners of two. Despite the fact that he "placed" in his previous race rather than won, the *Daily Racing Form* still said he would come in first, as did the racing program, a glossy brochure sold to serious bettors. Then, too, June 18th was John's forty-ninth birthday, which we took as a sign. Baby would be giving John a wonderful gift.

How great this was going to be! Back in the middle of the Belker season, a reporter for the *Detroit Free Press*, in a play on Baby's racing name, wrote that it would be a "real surprise" if he won. It hurt to see it. Now here we were with two predictions in black and white that he would come out in front. "How do you like *that?*" I told the other reporter in my head.

But again he came in second, by just a half a length.

We were now five races into the season, feeling extremely frustrated. We were *so close*. And it was still the general feeling at the track that Baby was a horse who should be raced, a runner and a winner. The problem, time and again, seemed to be faulty communication by the jockeys. Baby was like a difficult bull, and other than Terry, jockeys just couldn't control him. He would run right up to the rear of the horse in front of him, his nose literally in its behind, before the jockey could pull him back and coax him to run around the horse rather than try to go through it. And pulling a horse up at racing speed and asking him to turn to the side a bit and then regain his top speed—horses just aren't able to do that. Even so, Baby would come within inches of a win; he was that good. But it wasn't quite enough. If only jockeys other than Terry could keep him out of traffic trouble.

I knew Baby could be dropped into a lower level race, if need be—a high-level claiming race rather than an allowance race. I didn't like the idea of it, but it did provide a potential solution.

The morning after that fifth race, however, Pam said, "we've got a problem. His tendon is swollen." The tendons, fibrous cords in a horse's legs, attach muscle to bone. Like rubber bands, they have to be able to stretch and then snap back with each step. But when there's swelling, a tendon doesn't work right.

"We can inject him and go on," Jerry said, "or you can take him home and rest him and let it heal."

I didn't know what injecting Baby meant, but it didn't sound like a good idea. "It would probably get worse if we keep going, right?" I asked the private track vet, Larry Wales, who was standing with us.

"Yes," Larry said. "But it isn't very bad. It's not even bowed out. Most people would inject and keep going, although taking him home is also an option."

I ordered an ultrasound and learned it was tendinitis. Larry explained that Baby had only about 30 percent damage there, with a little too much stretching having occurred and a concomitant loss of some necessary tautness. But I had already made the decision to bring Baby home. I wanted him to heal naturally, not have his pain masked with a drug, get worse, and then heal after the season. I would bring him back next year.

Pam supported my decision. Although Jerry would have kept racing Baby, she was clear that I saw Baby as a pet, not an investment. And she herself wasn't driven by money, trying to talk me out of doing what I needed to do.

Baby came home on June 23rd. Scarlett pranced a floating trot for him as he came down toward the barn from the trailer. "Look, I don't have a cold anymore," she was telling him, and he honked to let her know how pleased he was at the news. All of the horses were bonded, but these two bonded in a way of their own.

Our farm vet confirmed that Baby's injury had a good prognosis without any major tearing or core lesions, and it felt wonderful to have him safe and sound in our backyard again, wonderful to know that he'd be there through summer and fall, then at Christmas and during the winter, rolling in snow. I was happy, too, that he was together with Scarlett and the others. Competing with my drive to win was my drive to nurture him, to see him relaxed and enjoying the company of the other horses in sight of my kitchen window. It was as if I had two gears—"win" and "love." But they were not like the gears of a car. In a car, you can't be in "drive" and "reverse" at the same time, whereas to a certain degree I was pulled in opposite directions when it came to Baby. At the track, as much as my mind was on the race, a part of me did rue that he was missing the idyllic life he was entitled to at home. And when he was at home, while my heart would burst at his simply enjoying life as a horse, running around the pasture and grazing contentedly, I couldn't help but wonder about his prospects and told myself that was okay because he truly did seem happy on the race-course.

So although I was glad to see Baby and Scarlett standing head to tail so they could shoo the summer flies from each other's face, while they loved to stand next to each other like that and fall into a kind of doze together, I knew the gears were shifting again. I had already started thinking that we were in an excellent position for next year. We had gone from coming in last in claiming races with Belker to almost winning allowance races. With the right jockey and no infections, we were going to see more wins. Scarlett would even be able to go back that summer if her health was deemed good enough.

We also were feeling good because just days before Baby arrived home we had received the news that Pat was in foal. Toward the end of May, we sent her to be bred to Baby's sire, Reel on Reel. Because Baby had won his first race and was losing others by very little, we felt we had a recipe for success and wanted another "bake." I suppose that at the end of the day, there was no doubt about it—our horses' wonderful life at home notwithstanding, we were caught up with racing fever. "Win" was a mighty powerful gear.

Some people had told me to wait till late January or February to breed Pat. Because all Thoroughbreds are given a universal birthday of January 1st, they said, it was important to have a foal born as early in the year as possible. A three-year-old racer born in January is going to have an advantage over a three-year-old born months later in the spring.

But the only way to get Pat into heat in the winter would have been to install a bright light in her stall in late fall or early winter to trick her body. Mares come into heat in the spring because of sunlight. It insures that when the foal is born the next spring, the grass will be green and lush with nutrients. Mother and foal will eat well, giving the newborn the best chance of starting life out healthy. I wanted Pat and her next foal to have that natural experience—the ability to eat rich grass and become strong before the cold weather set in.

It wasn't too many weeks after Pat came into foal and Baby came home that it was time for Scarlett to go back to the track. She had been recuperating for almost two months by then and was ready to start over with another sixty days of training so she could run some races in late summer and fall. But once she was back at the track, we learned she had a disease called azoturia, or tying-up syndrome. It's a condition, not all that rare, in which a horse's large muscles cramp horribly after exercise. In some cases it gets so bad the animal dies from it. Think of a bad charley horse, but instead of solely in the leg, it's in a horse's back, pelvic, and massive hind limb muscles.

I think it only started showing then because Pam had begun giving Scarlett Lasix to enhance her performance during timed works. One of the possible triggers of tying-up syndrome is an electrolyte imbalance, and Lasix affects electrolyte balance, too. Scarlett probably was always susceptible, but the drug pushed her over the edge.

Racing rules specify that a horse is supposed to

have Lasix only if she bleeds through the nose while running. But almost all the horses are given the drug. No one ever put a scope down Scarlett's throat to verify that she bled. I certainly never saw any blood come out of her nose.

We were able to keep her out of pain with muscle relaxants and analgesics, but clearing the tying-up syndrome was another story. We tried lots of treatments, none of which helped, and I was calling all over the country to see if anyone knew of a possible solution. Finally, a veterinarian at Cornell University, a Dr. Beth Valentine, said I had to take Scarlett off all forms of her usual carbohydrates and put her on alfalfa pellets with three cups of vegetable oil a day. She also advised me that a horse like Scarlett should never have a day off. She was always going to need to go out and do something so her muscle enzymes would metabolize properly.

To my amazement, not to mention the amazement of other vets on the case who had been more than skeptical, Dr. Valentine's instructions worked. Scarlett even ran three races in October and November. But she was still not completely herself—you could see she was a little stiff—and the best she did was to come in second in a race in November. That race, as opposed to the other two, was a full mile, so it was clear that she truly was a classic distance runner. But she was going to need more time to adjust to the new diet and come back to herself. The track would be closing for the season in a couple of weeks, and there were no more races for fillies, anyway. We decided to bring her home to regain her strength.

My time with Scarlett alone at the track had been somewhat different from my time there with just Baby. I visited her every single day, just as I did him. But she didn't whinny at the sound of my footsteps the way Baby did, although she did always pop her head out of her stall when I called out to her from the entrance to the shedrow. She never became aggressive as Baby did, either, although of course, Baby had been put on steroids.

Unlike Baby, Scarlett liked to snooze standing up rather than lying down all stretched out. And whereas Baby always wanted me to put my hands straight out in front of me, palms stretched and thumbs touching, so he could rub his head against them, Scarlett enjoyed pushing her face all the way down the side of my body, from my shoulder to my thigh, then pushing all the way back up, rubbing her entire forehead, down to her nostrils, as she went. She waited for me to brace myself by holding onto the bars of the stall door before she started moving because she knew that if I didn't hold on, she'd knock me over. Up and down, up and down she'd go, even rubbing her eyes against me in the process.

A lot of people don't let their horses do that. They say never to let a horse invade your space.

But I didn't mind the closeness. I liked it, actually. Scarlett never tried to bite or step on me. I was happy to be her rubbing post.

Along with letting her rub, I would brush her, or perhaps take a comb through her mane. Sometimes Pam, who always kept Scarlett's coat gleaming, would have the hair on her mane braided up with maize-colored yarn. Other times she'd braid her hair tightly overnight and then take out the braids the next morning, letting the curls adorn Scarlett's neck. She looked so pretty because she had a gorgeous neck, not too long or short. Everything about Scarlett, in fact, was conformationally perfect. If anyone ever commented, "This is what a Thoroughbred horse should look like," they'd be pointing at Scarlett.

The same couldn't be said of Baby. Stout, compact, and sturdy, with a shorter neck and a broader chest, he looked more ready for the football field than the track. But he felt bonded to me in a way Scarlett didn't. She, too, was born into my arms, and I was so thrilled to have in her my Secretariat souvenir. I loved to hug and kiss her. But for Baby, when I was there, the whole world went away. He'd rather be with me than another horse. Nothing could distract his attention. Scarlett was more independent, aloof. It wasn't that she didn't love me. She knew I'd swat a fly off her, do anything for her. But she didn't need me in the same way. If another horse walked by, she'd turn her attention away. I guess you could say Baby was a mama's boy, tough as he was, and that endeared him to me on a different level.

Shortly before we packed up Scarlett's belongings for the trip home, Stan Wyle came over to talk to me. I knew him in two ways: as the president of the HBPA board, representing Michigan's 1,200 owners and trainers, and as the owner of Reel on Reel, the sire of Baby and the foal with whom Pat was pregnant.

"Are you getting that respiratory drug from Canada?" he asked.

"No," I said. I didn't know what he was talking about.

He came very close and said conspiratorially, "Well, you need to get it. It helps them breathe better during the race, and the State Racing Commission lab doesn't know how to test for it. This guy comes around and takes your order, and then he makes the drug run to Canada."

I knew this was illegal, but Wyle wasn't somebody you argued with. I just said, "Okay, thank you. We don't really need it."

"Yes, you do," he said. "You should be using it." It was all for him, I realized. If his Reel on Reel progeny did well, it made his stallion look good. He could charge a higher stud fee. It gave me a sinking feeling that the president of the HBPA, whose job it was to make sure that things went as they were supposed to, was advising me to give my horses an illegal drug.

Still, I felt the year ended on a good note. Scarlett had shown the promise Jerry and Pam thought she would and was going to have all winter to become acclimated to her new diet. Baby was going to come back healed from his tendinitis and ready to tear up the track.

Our farm vet suggested that to build up Baby's muscles, which would protect his tendons, he start a regimen of swimming. There was an indoor pool for horses just two miles from our house, and Pam thought sending Baby there was a good idea because he'd return to the track with his muscles already built up some.

So starting on January 18th, 1996, Baby went into the pool every day. There was a ramp with a gradual slope that he'd walk down and then, holding his head just above the water, he'd start swimming. It comes naturally to horses, just like it does to dogs. Each time he came around, his eyes would widen as he looked at me, as if to say, "What am I *doing?*" He looked so adorable, like a great big dog paddling.

By that point, his tendinitis was essentially healed. I had been told he could start race training after four months at home, but this was now seven months later, and he wouldn't be starting with Pam again until March—fully nine months after his injury. I didn't send him or Scarlett to Florida that winter because I wanted to make extra sure about the tendon, and I wanted Scarlett to heal from a deep-cut biopsy that Dr. Valentine had ordered to make sure she really was on the right diet to treat her condition. Pam was okay with that because the first race wasn't going to occur until the middle of April, unlike last year, when the meet began in March.

In the meantime, both Baby and Scarlett did their usual winter frolicking—rolling in the snow and coming to the back door covered in white, waiting for treats. I'd go to the fridge and take out a bag of carrots, cracking them and handing them out. Finally, I'd tell them, "No more," but they'd stand there, beseeching me with their eyes like two dogs begging. So I'd go get some more and say, "This is the last time, now go out and play." Then I'd sneak off to the side of the kitchen where they couldn't see me through the glass and wait until they gave up and walked away. I couldn't bear to say no to them, but I could have gone through pounds and pounds of carrots before they felt they had had their fill.

I loved having this respite with them. At the same time, I knew this was going to be our year. Baby was doing wonderfully, and Scarlett was now going to get to race fully treated. Once training started, in fact, she went through her timed works beautifully, with no tying up, no stiffness, and on lab tests, all of her enzymes within normal range. I was glad in no small part for the money we stood to make. I had worked hard in my role on the HBPA board the previous year to get the state to pass legislation allowing simulcast racing, which meant people could now bet on Michigan races from other states, watching on screens at their local tracks. The purses, and our take, stood to increase dramatically. With the extra money to be earned coupled with Baby and Scarlett's fantastic condition, our stars were all aligned.

On April 19th, Terry Houghton rode Baby for a timed work, a good sign that he wanted to race him, so we were thrilled. Everything was in place.

A few days later, the HBPA had its monthly board meeting. The chair of the backstretch track committee, a trainer named James Jackson, said that the track was in really bad shape. Two horses had broken down on opening weekend and had to be euthanized. They might have run into a groove or dip, Jackson said. It wasn't clear.

It didn't really give me pause. I suspected those horses broke down because they weren't properly conditioned and were running with preexisting injuries. I already knew that official lameness exams didn't rule out injuries and that other owners and trainers didn't take the care I did, that people were running injured horses all the time. But *my* horses were fine and wouldn't get into trouble unless they were near the back of the pack, which was not going to happen because they were both so ready to win.

Soon after that meeting, Terry also rode Scarlett for one of her timed works. We were really in position. The best jockey at the track wanted to race both of our Thoroughbreds.

Pam had a race picked out for Baby on May 10th but had to scratch it at the last minute. It had been confirmed that Terry would ride him, but his schedule didn't allow him to take Baby on his last timed work before the race. Baby ran off with the jockey who did take him—the guy couldn't control him; few could—so there was not enough horse left in him to run at his highest speed just a few days later in the actual event. We were disappointed but not devastated. Everything still looked great, and to add to our high, Pat gave birth on May 15th to a beautiful filly we called Sissy, who looked very much like Baby except for a star between her eyes that resembled an upside-down Nike logo. Her official name was Surprisingly Reel. We were particularly thrilled because Reel On Reel fillies were doing even better in races than the males.

When I reached the track later that day, Bob Miller, a horse owner and trainer who had played for the Detroit Lions football team in the 1950s, said to me in his booming voice, "Looks like you have a runner." He had been watching Scarlett do a timed work.

Hearing that felt great. Bob had been in racing for more than twenty years. His opinions were very well respected. I felt swept up, as if in a joyous wave of hope. Both Scarlett and Baby were in for big wins.

A couple of days later, Pam found another race for Baby to take place on the twenty-fifth. The only kink was that Terry wouldn't be able to ride him; he was already committed. That was unfortunate because we would not have Terry's ability to control him, to keep him from ramming into another horse. But Pam secured Joey Judice, who also had a very good reputation, and in a timed work before the race, Baby and Joey matched extremely well. Joey handled Baby's bullish style as if he had ridden him many times. Pam, Jerry, John, and I were giving each other high fives.

Three days before the race, on the evening of the twenty-second, the HBPA board held another meeting and, again, James Jackson said the track was in bad shape, that there were uneven spots, gouges even, that needed to be resurfaced.

I reminded myself that James liked to talk, that he enjoyed the limelight. He would stand for emphasis, whereas all the other committee chairs gave their reports from their seats. Then, too, Baby had just had another timed work that very morning, and his jockey didn't say anything was wrong. Pam wasn't getting any feedback from

Jerry about something being wrong, either, and he rode Baby and Scarlett on the track every day.

But at the same time, two other trainers at the board meeting piped up and agreed with James that there were problems with the track. One of them said that half his horses were back at the farm, sore. That nagged at me.

The next day, by pure coincidence, I saw the track's general manager, Jay Fortney, in his suit and tie, talking to people at the maintenance building. He was finishing up and walking back to the track, and I hurried to catch up with him. We had a good relationship, even though he was "track" and I was "owners and trainers" by virtue of being on the HBPA. We had worked together on the simulcasting legislation.

"Jay, wait up," I called out. I told him there had been an HBPA meeting the previous evening and that for the second time, James Jackson adamantly expressed that the track was not in good repair and needed maintenance. "I have to tell you," I said, "we have a horse racing in two days and another horse slated to run the week after." Pam had picked out a race for Scarlett by that point. "I will not send out my horses if there's a problem with the track."

Jay was a big man, both tall and heavy. He breathed in, puffing himself up. "James Jackson ought to stick to training," he said. "That's what he knows. I used to be the superintendent for

Belmont Park in New York. If I can take care of Belmont Park, I can certainly take care of the Detroit Race Course."

I took him at his word. Belmont Park is where the Belmont Stakes takes place, the third "jewel" in the "Triple Crown" of racing, after the Kentucky Derby and the Preakness, in Maryland. It has to be maintained in the same condition as the Derby's Churchill Downs track in Kentucky. Also, Jay sounded adamant bordering on angry. And because I had a good relationship with him and the rest of the track management, coupled with the fact that it was easy to dismiss what James said as exaggeration, I had every reason to believe him.

So I let my concerns go and went forward again with the excitement that had been building all these months from Baby's last race the previous June, where he had been beaten by only a fraction of a length despite a stretched tendon. At this point he was going like a tiger, a freight train. We knew we were on our way to wins, first with him and then with Scarlett.

Baby's race date, May 25th, was during Memorial Day weekend, and the weather was a cloudless, summery seventy-eight degrees, so there were more people at the track than typically.

As usual, Baby let out his hello honk when I entered his shedrow that morning. I breathed into his nose (no treats—he wasn't allowed apples or carrots on race day), and brushed my nose and lips across his velvety muzzle, as usual. He seemed incredibly alert, right on the muscle. "Boy, he's ready," I said to Jerry. It was that same hopeful feeling as when Baby had come back from Florida. I knew how much swimming he had done all winter, how much fitter he was than horses who began to work out only when the track opened in March. I also knew that since this was to be a $10,000 claiming race rather than an allowance race, Baby's competition was not going to be fierce. Furthermore, Baby's last timed work before the race was a bullet work, meaning he ran the fastest and a bullet mark was put next to his name in the *Daily Racing Form*.

Baby himself was completely comfortable, with not a hint of nervousness. He knew the routine backward and forward—another romp in the park.

We walked with Baby, Pam, and Jerry up to the saddling area and, as usual, I told the jockey, Joey Judice, to come back safe and squeezed his hand. Then, while Pam was giving Joey instructions— "you know what to do, just stay a bit off the leader"—I put my hand on Baby's neck, moving it under his mane. "It's okay, Baby. You be a big boy. We'll be waiting for you. We love you." I was speaking softly; you don't want to be saying those intimate things loudly enough for everybody to hear.

I lingered just a bit, after which Pam gave Joey

a leg up, and Baby was paraded in front of the grandstand with the other horses while John, Pam, Jerry, and I went to take our seats, about eight rows up, along with Jessica and Rebecca, my parents, my sister, an aunt and uncle, and lots of friends—as usual, about twenty people altogether.

I felt on top of the world. It was the start of what was going to be a stellar year, with Baby about to win his second race and Scarlett poised to run her first race of the season the very next week. And we had a ten-day-old filly at home who would someday be making wins for us, too. It was like I had reached the top of Mount Everest. I felt so confident I even bet $200 on Baby that day, ten times more than I ever bet. We couldn't have been in a better spot.

The bell went off. It was the last race of the day, close to 6 P.M. We'd soon be getting our second win picture. The first was already hanging in the main hallway on the first floor of our house.

Baby was never quite a jackrabbit out of the gate, even at his best, but he came out sixth of twelve, a good enough position and just a length and a half off the leader. Going along the back stretch of the track, he slid into perfect position, with his head right off the flank of the first horse—exactly where Pam said she wanted him. The rest of the field was a couple of lengths behind.

About halfway through the race, Baby was

clearly poised to win. Despite my confidence, I could feel my heart beating in my chest—Baby hadn't even kicked into gear yet. Joey was still holding him back. John and I had our hands clasped together. Then, suddenly, almost imperceptibly, he drifted slightly off to the right—and stopped.

"Oh my God!" I cried out.

"Don't worry," Pam said. "The saddle probably slipped." She took my binoculars to get a closer view, then handed them back to me. "Here, look at him," she instructed. "You can see his front legs. There's nothing wrong."

That calmed me down. The vast majority of breakdowns occur in the front legs. Then Joey took off the saddle, which was in keeping with what Pam thought had happened. But he and Baby just kept standing there. The other horses had already crossed the finish line. Why are they waiting, I wondered.

Then I saw the horse ambulance coming out, a trailer painted white. Pam grabbed my arm—she didn't want me running onto the track. "It's going to be alright," she said. "It'll be alright. Come on. We've got to go."

CHAPTER EIGHT

"Oh, Baby, Oh, Baby." I put my nose right against his because I wanted to make sure he knew it was me. Just like with the plastic chair stuck on his head, with his first view of a grey horse, with anything that made him feel scared, it was always me. Then I threw my arms around his neck and lay my cheek against his, speaking in the same quiet, reassuring voice I had used so many times since he was born. "I'm here, Baby. It's Mommy. It's okay." I knew I had to stay calm so that he could stay calm. "I'll take care of everything, Baby. Don't worry."

Covered in sweat so profuse it turned into foam that cascaded down his neck and chest, he was trembling all over. But I took comfort in the fact that his eyes, widened with fear, had relaxed some. He recognized my presence. Better still, I saw that everything was okay because he was still standing on both his front legs, where nearly all fatal injuries occur. Also, there was no blood. It had to be something minor, although clearly very painful. Maybe there's a bone chip in a joint, I thought, or a pulled muscle.

We were together in Baby's shedrow, where the ambulance trailer had been brought. The back of the trailer was down, but I had run to the front, where a little door lets you into a very small area right by the horse's head. Larry Wales, the private track vet, was already in the trailer when I came on.

I can't remember exactly how we had made it from the grandstand to Baby. John and I, and I guess Pam and Jerry, too, climbed down to the bottom row, then went through a little gate where Pam had parked the golf cart that she used to navigate the roads on the backside. I don't know how many people climbed onto the cart with us. The guard wasn't checking IDs, as he usually did. He was just letting everyone through.

Along the way, we ran into Baby's jockey, Joey, who was holding the saddle. "It was like an explosion," he blurted. "The leg broke."

I looked at John, and he looked directly back at me. But as in a tsunami, what was clear, even familiar—it was a simple statement, after all— became jumbled with everything else ordinarily recognizable until, all caught together, the whole became a chaotic blur, with Pam and all of our guests running alongside us tossed into the flow.

"Joey doesn't know what he's talking about!" Pam shouted furiously. "He's not a vet. He doesn't know."

At some point Larry had caught up with us in his truck. "Jo Anne, do you want me there?" he asked. Usually, when the ambulance is called, the official vet at the track, the one from the Office of the

Racing Commission, is sent out to take care of everything. But Larry knew me so well. He knew I would take Baby home when he had stretched his tendon rather than continue to let him race. He saw Scarlett go through tying-up syndrome.

"Yes. Please. Thank you, Larry."

I don't know how he arrived at the ambulance before we did. "Jo Anne, it's not good," he said. I was still breathing into Baby's nose.

"We'll take him to Michigan State and fix it, whatever it is," I answered.

"Jo Anne, his leg is broken."

Larry didn't know what he was talking about again, like when he gave Scarlett the wrong antibiotic all through the previous spring. All you had to do was look at Baby to see that neither of his front legs was broken. "Larry, we'll take him to Michigan State. It's okay. Money is no object. We'll do whatever it takes."

"Jo Anne, it's really bad. It can't be—"

But I stopped hearing him. The foam—my God, Baby just kept shaking. "I'm here, Baby. It's going to be okay. Baby . . ."

Larry was interrupting me again. "Jo Anne it's not going to be alright. This is bad. We can't—"

I felt that if he wasn't going to do something he should just get out of the way. "It's *okay,* Larry," I responded, letting him know with my tone, calm but firm, that I was in charge. "We'll take him to Michigan State. We'll spend whatever's necessary.

We need to get a trailer." I knew we couldn't transport Baby in that one.

"Jo Anne, let me talk to you," Pam said from outside the trailer, so I left Baby for a moment and my mother came on to be with him. "It's all right, Baby," she whispered. "It's going to be all right." I had been composed to that point, but my mother's tender manner with Baby made me start to cry.

"Jo Anne, this isn't good," Pam said. There, outside the trailer, I realized just how many people had crowded around, not just my own family and friends but dozens of others from the backstretch. Ours had been the last race of the day, so nobody was in a rush with any horses.

Not you, too, Pam, I thought to myself. Don't *you* agree with him. She, more than anybody outside my family, knew what Baby meant to me. How could she say that? My eyes went again to the blur of people—people I knew, people I yakked with in the kitchen, backstretch workers I didn't recognize but who recognized me, perhaps because I was on the two boards, and had crowded around out of curiosity. Then I looked again at Pam and just went back in with Baby, my mother stepping off.

Bill Frank, the Racing Commission vet, was already on the trailer, whispering with Larry. I hadn't seen him step in. "Jo Anne, do you want a second opinion?" he asked.

I suppose I said yes because Bill looked at Larry and Larry nodded, and the two of them switched places. Bill palpated the tibia on Baby's back left leg—a very long bone that runs along the upper part of the limb—going up and down, up and down, with both hands, and then he looked at Larry and nodded and turned to me and said what Larry had tried not to say. "Jo Anne, it—the tibia—it's fractured." I must have had a blank look on my face because after a moment he added, "It's shattered. He can't be saved."

Why are you all against me? I wondered. Why doesn't anybody understand? All we have to do is take him to the hospital. It doesn't matter how much it costs. Even if the leg is broken, they can fix broken legs. Years ago, maybe no. But not now. This was the 1990s. I wasn't able to entertain the idea that there was a fracture they couldn't fix.

". . . can feel it, even though you can't see it," Larry was saying. He had tried not giving me the details to spare me, but he saw that neither Bill nor he was getting through. "It's in multiple pieces. I can't even count how many—"

We have to get out of here, I realized. We have to get away. "Don't worry, Baby," I said in a low, almost conspiratorial, voice, going down to his nose again. "Don't worry. I'm going to get you away from here."

I looked out of the trailer and once again saw all those people, but it was impossible to recognize anyone. It was like one of those dreams where what doesn't make sense makes sense and vice versa.

At some point—I don't know if Pam took my arm or one of the two vets came over—someone said, "He's in pain. He's in shock. Can you see him trembling? We have to put him down."

Until that point my thoughts seemed very logical to me. I had my charge cards in my purse. I could make the very sane, very practical decision to transport my horse to the hospital and save him. I just had to find a way to sneak away with him. Now, I felt numb, as if somebody had tied me up and gagged me. I needed to move, to get Baby onto another trailer and take him away, save him, but couldn't budge from the spot, couldn't scream. I had lost control, didn't exist anymore, was going with them. Someone was directing me, moving me, I don't know who, although I remember Larry saying, "Let me take care of it. You don't have to go," and I answered back, "I'm going, I'm going, I have to be there."

I turned to Pam, and she said something to Larry, and there was commotion as to who was going in what vehicle and who would be on the golf cart. To this day I don't know if I went in Pam's cart or someone's car. Maybe it was a car, but I don't know whose, and we were traveling, but I didn't know where, we could have been in my pasture driving a car, passing a lot of people.

Nobody was talking, and I don't know if John and the girls were with me at that point.

Then we stopped, and we were way behind the track on the acres and acres of fields, beyond which stretched some woods. We stepped out of the car, and on the far side of a field was a bit of a hill that we had to walk up. It was then that I saw the ambulance trailer, which snapped me to attention a little—Oh, I have to go to Baby.

He was already standing there, still covered in sweat and foam. Larry was there, too, and by that point John and my daughters were with me, right next to him. Some friends and family, I don't remember who, drove up with us but stayed at a respectful distance, maybe twenty feet behind.

It wasn't quite sinking in yet why I was there. Baby still looked so strong. When you think about it, for him to have shattered his tibia into an uncountable number of pieces and not to have gone down on the track, to take that bumpy ride back to the shedrow, out to the back acres, and still be standing—it took amazing heart, and strength, strength that possibly saved not just his own jockey's life but also the lives of the other jockeys and horses who were behind him and, had he gone down, could have tripped over him at blazing speeds and broken their own necks. His response to his pain was, literally, heroic. I understood that day in a way I never had before what was meant by the phrase, "the heart of a Thoroughbred."

"We have to do this now," Larry said, which pushed me out of my daze. The girls were patting Baby and crying, John was crying, and then Baby and I were alone together. "I'm sorry, Baby. I did this to you," I said, pressing my face to his wet neck and cupping his muzzle with my hand, kissing him over and over. "I failed you. This is all my fault. I'm so sorry." Then I breathed my scent into his nostril, whispering good-bye, wishing, crazily, that the gesture could breathe life into him, as it did five years earlier.

The hardest thing to do was to step away. I wanted to be able to stay with him and keep my hand on him, be touching him while it happened. But Larry said I had to step back because you never know how the horse is going to go down—it could rear or stumble toward you—and they don't want anybody caught underneath.

I watched Baby's face as the syringe went in, shuddering as I wept, looking for some sign of forgiveness. But by then Baby had gone some-where else himself. As soon as the drug entered his bloodstream, he sank to his knees, then rolled over on his side, in the position in which he loved to nap. I was grateful that it seemed relatively peaceful, Baby taking a last couple of deep breaths, his eyes still open.

I knelt down and kissed him again, after which Larry touched his eyeball to make sure there was no response.

I recall thinking that I wasn't going to be able to walk away from him. But I don't really remember how things went after that. When I had Baby to focus on, I could act, but now I was back in that trancelike state, as if I'd been hypnotized, functioning, but at other people's direction. I don't think there would have been any other way I could have left Baby lying there in the dirt.

I can't remember walking away, getting back in a vehicle, driving off the back acres, returning to the shedrow, saying good-bye to anyone, getting into our own car.

The only thing I remember is being with John in the parking lot outside the security gates. We were about to get on the highway, but John suddenly threw the car in park. We grabbed onto each other, and he was sobbing, and that brought me out of my trance to the point that I began wailing myself, rocking back and forth as we held each other.

"No, no, nooo!" I kept saying, and my wails turned into hysterical crying. I don't know how long we sat there. I don't know how we made it home, in fact. At some point John would have had to compose himself enough to drive, but my mind draws a blank about being on the highway. I didn't know where the girls were or how they got back to the house. It was a very selfish moment.

To pull into the driveway and see the "It's a filly sign" in pink for our ten-day-old newborn, and then the barn, stung like a hard, deliberate slap.

The barn had always been my source of comfort, a place of solace. I could go there, sit on the hay, and cry if I needed to. My horses loved me no matter what, and I drew fortitude from them. They exuded strength, a phenomenal power, with their unconditional love. It gave me peace, cure, comfort.

But driving up now felt like someone was hitting me, shaking me. It was physical, the knowledge that the barn would never again be the same.

I knew I had to go and check on everyone, Pat and the new foal in particular, but for the first time since we had horses, I almost couldn't bear to bring myself in there. Beauty and Pumpkin actually would have been okay because I left their stalls unlocked—they could have walked out into the pasture whenever they wanted and grazed, and the outdoor trough always had plenty of water in it.

But Pat, since she was nursing and confined to her stall with the newborn when I wasn't home, would need more hay, as well as water. A lactating mare needs a greater amount of food than usual, and she definitely would have drunk all the water in the two pails I had left her that morning.

I also had to clean the large foaling stall that Pat and the baby shared. Every time Pat gave birth, I heavily bedded her stall so both she and the baby would be as comfortable as possible. And

I couldn't stand the thought of a newborn foal lying in urine-soaked straw or anywhere near manure, so I always made sure the stall was picked up, freshened, and cleaned. You could even go in there and sit on the floor with the sleeping foal's head on you, or lie down right next to the little horse and cradle it. I felt it was especially important to keep the stall spotless because a tiny foal is in there almost all the time. You can't let it wander into the pasture when you're not home because it's not safe. What if a coyote came through the fence, or one of its little legs became caught in something?

I became racked with sobs all over again, thinking of how I had tended to Baby as a newborn just five years earlier.

All the horses were inside, even though Beauty and Pumpkin could have turned themselves out. A herd likes to stay together. Walking over to Beauty, the first horse I ever owned and the dominant one in our herd, I lay my head on her shoulder, still crying. A horse knows your emotions, just like a dog does, if not more. She tensed at first because my mood was not what she anticipated, and then turned so that her face was right next to mine. "What's wrong?"

Her muzzle became wet with my tears. "It's so bad, it's so bad," I told her. "We're not going to see him anymore."

The air from her lungs was pumping out through

her nostrils right next to mine, warm and alive, signaling her affection. "*I'm* here, I'm here," she was telling me, but her scent, so familiar—each horse has her own scent, like people have—wasn't bringing me the comfort it usually did. Not even the beautiful feel of her velvety muzzle as I rubbed my nose and lips against it could console me, not her ears up and pricked forward in her sweet, anticipatory way. Pumpkin tried to help, too, but Beauty told her not to come near, laying her ears down flat to warn her, and all she could do was slink back to her stall.

Then I had to enter the foaling stall, which I dreaded. How was I going to be able to face Baby's mother and his ten-day-old sister—and not just a half sister like Scarlett but a full sister with the same sire and dam? I couldn't even bear to call her by the barn name we had given her, because "Sissy" referred to the fact that she was *Baby's* sister, and now she was full sister to no one.

To be able to be in such close proximity to a newborn foal, with her rounded head and coat as soft as that of a newborn kitten, and the way a baby horse tickles you with her curly whiskers when she walks up to smell you inquisitively, her long lashes fanning out—normally, that would have been such a privilege, such pure delight. A horse will never be that way again after its first couple of weeks. Yet there was no joy for me, no comfort, even though the same blood coursed through her veins as through Baby's. In fact, it made it harder that she looked so much like him.

When I opened the gate to her stall, she at first just stood there and then came over to me on her long, spindly legs, her little tail only six inches long. Ordinarily, I would have immediately been on my knees hugging her, smelling her breath and enjoying the precious scent of milk on her mouth. But in my grief, it was all I could do not to avoid her. It wasn't fair of me. I just couldn't help it.

Pat was pacing, which was easy to do in that big stall. She was tense because of my odd behavior. I went right to her head and cried some more and ran my face down her nose to her muzzle and buried my own nose there.

Her breathing out increased, not in the almost rhythmic way Beauty's had in order to comfort me, but more erratically, and with more effort, or intensity. She was considerably more nervous. As a Thoroughbred, she was naturally edgier than Beauty, a Quarter Horse. I told her we had lost Baby and began crying much harder. After all, we were both mothers to him.

And then I looked up, and there was Baby's stall right across from Pat's, next to Scarlett's, with the photo there of me standing by him the day Scarlett was born, when he felt forlorn that she was getting all the attention and I went over to give him a kiss, telling him he'd always be our baby. "I'm here, Baby," I had told him. He was just a year old then.

As perfunctorily as I could I went through the chores—dumped the old water, filled the pails up again, brought over more hay, mucked out the soiled straw, picked up the manure—and then walked out as quickly as possible. Seeing the reminders of Baby made me feel literally nauseated. I had to leave his house, their house.

I didn't know how I was going to keep doing this four, five, six times a day, every single day, the way I had now for so many years. How I was going to work on imprinting with Sissy—getting her used to being touched by people, working my hands all around her body while talking sweetly and quietly to her; getting her accustomed to strange objects so she wouldn't spook? How I was going to come down to the barn to turn her and Pat into the pasture, so important so the foal can run around and build strong bones and muscles, and just as important for the new mother to get back into shape? How was I then going to come back down a while later to bring them back into the barn so the flies wouldn't drive them crazy?

Once I was back in the house, everywhere I looked, there were pictures of Baby. There were more pictures of my horses, in fact, than of my daughters. The girls understood that. I had waited longer for the horses.

As I walked about, I was looking at pictures of Baby in the pasture, Baby as a baby, on the refrigerator, on the hallway wall, in the great room. There was Baby's win picture hanging prominently.

At some point, the girls arrived home, but what happened after that remains shrouded. I do know I had a fierce headache, feeling like my head was going to burst. I went upstairs and curled into a fetal position on the bed, hiding under the covers even though it was already late May and still light out. I wanted to disappear, to not exist, to not have to think, to recall, to feel. I couldn't take what had happened, what I had done.

I slept on and off, waking periodically to wonder to myself whether what had occurred actually did happen, then regaining more consciousness until the "Oh" set in again within seconds and the pit in my stomach grew and my head continued to hurt and I didn't know what time it was even though I kept looking at the clock.

Toward early morning, as the first hints of light seeped through the curtains and in some faraway place I was wondering whether you could make something unhappen, it hit me. "Oh my God, how did I *leave* him there, in the dirt, in the dark, on those acres of death? The truck was going to come and pick him up—it was too warm to have too many horses back there at once—and what if it came right away? They would take him and grind him up.

I still had a pounding headache and had not wanted to get out from under the covers, but rousing myself from an inability to do anything or think coherently, I darted from my half-conscious state. John had not come up to bed. We were each in our own world, so I went running down the stairs to him in the great room. He, too, was awake. "We can't leave him there," I started shouting. "They'll take him to the rendering plant. We've got to get him out of there. I'll call a transporter."

Because it was a holiday weekend, it was going to be hard to find somebody, but I needed that task. I needed to keep taking care of Baby, and to make sure the track did not get to decide what to do with him. I had already made the most awful decision for him in listening to Jay Fortney instead of James Jackson. I had allowed my head, my desire to win, to obscure something in my gut. But the track had also made the most awful decision for Baby in not spending whatever money it would have taken to keep the racecourse safe. It wasn't going to get to make this choice, too.

It was too early in the morning to be making phone calls, and besides, I knew I had to get down to the barn. Again, I performed my chores there robotically, just wanting to check things off in my head as I went through the motions and get out of there as soon as possible.

When I came back to the house, I got on the phone, early as it still was, and started making calls until I found a transporter that could reach the track that morning and take Baby out of there. I also called Michigan State University, which takes in equine emergencies twenty-four hours a day. They have a pathology department and perform necropsies there, the equine version of autopsies. My legal background as a court reporter had already kicked in, and I wanted to be able to prove that track conditions killed Baby and not some kind of conformational problem that had never been detected. After that, I'd give him the end he deserved—cremation, rather than being ground up at some rendering facility.

John was going to have to direct the transporter on the back acres. It's kind of a maze at the track, and it was necessary for him to meet the trailer in the parking lot, sign the driver in, then lead him to Baby.

He left right away, and as soon as he did, I began to wonder whether Michigan State was the best place in the country to look at Baby's leg. I didn't want anybody second-guessing what had happened to him.

Making a couple more phone calls, I decided the best person was a vet named Susan Stover at the University of California, Davis, largely because California was the only state in the country that required every horse who broke down on the track to have a necropsy, and the horses were often sent to her. Moreover, she had published the most research papers on catastrophic racetrack injuries. But I would have to ship the leg. So I called Michigan State back and told them I still wanted a necropsy but that I wanted the leg sent to U.C. Davis.

While I was waiting for John to return home, I was extremely touched to receive a number of phone calls from people at the track, some of whom I didn't even think had my home phone number and, more importantly, would have seen something like a horse breaking down as all part of the business. I'm quite certain, in fact, that I was made fun of behind my back for all the love and attention I lavished on Baby. But they understood my attachment to him, and that gave their calls all the more meaning.

One came from James Jackson, who had somewhere between forty and sixty horses that he trained and had little time to offer me condolences. But he went out of his way to find my phone number, probably from someone else on the HPBA board, and told me how sorry he was. "I want you to know," he said, "that I am with you if you ever need me. I know the condition of that racetrack, and I know what caused your horse to break down." It was particularly meaningful because he could have said "I told you so," as he was the board member who kept sounding the alarm that horses were breaking down with increasing alacrity.

Others phoned, too, but I can't remember who they were, I was so distraught. Each call would start me crying all over again.

At one point, I heard a car, and I was sure it was John coming home from the track. But it was Pam and Jerry. Pam was crying. Jerry looked stricken. You could see the compassion in his face, and we all hugged.

"In all my years of training," Pam said through her tears, "I have never had a horse of mine break down on the track. Never. I can't believe that of all those horses, of all those owners, the horse that it would end up happening to would be yours. It's so hard to understand."

As we were crying and talking, John pulled up. This poor man had had to go to the track himself—I couldn't bear to go back—and see Baby lying there.

John is a man's man. He had been a sports jock when we were young, and he was always the person you could lean on. He had held it all in at the track that morning. But, he told me later on, when he and the trailer holding Baby branched off in different directions once they were on the highway, he lost it.

That was the state he was in when he drove down our driveway. Getting out of the car still teary-eyed, he walked up to me and, in front of Pam and Jerry, threw his arms around me and cried even harder. A lesser man would have tried to hide his emotion. But John wasn't ashamed that he loved, and I loved him all the more for that.

Pam and Jerry left soon after, but before they did, I told Pam that I would be arranging for Scarlett to come home as soon as possible, that we were officially out of racing. She started to say that maybe I wanted to think about that a little bit because Scarlett was doing so well and was due to race the very next week but that it could be postponed if we needed more time. Jerry, who was head over heels for Scarlett, enthusiastically pressed for her to continue. But I told them no, that I would never again sit in those stands and watch a horse of mine—or any horse for that matter—come out of the gate. How many other horses were dying out there that I didn't even know about? It was a moment too late, but I had learned my lesson.

They still told me to think about it, that I had time, before they drove away. But I had never lost a close family member before this. I even had both my parents. And I lost Baby because of my own poor judgment. I would never take that risk again.

Once the car drove out of sight and John and I started walking back to the house, I realized I had in my hand a ziplock bag with a piece of Baby's mane and one of his shoes, still grouted with the sand from where he pulled up. I don't remember Pam putting those items into my hand, although I had called her before John left for the track and asked her to please get them for me before Baby was removed.

I was glad no one had cleaned the sand from the shoe. I wanted it just the way it was, never opening the bag, even to this day, but always keeping it with me. If I was sitting at the kitchen table, it was next to me there. If I was watching television, I would set it down gently on the couch with me. When I went to bed at night, it stayed on my end table. Eventually, the shoe came to rest by my computer mouse. I am looking at it now. Pieces of sand have fallen to the bottom of the bag.

Scarlett arrived home two days later. As usual, the whinnying and neighing began as soon as the trailer pulled into the driveway, and it was then that I realized that what I thought would feel therapeutic, like pure relief, would be yet another reminder of my grief and all I had done wrong.

I *was* relieved. The track was a dangerous, lawless place, and I had already started making noise about its surface before Baby's death. Someone not wanting things stirred up might take revenge, so I knew I needed Scarlett out of there fast. But the relief was by no means unalloyed. Each one of the horse's voices was unique, and the clamor was euphoric, with bellows of joy coming from deep within. But there would be no distinct foghorn of a sound, no Canadian goose honk, joining in with the others. Scarlett's presence without Baby was further proof that I had failed, that all my dreams of winning played out as mistakes, bad judgments. The missing voice, so pushed into relief now with Scarlett's whinnies breaking across the field, echoed to me my defeat. Rather than putting the horses first, I had plunged ahead blindly, leaving their lives in the balance with disastrous, unfixable consequences.

Once I had Scarlett in her stall, she blew into Beauty and Pumpkin's noses and vice versa, only driving home the point further. "I *told* you it was her," Beauty was saying to Pumpkin as she confirmed it by exchanging breaths, but next to Scarlett's stall was the empty one, the one that should have had her brother. It represented what I hadn't been able to do—keep Baby safe, even though I had promised him that much five years earlier, when he was born. I couldn't even follow through for five years. What I had done felt like child abuse ending in the worst way possible. There could be no repair, and I would never again be able to know the complete solace I had always felt with my horses—hearing their rhythmic munching, watching them bond, graze in the pasture. That lack of perfect contentment that I finally achieved when we bought our little farm and first horses was going to haunt me forever. That was my sentence. Was Pat waiting to hear Baby's voice along with Scarlett's, I wondered.

The two had been coming and going together for some time.

Everything became a reminder. When I turned Scarlett out, I should have been turning Baby out, too. I could see the two of them playing together in the pasture, but his figure was a ghost, a memory.

The walk from the house to the barn was down a slight incline, and every visit there I felt a heaviness in my chest. The downward slope felt like the physical truth of what I was experiencing, each step drawing me lower emotionally as I crossed into the barn and had to see his empty stall. I continued to cry as I tended to the barn chores, but just as often my eyes were dry and I could feel a numbness and a gnawing in the pit of my stomach.

John, like I, was aggrieved, but it soon became apparent that we were at odds in how to cope with Baby's death. For the longest time, he could not even drive down the expressway that went past the track, even though we used that road regularly. You could see the track from it, and he couldn't bear that, so he would drive miles out of the way to avoid the view.

But I was back there within four or five days. I felt that if I didn't do something—prove that the uneven track surface killed Baby—that if too many weeks passed, my role on the HPBA board would be diminished to the point that I wouldn't be able to effect change, that I'd be forgotten. That

Baby would be forgotten. I had to act fast. They were not going to just gloss over this and let other horses die. Yes, I had wrongly trusted Jay Fortney in his suit and tie rather than James Jackson and the others in their horse clothes who had been complaining, saying things were worse on the track than ever. I mistook Jay's dress for class, and because he was the track's general manager and was browbeating me when I questioned him, I backed down and put my trust in the wrong person. But if I just went away quietly, Baby's life wouldn't have meant anything.

John was irate at me for my decision, horrified. "How could you go back and have anything to do with those fuckers," he asked, "for those people who care nothing?"

A child's death is one of the top stressors in a marriage, often leading to divorce. One parent wants to try to leave the death behind. The other wants to investigate, bring the wrong doers to justice and make sure it doesn't happen to others. That was John and me, and if it didn't push us to the brink, it pushed us as far from our zone of comfort with each other as we had ever been.

He didn't want to hear a word I had to say about the track. When it was time for me to leave for a board meeting, he would make a face and roll his eyes, clearly showing his displeasure. I was alone in my quest to make good on Baby's death. I could not have handled it John's way.

Yet it was unfathomably difficult to go back there, in no small part because I wasn't getting any real sleep those first couple of weeks. I'd wake up well before dawn and think, "This didn't happen," followed by a moment of peace. But then reality would quickly sink in, and I couldn't fall back.

Each time I reached the track parking lot, I wasn't sure I could manage. I'd sit there crying for long intervals. But I knew I couldn't go to the backstretch like that, that I wouldn't be taken seriously. So I would compose myself and walk briskly, confidently, inside. The board understood that I was not going to continue in racing. But they were happy to have me stay on and try to improve track conditions. Horses into whom they had sunk considerable time and money were at risk.

I also started writing letters to the State Racing Commission, goaded on by the increasing number of breakdowns I was learning about by dint of going to the track every day—other tibia fractures, pelvic fractures, fractures of the humerus, or shoulder bone, fractures that should have been exceedingly rare. There were specific rules and regulations on what had to be done to keep the track in the best condition, to avoid situations in which a horse could place his foot on the surface at thirty-five miles an hour and fall victim to a catastrophic injury, and I knew those who ran the operation were in violation. I would talk to people in the kitchen, and they would tell me that there was equipment to maintain a safe track, keep it level, but that, for instance, a certain piece of equipment was broken and hadn't been fixed in years.

I began building a case by creating a form, or survey, to compile a record of the horses that died out there and left copies at the receptionist's desk in the office of the HPBA board. Trainers started to fill it in, answering questions such as whether any of their horses died during a race that season or suffered a catastrophic injury during morning training.

While collecting my burgeoning statistics, I asked in my letters to the Racing Commission, "What is being done to insure an even track surface?" quoting from the official language of the general rules of racing put out by the State Department of Agriculture.

I received few replies, all of them vague. "Thank you for your letter. We appreciate your concern."

One day, while I was writing one of my letters, we received the call that Baby's ashes were ready to be picked up. We had already received the necropsy report and learned that Baby had been biologically sound and that nothing about his conformation would have caused his fatal injury. When I told the veterinarians that the jockey said it was like the sound of an explosion, they said that was typical for a tibia shattering. The tibia is massive—one of the largest, densest bones in the body. When you do research on the tibia and put it in a vice and squeeze as hard as possible, they told me, you still have a hard time breaking it. In other words, it was apparent that it took the force of Baby's foot stepping at lightning speed onto an improperly cushioned track surface to torque his leg and destroy it.

I don't know what I was expecting when we went to retrieve the ashes at Michigan State; something somber, funereal, I suppose. So I was surprised when the girl behind the desk didn't say anything like "I'm sorry for your loss" but, instead, just reached for one of several containers on a shelf next to her. It looked like one of those five-gallon, white, plastic ice cream tubs. When she set it on the counter, we could hear a distinct clinking inside. Cremations do not just contain ashes. They also contain little pieces of bone. On the top, in black magic marker, was the date Baby died and his formal Jockey Club name, Reel Surprise.

I hugged Baby to me, my knees almost giving out from a new round of grief, and John and I staggered out to the car. It was just like being at the track right after we had Baby put down, and we were holding him between us and sobbing, grabbing on to each other.

"I don't know about you," John finally said as

the heaving of our shoulders subsided, "but I need a drink."

"I do, too," I told him.

It was only about 10:00 or 11:00 in the morning, but because we were in East Lansing, a college town, it wasn't hard to find a bar open.

"Are you ready?" John asked.

"No," I answered. I can't leave him."

"Take him in," he responded. So on a chair between us sat Baby, who I knew loved me as much as he loved his own dam, finally getting to "have" the drink with us that he didn't get to have when he won his first race and I wished he could have been there celebrating. Once we came home, we set the big, ugly white tub on the coffee table, where it sat for an entire year.

As the weeks wore on, I conducted more and more research. I learned from a man named Steve Wood, the superintendent of the well regarded Santa Anita track in California, that on top of a hard limestone track base, there were supposed to be so many inches of clay, and on top of the clay, so many inches of a very specific blend of sand and silt that would let water run off. Never, ever, was a horse's foot to break through those inches of clay and sand and strike the limestone, which was like cement. The soft cushion on top was supposed to be uniformly thick enough all the way around the track, and all the way from the rail on the inside to the track's outer edge—some 90 feet.

But it wasn't. The protective cushion at the Detroit Race Course was much higher near the inside rail. That's why jockeys preferred not to run right alongside that rail, even though it would have been the shortest distance around. In fact, most of them tried not to run within five feet of it. Too deep of a cushion would slow a horse down, like trying to run on heavy sand on the beach.

Just how deep the sand-clay cushion was at the rail no one knew, and it also wasn't known why so many horses were breaking down. To find out, I convinced the HPBA board to pay for an independent evaluation by Steve Wood himself. Along with being the superintendent of a top-level track, he was the vice president of the International Race Track Safety Board.

Steve agreed to come to Michigan for a fee of a few thousand dollars—a lot of money for our board—and do an inspection himself.

Part of what he told us was just what the jockeys and trainers already knew through experience. Near the rail, the combined layers of clay and sand were as deep as ten inches.

But what came as a shock to all was that out a ways, the clay-sand cushion was sometimes only a quarter inch deep, much too shallow to protect a horse's leg from the hard limestone surface beneath. The whole of it was supposed to be on the order of six inches. While the jockeys and trainers were aware the horses could run faster there than they might have anticipated, they had no idea just how dangerously thin the soft, protective layer had become. It explained to them why they might have had at least one, if not two, horses die on the track that season but hadn't lost any for five seasons before that. Routine maintenance had deteriorated to an astonishing degree.

Worse still, Steve found, the limestone was a mess. In spots it came up like waves. In other areas there were dips and gouges. No wonder horses were now breaking down in record numbers. They were running on just a sliver of soft material above a hard surface in complete disrepair.

Steve told us that industry standards called for measurements to be taken in several spots around the track every single day—and posted for everyone to see. That way, if the cushion were deeper in one area, bettors would understand why there was a bias in where the horses were being run. They could then use the information in handicapping winners.

But our track never checked to see that the racecourse clay-sand combination was of a uniform consistency and depth all the way around and all the way across. Workers would drive harrows and graders around, but no one ever followed up by taking measurements to determine whether that made the track level. We didn't even have a track superintendent, let alone someone to take measurements.

Steve recommended that the track be shut down for two weeks for the necessary repairs and that two weeks be added to the end of the season so no one would lose any money. If the night lights were used and work went on twenty-four hours a day, he said, the waves in the limestone base could be shaved, the valleys filled in, and then an even layer of clay and sand installed and leveled. After that, he said, there would need to be daily track maintenance. The top layer of sand would naturally drift toward the center, toward the inner rail, since the track was built on a bit of a slant for rainwater to drain off.

Steve put his recommendations in writing for the HBPA board to file with both the track and the State Racing Commission, and when we presented them, to our great surprise, the track agreed to do the work. We couldn't believe how easily the higher-ups acquiesced and were thrilled that our efforts were going to bear fruit. Even the trainers were glad, despite the fact that they would not be earning any money for two weeks. Too many horses were going down.

A week later, the HPBA board paid for Steve's assistant, Danny Houck, to fly out from California and oversee the repairs, but Danny soon called me and said, "I don't know what to do here. I've phoned Steve for advice because they are *not* repairing the base."

It turned out the track heads were now saying

Steve wasn't qualified to evaluate our track because he was from California, where tracks are built differently to accommodate different weather conditions and, further, that they had never agreed to make any repairs. They said they would spend three days smoothing out the soft top layer but were not going to touch the base, which of course was going to leave the larger problem unsolved. They also refused to take measurements.

When we brought this up to Steve, who had supervised the building of tracks from Argentina to Hong Kong, in all kinds of climates, he responded in writing: "It does not matter if you are from the east coast, west coast, or the North Pole. Irregularities in the limestone base were visible to the naked eye of either an expert or nonexpert . . . it was quite obvious there was a problem."

From those in the Racing Commission, whose salaries depended on money being made by the track, we received no communication at all.

By that point—the middle of July—more horses had died on the track than had died all through the previous season, which lasted through Thanksgiving.

"Why are you still sending your horses out there?" I would ask various trainers.

"Jo Anne," they answered, "you can take your horses home. This is something you did extra. But it's how I make my living, how I pay my mortgage. My kids go to school here. I can't just pick up and go to another track."

I wasn't having an easy time of it emotionally. It was impossible for me to walk down Baby's shedrow. If I went to see a trainer because his horse didn't finish a race and I wanted to find out why, I would just look down when I passed the gravel road where Baby's stall had been. He was on my mind all the time. I think what drove me was not so much vengeance as incredulousness. How could this happen to my horse—and still be happening to other horses—with everyone now having no doubt about what was wrong but not lifting a finger to fix it?

Yet every day I had to steel myself, have a cry before getting out of my car, reapply my makeup, and then go back there business-minded so I would be taken seriously. Otherwise, people would have told me to get over myself, that what happened to Baby happened to horses all the time. It would have been seen as *my* issue rather than as an endemic problem.

And the problem was much worse than I imagined. I had started asking trainers and others what happened to all the horses who went down, since I knew not all of them suffered a life-ending injury. Sometimes these conversations would take place in a local bar that we would go to after board meetings. Sometimes they'd occur right at the rail.

"Oh, I got rid of it," they would tell me.

"What do you mean?" I'd ask. "I just want to keep my records straight."

"Oh, it went to auction."

"Auction?"

"Yeah, the meat buyer took it. I got eighty cents a pound."

I still wasn't quite getting it—I continued to have it in my head that the horses were retired to a farm, or rehabilitated somehow—but the more people I talked to, the more I began to understand.

When horses at the track broke down, they generally weren't taken somewhere for recuperation. And when they experienced a catastrophic injury, they usually weren't put down humanely with an injection, as Baby was. Almost all who could no longer race were sent to a slaughterhouse, and the owners would receive money in return. Their horses would be killed and sold to actual butchers where horsemeat was legal—France, Belgium, Japan. All the little euphemistic blurbs printed with each set of racing results for horses who did not make their way around the track—"broke down," "vanned off," "DNF," for "Did Not Finish"—they all meant the same thing.

People explaining to me that a particular horse was removed would freely use terms like "kill pen." They were all fine with it. It was part of the economics of racing. Why not earn a last few hundred dollars on a used up horse rather than lose money on the horse by chemically euthanizing it or paying to board it somewhere where it could graze on pastureland and be given a nice retirement?

I started to realize that what I thought was abuse—Simply Darling being fed her sweetened grain all at once, the little filly with the bleeding welts—was nothing compared with this slaughter pipeline. It came over me gradually until one day, when my understanding reached a tipping point, I felt dizzy, like I needed to hold onto something. How could this be going on? I had had so much fun here. I laughed in the kitchen, kidded around at the rail, and these very people with whom I had been cavorting were giving their horses horrible ends. I needed to do something.

I found antislaughter groups online who were trying to get the word out. I'd be at the computer and have to stop and look away. The horses, I learned, are crammed together, forced down tight metal chutes, one after another, no matter what their condition, whipped and beaten to make them go faster even if a leg is broken. Then they end up in a metal box and are hit in the head with a retractable bolt that is meant to knock them unconscious. But because horses are naturally head shy, they keep trying to move out of the way, so the bolt shoots out again and again, going into their heads but not killing them, after which they are hoisted up on a chain by one of their hind legs and a sharp blade slits their throats. I couldn't read it all at once, or look at pictures of horses in kill pens starving and thirsty while they waited for a week or more to be sent to a slaughterhouse, often in cramped trailers meant only for hogs and cattle so that they had to bend their heads very low for the entire journey.

It made people pressing me to take Scarlett back to the track all the more preposterous. "It won't happen again," Frank the Greek said to me, referring to Baby's tragedy. "She's sitting on a win. She's on her way." When he found out I now had a full sister to Baby, too, he tried to talk me into racing her as well.

Jerry also had a hard time letting it go. While Pam knew that I wasn't going to change my mind, he would say to me sometimes, "You know my plans for Scarlett. There's the two-hundred-thousand-dollar Sire Stakes Race in October." That's how perfectly made Scarlett was for racing. She was the equine version of the most beautiful actress you can think of, like Julia Roberts or Angelina Jolie on the red carpet.

Scarlett's promise was so well known that even people with whom I was barely acquainted tried to talk me into racing her. "Are you ready yet?" they would ask in the kitchen.

I would never be ready. It was so painfully clear that the track's being dangerously uneven was only a small part of the problem. I didn't want to have anything to do with this activity anymore, this so-called sport in which the "athletes" were treated like decks of cards or dice—gambling devices thrown away once they were "used up."

Even those trainers who treated their horses well inadvertently played a part in racing industry practices. Although such trainers made sure to find a place for all their Thoroughbreds who could no longer race, I knew it couldn't be true for a horse they dropped into a claiming race that was then bought by someone else. That horse probably went from cheap claiming races to the slaughter-house. These trainers did care. One or two would even cry when their horses broke down. But like others who cared—and there *were* people on the backstretch who truly didn't mean any harm—it was easier to look the other way, pretend it didn't happen, accept on blind faith the assurances of those who obfuscated the truth by saying they'd find a broken down horse "a good home" or "take care of it." I couldn't pretend anymore. The thought of it all turned my stomach.

In the meantime, wrangling with the track and the Racing Commission went on through the entire summer and early fall, with me continuing to write unanswered letters asking why these entities were not adhering to the rules and regulations for track safety, why the track was not even taking measurements. Finally, in October, I and the rest of the HBPA board found out that the track had hired its own independent evaluator, the track superintendent at prestigious Belmont Park in New York. His final report was more scathing than Steve's, stating that it would take $595,000 to repair the track. Even with that, however, no improvements were in the works.

It was then that I decided to hire a lawyer. I wanted it acknowledged that beyond my own clouded judgment, it was a financial calculus that killed Baby. He deserved that. By forcing that truth out, I could save him, or at least something of the dignity he deserved. Even more important at that point, I needed to try to protect other horses from the same fate. I knew that if someone else had owned Baby, he would have ended up at a slaughterhouse, where, abandoned, he would have met a frightful end.

Every horse, utterly dependent on its owner, understands what it means to love and to feel loved and to bond with other horses and with people. Every horse is by nature cautious. Every horse loves to roll in the grass, to shake out the snow. By working to save them going forward, I was in some way saving something of what I so loved about Baby.

CHAPTER NINE

Having been a court reporter for years, I should have known what a difference hiring an attorney would make. Through all my months of writing letters to the State Racing Commission, making phone calls, attending HBPA board meetings, and meticulously monitoring the injuries and deaths of Thoroughbreds on that form I had designed, I had gotten nowhere. But then I brought Bill Mitchell onto the case after researching who would be the best lawyer to represent me. Within weeks, the Racing Commission, whose job it was to make sure the track adhered to laws regarding safety for the horses, set a hearing date for December 10th. They subpoenaed dozens of people, including track experts, trainers, HBPA board members, veterinarians, even the track executives. These people were served not just subpoenas but subpoenas *duces tecum*, meaning they were to arrive at the hearing bearing supporting documents.

How glad I was to be served my own subpoena one day at the HBPA Board office. Now, finally, all the documentation I had been amassing could be used to make the track do its job.

William Mitchell III, outspoken, determined, and unfazed by controversy, came to me by way of the new president of the HBPA board, who had been elected just weeks earlier. I knew a lot of attorneys, but the board president knew attorneys who knew the racing commissioner, who had been appointed by the governor. He knew attorneys who knew the track executives. He also had a really warm feeling for his horses and so understood how much I loved mine. And he, too, had lost one of his most promising Thoroughbreds to the track, a young filly whose two front legs literally broke off at the knees during morning training that year on the uneven racing surface.

Bill Mitchell, my lawyer in the suit against the track.

Bill had not been a complete unknown to me before then. A top criminal trial attorney both sharp and jovial, he was on TV all the time. I liked that he was a trial lawyer interested in high-profile cases and, just as important, I liked that he used to own racehorses himself. He really understood the inner workings of the track and the legal responsibilities of the various parties involved.

Bill and I agreed that I shouldn't start by filing a lawsuit but, rather, that he work to force the necessary repairs to the track to stop the maiming and, in addition, arrange a settlement for the loss of Baby. We assumed a settlement would be easy to reach. The evidence on what happened to Baby was so strong.

To this day I don't know what Bill did to get things moving so fast. If someone smoked in a shedrow, the Racing Commission didn't hesitate to fine the person fifty dollars. But enforcing rules that would cost the track money—that it had not wanted to do.

By 10 A.M. on the day of the hearing, the room was packed. I didn't expect it to be jammed, but even the press was there. I wore a simple black dress with a black jacket—the same outfit I wear today when giving speeches about racing as a slaughter pipeline.

"I'm going to be busy," Bill said to me when he found me in the crowded hearing room. "I've got to talk to a lot of different people. But I'm here."

I couldn't wait to be called to give my testimony after all those months of trying to get the attention of the racing commissioner. I had my written statement and all my other exhibits in order—minutes of board meetings, copies of letters to the commission going all the way back to May, my own horse's veterinary records to show he was sound, and my continually growing list of horses who had died on the track.

But hours passed as I and everyone else sat there, waiting for the hearing to start. Private meetings kept taking place in various small offices—I'd see Bill go in one room with the racing commissioner and some of his deputies, then exit that space and go into another with the owners of the track.

Finally, there was an announcement that there would not be a hearing after all. The track had agreed to begin the repairs recommended by its own expert from Belmont, the one who had said the fixes would cost almost $600,000. Beginning as soon as possible, weather permitting, they would start the first of two phases: completely rebuilding the limestone base—not patching it but rebuilding it. They'd also add the necessary soft cushion. The work would be done from the rail all the way to forty-five feet out, which would be wide enough since we never had eighteen to twenty horses in a race, like the Kentucky Derby does. At most we'd have eight to ten, sometimes twelve.

Phase II, the repair of the track at the two starting gate shoots—short areas on which the horses must run when they break from the gate in order to enter the oval of the racecourse—would take place later in the year.

We won! I couldn't believe it. Just like that, the track was going to be fixed. It was too late for Baby and all the other horses that had died throughout the season, but at least going forward things would be different. I couldn't wait to call John to let him know that my doggedness had paid off. I couldn't wait to come home and tell the horses. For once I'd be going to the barn with good news instead of just misery that Baby wasn't there.

Mostly I wanted to tell Scarlett. She was my direct link to Baby, even more than Sissy. Although, unlike Sissy, she was only his half sister, she had lived at the track with him, raced with him, trained with him, traveled to Florida with him.

I also knew she'd be leaving again soon, right after Christmas, in fact. I had signed her up for eventing, and she'd be boarded and trained at a facility twenty minutes away, in Ann Arbor.

It was not an easy decision. I loved having her near me, just enjoying herself in the pasture, enjoying being a horse. I also loved watching Scarlett and Sissy play together now that Sissy was big enough to be let out into the pasture with a barn mate other than her mother. Scarlett was still a young horse, only four, not even an adult yet, and had lots of young-horse energy, whereas Beauty and Pumpkin were old by then and didn't want to tear across the pasture with a weanling. Pat was not going to play tag, either.

Scarlett and Sissy would roll in the snow, get up and shake, then run together, their heels kicking in the air. It was beautiful to watch, if bittersweet. Here was a still-growing replica of the adult-size Baby cavorting with Scarlett, just as he had. The bonding between them was almost as intimate, as tender. It was a time-warped re-creation of what I remembered so well about Baby and Scarlett, one in which Scarlett had aged but Baby was still only months old.

Does Scarlett know this is Baby's sister, I wondered, in addition to being her own half sister through Pat? Does she recognize something about Sissy's scent? Or was I superimposing all this on the scene because of my missing Baby so much?

But while seeing them enjoy each other's company tugged at my heart, I was not able to quell my competitive drive. Scarlett simply was too perfect not to perform, not to be shown off.

I would watch her floating trot out back—her movements were so fluid that it appeared her feet weren't even touching the ground—and feel torn between needing her close to me and needing to let her reach her potential. Looking back, it was probably a foregone conclusion even before I realized it. Her potential was going to win out. I wasn't capable of nurturing a Secretariat snow globe, as I once thought I was. Even with Baby's death, having had my competitive nature stoked after it had lain dormant for years once my daughters stopped skating and dancing, having laid bare that very spot in my core where love and striving were one and the same, I had no choice but to send her out to shine, to win.

If you looked up "Thoroughbred" in an equine book or even a dictionary, the illustration would have been a likeness of Scarlett. She was so wonderfully proportioned. Everything hit the ground right. There was not an ankle bone that was too long or a leg that toed in. She had not too long or short of a back, not too short a neck to support her head. She also had huge dinner-plate feet, perfect for digging into the ground on a jump in order to get lift, and perfect for landing, for absorbing the shock over the widest area possible.

I had thought hard about the discipline in which to have her trained before settling on eventing, which is sort of like a triathalon for horses. It combines dressage, in which a horse is judged on performing difficult but flowing movements without any apparent communication from her rider, almost like an equine ballet; cross-country jumping in varied terrain; and show jumping, a high, fast kind of jumping in which rails set in shallow cups aren't to be disturbed and at which Scarlett, with her perfect conformation, would excel.

I thought she would particularly love the cross-country jumping. The obstacles are set out, maybe fourteen within three-quarters of a mile in the easier competitions, each two to three feet high. But as the competitions increase in difficulty, covering more than two miles, the patterns become more difficult, with as many as forty obstacles to pass and higher jumps to make. The obstacles themselves get wider, too. Whereas at first the horse might have to jump only over a log, later she'll have to clear things like a car, or a picnic table, flying five to eight feet through the air after taking off. The horse has to go faster in more advanced competitions, too, with penalties not just for lagging but also for refusing to jump. Scarlett would love the outdoor courses where she would be able to open up and run between jumps.

She would also excel at it. When she was only two, she had been out in the big pasture grazing alongside Baby one day when, without her noticing, he walked out of sight. Suddenly, not knowing where he had gone, she grew frantic and started calling to him, deep belly whinnies in which you could have heard the alarm way down the road. But Baby wasn't down the road. He had simply walked back into the barn and didn't answer her, probably figuring, "What's the big deal?"

I could see Scarlett building up a panic and running back and forth behind the pasture's fence. She thinks he got out, I realized, and was wandering who knew where. Finally, desperate, she spun around and went tearing directly toward the fence, five feet high, to get to him. "This is it," I thought. "She's going to go straight into it and fracture something." Now my own mind was in a panic. But instead, she took off and sailed over the boards, tucking up her front legs close to her chin and never even coming close to touching the fence top.

Now out of the pasture and in our front yard, having escaped, she began looking for Baby, still bellowing to him. Perhaps sensing that her call was further away than before, he finally honked back. At that, she spun around and came flying to the barn, entering through its front door rather than from the pasture.

With great relief she switched from whinnying to nickering, from "Where *are* you? I can't *find* you," to "It's you, it's you. I was so worried about you. Don't do that to me anymore." The two were immediately nose to nose as usual, continuing to live in the moment, as horses do.

What I realized, remembering that incident, was that Scarlett could definitely compete in anything that involved jumping. A lot of horses leave a leg dangling as they jump, or both legs, and hit the obstacle, whether it be a rail or other object. That's why, when training, they start out simply walking over poles laid out on the ground, then proceed to jumping obstacles only a foot high, and get to five-foot fences much later. But not Scarlett. At two, without any training, she already had it down.

Between the jumping, the running, and the dressage, horses who compete at high levels of eventing must be sound and more physically fit even than racehorses, who use only one set of muscles over and over as opposed to the muscles throughout their bodies. That appealed to me. I also liked that winners at most levels get ribbons. Money doesn't change hands until a horse gets to the very highest levels. And even at those levels, I learned when I probed, there were no scandals, as there often are when you mix horses and money. Eventing doesn't involve plying the horses with drugs. It doesn't involve sending horses to slaughter; it's a clean activity, a sport in the Summer Olympics, even.

In fact, I came to learn that rather than "going through" their horses, eventers more often than not really bond with them. When it comes time to move on to another horse, say, because the current one is not able to go to the next level, an owner generally doesn't dump his animal for the highest price he can fetch. He tries to find someone who needs a lower-level horse by talking with fellow competitors.

I can't say the conditions at the training facility where I boarded Scarlett for her training in eventing were perfect. I was nervous to send her away after Christmas. One problem was that Ann Arbor was a drive in the opposite direction from my court reporting work, so I knew that while I'd make it a point to go see her several times a week, I wasn't going to be able to get out there every single day. Also, there was no grass in the paddock where Scarlett was turned out for free time, so she couldn't graze.

But she was such a spirited horse. I really couldn't see keeping her confined to our little farm. And eventing seemed like such an all-around workout. If I were a horse, I thought to myself, particularly an athletic horse like Scarlett, that would be the kind of competition in which I'd want to engage.

Having Scarlett in a new pursuit and having to worry over her also gave me some relief from thinking about the track non-stop, selfish as that might have been. But the relief was meager at best. Although the track was closed for the winter, I still had to attend HBPA board meetings, more of them than usual, in fact, in preparation for the racecourse's resurfacing. It was hard to be there. I couldn't bear to look at the exact spot where Baby had pulled himself over. I understood, in a way I never had, why people put crosses at spots along the highway where loved ones have died in crashes. If I could have marked Baby's spot in some way, I would have.

Not until February did workmen begin removing the top, cushiony layers of the track. During board meetings, we'd see massive pieces of equipment out there on the racecourse, followed by growing mounds of clay and sand in the customer parking lot, which was paved, unlike the trainer/owner lot. The cushion materials would be reapplied to the track once the limestone base was rebuilt.

Toward the end of March, the board was told that the base was ready. We were asked to walk the course and approve it before the soft materials were added back.

But approval was out of the question. Every so many feet, you would step in a hole so deep it literally swallowed your ankles. Extending down eight to ten inches, it buried a man's entire work boot. The company hired to do the work had not had those heavy rollers go over the track to make it compact, as is done on highways.

The holes weren't the only problem. There were extended grooves, maybe five inches deep but three to four feet across, that had been created when water eroded some of the limestone. Water drainage had been set up improperly, with some areas more heavily drained than others.

The track did go back in and have the compaction executed properly to get rid of the holes, and also fixed the problem with the ditches. But we had to fight them tooth and nail to do it.

And that wasn't the whole of it. When the cushion material had been picked up from the customers' paved parking lot, the graders went too deep and took up asphalt along with the clay and sand. The workmen were supposed to have sifted through the top layer to remove all those pieces but did not. The track cushion now had big chunks of asphalt mixed in. Hundreds of thousands of dollars had been spent, with no one working for the track monitoring the progress. It took more haggling, with the HBPA board's finally bringing out the track's own independent consultant from Belmont Park in New York, to force the sifting.

The racing season was finally allowed to start once this correction was made, but there was already talk by the track that it didn't want to pay for Phase II of the repairs—fixing the shoots that led from the starting gates to the oval. It was a staggering combination of incompetence and corruption.

I wasn't too worried on that score, as once Bill became involved, tremendous headway had been made in getting the track to fix the racecourse despite its trying to shrug off its responsibility at every turn. I figured his involvement would force their hand with the shoots, too. But he had not been able to bring the track heads to the table to offer a settlement for Baby's death. I thought it would be easy once the track agreed to make the repairs to the racecourse. I thought their willingness to fix the track surface was an admission that something was wrong, the definitive proof we needed to make them own up that they were liable and settle rather than go to court. I was wrong. In

May, with no movement on that front despite Bill's many requests to meet with the track executives about Baby, he and I started discussing whether to file suit.

Don't do it, people on the board, as well as others, warned me. They said they had never known anyone who sued the track and managed to see the case through to the end, let alone win. "Their attorney will take your suit and file a motion to dismiss every other week," I was told. "They will keep hauling your lawyer into court. They will drag it out for years, to the point that it will cost you so much money you'll finally go away."

Moreover, they couldn't consider joining me in the suit even though many of their own horses had been maimed, and many more still had to be put down. The track would blackball them, refusing them stalls and banning them from the premises. And because racing was their livelihood, they couldn't afford to take that step.

Incongruously, in the middle of my deciding what to do about a suit, Scarlett entered her first competition. It was just a dressage event rather than a three-pronged eventing competition because the trainer wanted to see how she was going to fare. She had never done anything but race, and, the trainer wondered, would she be able to get on with a lot of horses in an entirely different arena?

The trainer needn't have been concerned. Scarlett

won. She did so well, in fact, that someone came up to me after the show and offered me $15,000 for her.

In truth, I can't say I was terribly surprised. Stepping off the trailer, she had the same air of confidence she had about her at the track, the "look of eagles," as they say of class Thoroughbreds. She was good, and she knew it.

Others did, too. During the winter, a world-class coach visiting from Virginia who had been watching her train wanted me to send her to him for more elite preparation. I refused. I would have been able to see her only a few times a year and, having already lost one love, I was not going to give up my life with another.

Scarlett's success, juxtaposed against having to make the decision about whether to file a lawsuit on Baby's behalf, was made more emotionally fraught by the fact that this was May. May 8th would have been Baby's sixth birthday. And May 25th, the anniversary of the day he died, loomed like an approaching eclipse. The previous year, that date had been filled with such promise, such excitement. Now, the grief was just as intense as ever, but people were going to expect me to have gotten over it, the way they want people to get over the death of any loved one once a year has passed and a Christmas, a birthday celebration, has come and gone without the departed person. Yet I would still wake up sometimes wondering for a moment whether it was all a dream. That's how close it all still felt—not just that awful day but his whole life.

Like a movie reel running through my head, I thought of how the vet teased me by saying "you've got a problem" when Baby was born because I had gotten the gender wrong, of how I blew noisemakers in the barn to desensitize him to startling noises, of his honk, of how he stuck his nose through the "prison" bars at his first training facility.

On the afternoon of May 25th itself, John and I sat in the great room, the clock ticking interminably while I looked from Baby's ashes back to the clock's slow-moving hands. The room was unbearably quiet—John and I said nothing to each other—but inside I was roiling, as if it were happening all over again. I felt swept along as if struggling in overwhelming waves—we were once more waiting at the picnic table outside the stalls on race day, sitting in the stands—until the moment arrived, 6:20 P.M., and as though swallowing too much water, I was gasping, then a zombie again, the breath knocked out of me.

I went up to bed, although it was still daylight, to cry and bury myself under the covers for not having been able to stop it, to stop time, holding the bag with the horseshoe and the piece of his mane in my hand rather than putting it on the end table, as usual.

Three days later, on May 28th, Bill filed suit.

I remained in an emotional well through most of June, finally sprinkling some of Baby's ashes in the pasture where he used to like to walk and putting much of the rest of them in a beautiful stein that I turned into an urn and kept in my office.

The *Detroit Free Press* covered the story of the suit—"Horse owners sue Ladbroke," the headline read. (The official name of the track owner-ship was Ladbroke Racing Corporation.) "Reel Surprise was injured May 25, 1996, during a race. . . . The lawsuit contends Ladbroke knew or should have known that the track was unsafe and should have made repairs. . . . Ladbroke officials did not return calls."

The track, in a veiled threat to Pam, told her to "control your owner." They also wrote a letter to the HBPA board saying they reviewed the board's bylaws and that I didn't meet the requirements to be a member and, further, that I should not be on the board at any rate since I had a lawsuit pending. To my great relief, the board wrote back that it was well aware of its own bylaws and that I was properly seated as a member and would remain so.

Through all of this, I continued to see horses break down and be carted off, not at the rate at which breakdowns occurred before the track was repaired, but horses sustained injuries all the time even on an even track surface, especially horses in the cheap claiming races for which our track was especially known. So many had already been running for their lives for some time, having been shot up with drugs to mask the pain of fractured ankles and knees and other problems and were on their last legs, literally, before being shipped for slaughter for a few hundred dollars while different horses took their place to keep the gambling money, the money that paid everyone from the jockeys to the track executives to the Racing Commission, flowing. How, I kept wondering, was I going to save them? How could I stop the slaughter pipeline?

I had learned through Scarlett's entry into eventing that Thoroughbreds were the breed most sought not only for that discipline but also for dressage and hunter-jumper competitions, or at least Thoroughbreds crossed with a heavy draft-type horse to create what is known as a Warm-blood—an animal with the musculature of a draft horse but the grace and speed of a Thoroughbred. And I knew that many horses sent to slaughter did not have unfixable injuries but were simply too slow for racing, or had slight injuries that required only a couple of months of rest, for which owners were unwilling to pay. I knew, too, that many of these horses were three or four, the age at which trainers in the various sport disciplines *start* working with their charges.

What I couldn't figure out, however, was how to

connect the two worlds, the racing world and the sport discipline world. If people in dressage or eventing could have come onto the backstretch for themselves, they could have easily picked out horses slated for slaughter. Thoroughbreds going to slaughter who would have been perfectly suited for those other disciplines would have been much, much less expensive for sport horse people than Thoroughbreds who hadn't been "spent" in racing, even if the buyers had to pay a little more than the kill buyer's fee. But the backstretch was a highly restricted area. There was no way in which the eventing world was going to get carte blanche permission to go "shopping" there.

The answer came to me by a fluke. I was standing at the rail one day, and a trainer asked if I would come back to his shedrow and take a look at one of his horses. I didn't want to go. I was constantly being approached by trainers who wanted me to get back into racing, offering to go halves on a horse with me so they could make some money as an owner in addition to the money they made on training. But I felt a responsibility to hear the trainer out. One of my main purposes for staying on the board was to remain visible, to continue to be a presence at the track both to figure out a way to save horses as well as to keep abreast during the lawsuit.

When we arrived back at the shedrow, the trainer brought out of a stall a drop-dead, gorgeous gray gelding, 16.2 hands tall—a perfect height, I knew, for sport horse people. I waited for the trainer to give the usual spiel, but he took me by surprise.

"Do you know any of those jumping people?" he asked. It brought to mind a picture of people on pogo sticks. "Do you know any of them who would want a horse like this? He's totally sound, but he can't run a lick."

The man knew the alternative. And although he needed to sell the horse one way or another, he recognized the pure waste of sending it to slaughter.

There was no doubt about my being able to find a buyer. Not only was the horse the right height, but people in the sporting world love grey horses, and greys make up only a small percentage of Thoroughbreds.

I approached the horse to see if he was going to jump out of the way, if his eyes would go wide. But when I touched his neck, he remained quiet. There was no prancing or trying to avoid me. He had not a bit of fractiousness in him.

"He'll try as hard as he can," the man was saying. "He really wants to please—"

The horse stood quiet, docile, as I bent down and ran my hands along his legs to check for injuries, agreeably smelling the top of my head. "Who are you?" he was asking. He reminded me of my own horses, so easygoing he was.

"Let me ask around," I said, especially excited because it seemed there was absolutely nothing wrong with that horse. "Can you give me a few days?"

"Yeah, sure," the guy answered.

As soon as I arrived home, I made a few phone calls. "We've got this horse at the track, grey, appears sound, really sweet disposition. . . ."

Two or three days later, when I went through the track kitchen to get to the backside, as I did every single day, people started coming up to me. "Would you go with me to my shedrow and take a look at this horse I have?" "Do you think one of those jumping people might want my horse?" I couldn't go twenty feet without someone stopping me.

It turned out the gray horse had sold. When I had made phone calls from home to see who might want it, I gave the trainer's number. Some-one had called him and struck a deal. The price of horsemeat could fluctuate down to thirty cents a pound—$300 for a 1,000-pound horse—and if someone were willing to pay him $500, or even $1,000, it was definitely worth it for him to sell it to that person instead of to the kill buyer, who would either take it to auction or straight to the slaughterhouse. Then, too, not everybody on the backstretch felt fine about killing horses; it was simply an economic necessity. If they could assure the horse a second life while turning a

234

profit, it was preferable to them on both counts.

More people approached me when I reached the rail. "Do they only want geldings? I've got a mare. Would they buy a mare?"

"Sure, they'd buy a mare," I said. Those in the sport disciplines did in fact like mares, not just for competitions but also for breeding. They could breed the mare to a draft horse and make their own Warmblood instead of paying tens of thousands of dollars for one. Even a mare who was too injured from racing to participate in a sport could be used for that purpose.

Another would ask, "They probably don't want a horse with an injury, right?"

"Well, it's possible. What's wrong with the horse?"

I was literally bombarded that morning, and somewhere in the space of about ninety feverish minutes, it came to me. I could save horses by connecting the two worlds in some kind of systematic way. It was so isolated back there behind the track, but the solution seemed obvious once others had connected the dots for me. I could be the middleman who wouldn't take any commission on the sales. That way, if it was later found out that the racehorse couldn't event or breed or otherwise prove useful in the sporting arena, no one in the sport disciplines would think I was in cahoots with the trainers trying to unload their horses for more money than they'd make sending them to slaughter. Just as important, the trainers wouldn't think I was getting a cut of their take.

My mind started racing. I needed to collect the names of people in the sport horse disciplines who were interested in finding out when a suitable horse from the track might be for sale, then get those names to the backstretch. How to do it? I literally lost sleep thinking about it.

Finally, I decided the best approach would be to write an article. Each discipline has its own newsletters, which are always looking for stories. And when I went to the editors of these publications, they all agreed to print an article I prepared called "Looking for a Thoroughbred?"

> If you have considered purchasing a retired racehorse but were not sure how to make contact with their owners or trainers, you may now have your name and telephone number placed on a list . . . you may indicate your price range or other particulars such as height and sex . . . There are no commissions or fees involved in this service . . .

Even the *Equine Times*, a four-state monthly newspaper that went to my market as well as to people involved in Western disciplines, a whole other world from the English disciplines like eventing and dressage, printed the piece—on the front page.

The phone immediately started ringing off the hook. I began typing up a list, adding to it every day, and making thirty new copies each day at the HBPA office. I'd put them in the track kitchen, at the timer's stand near the rail, where the clocker stood for horses who did timed works, in the men's bathroom. "Could you stand here for a minute and make sure no one comes in?" I'd asked someone passing by. "I just want to tape a couple of these on the wall."

Each day, along with adding new sport horse people to the list, I'd subtract any who had already connected with a trainer and bought the horse they were looking for. I'd have to take down all the lists I put up the previous morning and put up the new copies.

It took off like crazy. Trainers would rush up to me. "All the lists are gone. Do you have any more?"

Those in the sport disciplines also kept the pace brisk through a kind of passive word of mouth. "Where did you get that horse?" someone might ask another. "From the track," the person would respond, piquing their interest.

As terrific as this was, it didn't all go off without a hitch. Sometimes a trainer would say to me, "I called people on the list about my horse, and no one wants it. The trailer is coming by at such and such a time. If no one buys it by then, it's going on."

Frantic, with maybe two hours left, I'd start to call people myself. Maybe the guy had an outdated list, or maybe he didn't make calls to all the people who might be a match.

Without lying, I did everything I could to make a horse sound as appealing as possible. If a bay, or reddish horse, had no white markings, which are desirable in the sport discipline world—they call the white spots "chrome"—it was considered ho-hum. That was Baby's coloration. He had had only a few white hairs between his eyes. But I never said "no markings" for such horses when talking to potential buyers. Instead, I'd tell them, "Oh, he's the cutest horse—plain-brown-wrapper bay."

Sometimes I found someone who *would* buy the horse. I'd run from the HBPA office back to the trainer and front the money by writing him a personal check. He could have cash in two hours from the kill buyer. He couldn't afford to trust me that some person entirely unknown to him would follow through. Only if he had the agreed-upon fee in hand would he consent to hold onto the horse for two days until transport could be arranged.

I, in turn, had to hope that the buyer would show up. Fortunately, I never had a situation where someone didn't. I had to meet each of them at the gate since they wouldn't have been allowed on the backstretch without my signing them in.

Sometimes, when I was going down the list making phone calls, someone would say, "It's not for me, but let me call somebody who I think the horse might be right for, and I'll call you back." While waiting, I'd see the truck coming. I'd literally have minutes to save a horse from death. Sometimes I was successful, but there were plenty of times that I wasn't. I needed two more hours that I didn't have.

I bolstered my efforts by walking up and down the shedrows with the horses-wanted list. These were hot days, in the nineties, with high humidity. "I know you're busy," I'd say, "but maybe your wife would make a call. These people pay a lot more than the kill fee. Why not get a couple hundred dollars extra?" Some trainers refused to deal with me. They would just let a horse go to the kill buyer rather than go through the trouble of dialing a few phone numbers.

Coming to terms with who so many of these people really were was one of the most difficult aspects of the struggle. I had worked so hard in the beginning to cultivate friendships with people on the backstretch. I had wanted to be "in," and on some level I was. But so many of those very same people, I learned more and more, couldn't have cared less about horses. We had absolutely nothing in common. Yet I couldn't show my dismay, my anger, my grief. All the while, while working alone with no one else back there to help, I had to remain chipper, friendly, acting as though my heart wasn't broken about Baby, about all the other horses at risk. Making it harder still was that every time I couldn't keep a horse from the kill buyer's hands, I experienced it as a personal failure. I berated myself for not having done more.

I always remembered the horses I wasn't able to save much better than the ones I could. It was not hard to see Baby in each horse that ended up on the truck, whether or not it had his coloring. Sometimes it was the hooves, like iron rather than the seashell-like hooves of most Thoroughbreds. Other times, it was the way the horse's eyes were set in his head, the slant of the shoulder, or the massive rump muscles. Some horses had Baby's bushy, fly-away mane. Often, it was simply the way a horse would react to me as I examined him—smelling my hair or blowing into my nose. Those were signature moves of Baby's.

Once the horses were jammed onto the huge trailer, they stopped being treated like living beings. Without food and water, they'd be forced to wait while the summer sun beat down on the vehicle's metal exterior, pawing, beating each other, literally dying of thirst. They were now meat, and even minimum animal husbandry was refused them. Some were lame, like Baby. They were going to go through the entire slaughter process with a broken leg, in horrific pain, rather than undergo chemical euthanasia.

If there had been any doubt about their ultimate fate, it was erased when an article came out in the *Daily Racing Form* that August about a racehorse named Exceller. A very famous racehorse, Exceller had run in the late 1970s and was best remembered as the only horse to beat two Triple Crown winners. Such a feat had been unheard of.

He retired in 1979, going to a farm in Kentucky to stand at stud. In 1991, he was transferred to Sweden to continue breeding, and when the *Daily Racing Form* went to check up on him for a "Where Are They Now?" column it used to publish now and then, the reporter found out they were several months late. He had been sent to a slaughterhouse that April.

That's when I realized it wasn't just cheap claiming horses at our crummy track who were being sent to their deaths. It was pervasive. Even this famous horse, who had no doubt earned his various owners more than a million dollars, was slaughtered at the end of his stud career rather than allowed to live out his life in peace.

I couldn't talk about this to people on the outside. If I had spoken about slaughter publicly or even about the concept of "rescuing" horses, I would have been forced to resign from the HBPA board and lost my track license, and that would have been the end of my ability to help save the

Thoroughbreds. The board was okay with me trying to improve racing; it would not have been okay with me impugning its members' bread and butter.

On very bad days, when the truck left full, I would go straight to the barn upon arriving home because there I could just sit on the hay and wail. I couldn't cry in the house because John had been opposed to my going back to the track from day one. He would have been even angrier at me if he knew the degree to which it upset me.

The horses never got used to my crying. They hated for me to sob like that. It made them nervous. Tense, they'd prance, move around, bump into each other in the run-in attached to the barn. "What can we do to help? What can we *do?*" They wanted the herd secure, relaxed, not like this, not with one of their own in distress.

If I could compose myself and remain calm before going in, they did better. I'd gently cry on their shoulders, breathe in their scents. Interacting with them, even sadly, was better than just sitting on the hay weeping uncontrollably.

Poor Sissy. She took my moods the hardest. Still only a yearling but already having shown clear signs of her temperament, she was skittish and had a difficult time coping. It was my own fault. In my grief over Baby when she was born, and because physically she was such a searing reminder of him, to my discredit, I couldn't bear to bond closely with her when she most needed it. I hadn't done all the work with her that I had with Baby and then Scarlett—blowing New Year's Eve noisemakers in the barn, waving white sheets, setting out pieces of plywood for her to walk over. My not having worked to desensitize her to unexpected sounds and sights made her more afraid of things in general.

An unusual noise would send her running. If I was walking her down the road and someone started a lawnmower in the distance, I'd have to have very strong control of her lead line and really talk to her—"It's okay, Sissy"—scratching her neck all the while so she wouldn't try to bolt. I could see her muscles tense. To this day Sissy is always ready for flight, in no small part because of the attention I failed to give her when she was very young.

I had little time to devote to her emotional maturation even when I might have felt more ready. Working to save horses became increasingly difficult as fall arrived and the racing season was coming to a close. Trainers needed to dump the Thoroughbreds who certainly weren't going to win anywhere else if they couldn't win in Detroit. It was killing me. If I saved fifty horses that year, probably 150 went unsaved, the greatest proportion of them in October and November.

I was exhausted, physically as well as emotionally, making too many trips to the bar across the street from the track to try to erase all the hours I spent in what was often an unsuccessful attempt to save an animal. Adding to the strain were the trips toward Detroit in one direction to continue my work as a court reporter and then, three to four times a week, in the opposite direction after work to go visit Scarlett in Ann Arbor.

As tired as I was, however, it was always such a pleasure to see her. As soon as I exited the car she'd know I was there, as the parking lot was right next to the pasture where they'd turn her out. I'd call her name, and up would come her head. Once she ran to me at the fence, I'd scratch the big groove between her cheekbones, where flies might bite. She couldn't relieve the itching herself because the indentation was too deep for her to reach by sliding alongside an object. If we moved inside the barn, I'd scratch her neck. She'd tilt her head up and turn it almost with a sigh, the way someone might sigh if you were scratching a part of their back they couldn't reach. "Mmmm, get that side a little more." She'd swing her head up over my shoulders and the top of my own head, then swing it back again for another scratch on the other side.

I was so happy to be surrounded there by the other boarders, who also adored their horses and who never would have thought to "get rid of" them. So different was it from track culture. I loved grooming Scarlett in the barn, in like company. We'd all share stories about the cute things our horses did, their special traits. People didn't talk about horses lovingly at the track.

Making it better still was that, to my great delight, Scarlett had a wonderful surprise in store. At the very end of the season, just before Thanksgiving, her name was announced at an awards dinner as the champion novice horse of the year in eventing for the entire state of Michigan. It was as if she skipped a grade, going straight over "beginner," the first rung on the ladder, to "novice." And not just reaching "novice" but advancing to the pinnacle. Some horses stay in "novice" eventing for three years before being ready to move on to the next level. Her winning was that much more remarkable because it was straight off the track, where all the horses do is run counterclockwise, throwing off their muscle balance.

I had had no idea how successfully Scarlett had been competing, as I hadn't been counting the points she was racking up at shows throughout that summer and fall. It was tremendously over-whelming to hear her name called out, then to go up in front of almost 100 people to be presented with her two-foot blue ribbon and a blanket for her with the word "Champion" embroidered on it. It was affirmation that everything I thought of her, that I knew her to be capable of, was true. I had known that everything I believed about Baby's abilities were true, too, but he never really had a chance to prove it because I kept choosing the wrong circumstances for him. If I had felt comfortable bursting into tears, I would have. Hardly anyone in the room knew anything about Baby. I was elated and rueful all at once.

In fact, as proud as Scarlett made me, and as much as I wanted to continue to make right on Baby's death, I was feeling drained by my own regrets, as well as by the goings-on at the track, to the point that I decided not to return the next year. I just couldn't bear any more witness to these killings as business decisions, couldn't bear to hear people say it didn't make any difference that the horses were whinnying for help while crammed inside the death trailers because "they were just going to die, anyway," couldn't cope with continually seeing before me the images of those horses I hadn't been able to save, each one, like Baby, another of my failures. I made it through the last couple of weeks of the racing season by counting down. "Ten more days, nine more days, eight more days . . ." Soon, I'd never go back to the track again.

CHAPTER TEN

I spent the winter healing in the barn, the decision not to go back to the track made easier by the Detroit Race Course's announcement that the coming 1998 season would be its last. The higher-ups had been hoping to install slot machines and transform the racecourse into a racino. But the state of Michigan turned them down. Casino Windsor had already opened just across the river from Detroit in Canada, a true Vegas-style casino just thirty-five minutes away. And downtown Detroit, just twenty minutes along the expressway, was due to get three casinos, approved on a ballot by popular vote. All these new casinos, very powerful with a lot of money to throw behind their claims to the local territory, were never going to let a racino materialize. The track would be closing.

Two years earlier, I had worked very hard to procure slot machines for the racecourse, pushing for it as a member of the HBPA's political action committee and even participating in a press conference held in the state capitol. My personal stock with the track's higher-ups had risen astronomically. "I never want to be on the other side of you," Ladbroke executive Bill Bork said to me at the time, pleased with my presentation. Now here we were, exactly in that position. With my suing the track, I couldn't be more on the other side.

The decision to close helped explain why Ladbroke dragged its heels fixing the racecourse and did such a shoddy job of overseeing the repairs. It had no doubt already known that it would be shuttering its gates.

My wish to make right on Baby's death notwithstanding, my resolve never to return was only strengthened by the news. Rather than feel I could handle trying to save horses for just one more year, I knew that an imminent permanent closing would mean the need for trainers to get rid of more horses than ever—a number I would find too overwhelming.

Michigan had always been a racing state, with a lot of trainers who actually put down roots there rather than travel nomadically from track to track throughout the country, as many do. In the 1950s, the Detroit Race Course was considered one of the premier tracks, right up there with Churchill Downs, so to work there had once come with a certain prestige. Once the track closed, trainers who had made their homes in Michigan would not take their horses somewhere else; they would get out of the business—and get rid of their Thoroughbreds as expediently as possible. I had already been through a season during which I lost more horses than I saved. I knew that in this climate of trainers needing to get rid of even sound horses, my efforts would be futile. Besides, I had already exhausted potential sport discipline buyers with my articles in local newsletters. There was no one else to tap into.

Taking care of my own horses at home had the effect of a tonic. Being near them warmed me, and I could feel my depression lift some. Just grooming them, letting them in and out of the pastures, scrubbing their water pails, removing debris from the crevices at the bottom of their feet—it all proved restoring.

Scarlett wasn't there. She was training through the winter, which was fine with me since she had done so well the previous year, and I continued to visit her several times a week.

But in the barn I still had Beauty, Pumpkin, Pat, and Sissy. Sissy, now going on two, had grown to the size of a bull moose. So muscular and strong boned had she become, like Baby, that you would not immediately have perceived her as a filly. And with her forelock perennially covering the star on her forehead, and her bushy mane and tail, which, like Baby, she had inherited from Pat, she looked uncannily like him, down to her iron hooves.

While I tried to bond with her, exhaling into her nose and giving her treats, it did not bring me comfort that she looked like her brother. Instead, it was a reminder of what I hadn't accomplished despite my having gotten the track fixed and saving dozens of horses. I was never going to bring Baby back, never going to fix what I had done to *him*.

Sissy was the only one of the four who elicited in me mixed emotions. The others were pure joy.

Beauty, my very first horse, I had already had for almost fourteen years, since 1984. We bought her even before we closed on the house. I loved to ride her, and she loved to be ridden, so it was easy to go on the spur of the moment. It's difficult to get most horses away from the herd. But Beauty was never barn sour, meaning unwilling to leave her mates. For her it was a treat to quit the barn, the pastures. "Come on Beauts," I'd say. "Let's go visiting." It didn't matter how many days had passed since I had last ridden her. She never acted silly and bucked, or raced off, the way some horses do when they haven't been mounted in a while. She never needed to be warmed up with lunging—having the "vinegar" taken out of her by being exercised in a circle on a thirty-foot line with a lunge whip with which you strike the ground if a horse refuses to move. I didn't even need a saddle. I could just grab a bridle and throw it on. She was only 15.2 hands high—easy.

Beauty had a naturally fast walk, which I like in a horse, and as she moved away from the house, the other horses would all call out to her while running around in the pasture, going crazy that one of their own was leaving. But she'd just keep going. Baby had been the same way. I loved it because it made me feel they'd rather be with me than with the rest of the herd. Once in a while Beauty would whinny back to the others, but not as a rule.

On the main gravel road near the house, a lot of people have horses in their backyards, so sometimes I'd go riding with a neighbor. But more often, we went ourselves, and the world disappeared.

Winter was such an especially wonderful time to ride her, as long as there was no ice. Her body kept me warm—it was like sitting on a heater—and if it was snowing, her all-black hair would become covered in white, making for a beautiful apparition. We never galloped but rather just enjoyed the sights in the woods, perhaps a deer running or birds foraging for food. With no leaves on the trees, you could see far into the distance.

As a Quarter Horse, Beauty would grow a very thick winter coat, heavy and furry, and I would open my fingers and push them along her neck, feeling the warmth coming off her body. It was fun to move my hands through her wooly covering, and when we'd come home, I would just hop off. Beauty was never even sweating, as we only walked, never trotted.

Nobody was ever more glad to see Beauty return to the barn than Pumpkin. Our second horse, Pumpkin had been advertised in the paper for $400, saddle and bridle included, and when we went to see her, it was clear she was starving. She had on her heavy winter coat of hair, but even through that, each rib was easy to see.

It was December 1984, the same year we brought Beauty home. A bucket of water for Pumpkin to drink had frozen over. At the same time, the ground remained soft; she was standing in mud that rose well over her feet.

After calling the vet to come give her a pre-purchase examination—she looked so bad that I wondered whether she might need to be put down—we took her home on Christmas Eve. My neighbors told me years later that when we first brought Pumpkin to the barn, they thought, "Jo Anne has got to be crazy." She was so very skinny and miserable looking. But by the next May, after Pumpkin shed her winter coat and had already been well fed for months, her new coat had the look of satiny, polished mahogany—a deep brown with orangey highlights.

That beautiful, docile horse—part Morgan and part Quarter Horse, the vet thought—became the one on which my daughters' friends would ride if they had never been on a horse before. She would canter for Jessica and Rebecca, but if Pumpkin knew you didn't know what to do, she wouldn't go faster than a walk.

Lowest in the pecking order, she was particularly attached to Beauty, who was definitely the leader of the herd. Pumpkin depended on Beauty; it had been just the two of them for years. Often they went out together, me on Beauty and one of the girls on her. But if I went out alone, she, more than any of the others, would run around and whinny. We'd hear her in the distance, and neighbors would tell us she whinnied from the time we left until the moment we arrived back home, beside herself with worry.

It wasn't as bad once Pat came to stay with us and Baby was born, but Pumpkin never became truly comfortable with Beauty's leaving, even for very short periods. "Is it really you?" she'd say with her scent, blowing into Beauty's nostrils upon her return. "I'm so glad."

Now thirty-one years old, Pumpkin was retired. With Jessica in medical school and Rebecca away at college, she didn't get ridden anymore, nor did she need to. It was her time just to eat and enjoy the sun on her back. But she was my connection to my daughters; I loved having her with me. Always gentle, she had absolutely no bad habits. She loved apples over carrots, and I was happy to oblige. I was happy to put a fan in the barn near her in the summer, happy to do whatever I needed to let her know she'd never lack for anything, the way she once had.

When Pumpkin and Beauty had first come to live with us, I loved listening to them munch their hay in their stalls at last check every night, around ten o'clock. It was so relaxing. I knew they were safe. They were eating. They had everything they needed. I could go to bed happy and sleep well, comforted that despite what had happened to Pumpkin, I had been able to save her. The world then was a good place.

It was what I was trying to re-create, at least to some degree, in the winter of '98, and I thought I was succeeding. Not only did I have Beauty and Pumpkin to complete the picture, and "little" Sissy, I also had Pat, the mother of my "children," who herself had been through a lot. Although she was such a large horse, almost sixteen hands, she was so very people-oriented, a true pet. You would never have been able to guess that she had been a racehorse before she became a broodmare. But Don Shouse, her owner before me, had indeed raced her until she was found to have bone chips in her knee and could no longer run, which was why he turned her into a mother.

She had actually broken her knee during a race. When she became mine, I had the vet x-ray her to see if we could take out the pieces of bone, but by then her body had already reattached them. It was too late. You could even see protrusions on her knee.

Pat wasn't in pain, but, like someone with arthritis, she did have some restriction of movement, which worsened as she grew older. It didn't hamper her activity when she had Baby. She could still run around the pasture freely at that point.

I enjoyed making sure Pat and the rest of the

herd were always cozy in the barn, closing the barn doors if it grew very cold and always checking to be certain they all had lots of bedding. It was such a comfort to be in the barn with all the horses chomping on their hay, everyone healthy. Such solace. And it was easy to enjoy because I wasn't coming home after work every day to an answering machine full of messages from people wanting to talk to me about buying a horse.

But sometime in March, I did receive a call that put everything in a different light.

A man named Jeremy Bricker phoned out of the blue and told me he knew of me because people at the barn where he boarded a Paint horse—a multicolored breed—had talked about me. But he couldn't find my Web site online, he said.

I barely was using e-mail at that point, let alone designing Web sites. I was still faxing virtually all of my communications, and I told him so.

"I would like to help you," he said. "I think what you're doing is really good. You could reach the world if you had a Web site. Your search for people who want these horses wouldn't have any geographic bounds. I'll create the site, design it, and maintain it. It won't cost you any money. It would be my part to help you help the horses.

"You wouldn't be limited to lists of people with descriptions of horses they were looking for," he added. "You could take pictures of horses that trainers were trying to unload and put them on the site so people could *see* available horses for sale. That would pique interest in Thoroughbreds that didn't match the wish lists of potential buyers."

A soon as he said "no geographic bounds," I realized I had never truly been healing, never making real peace with my decision to keep away from the track. I had simply been feeling defeated, knowing my efforts would be only a drop in the bucket compared to what was needed.

I was back in before he finished his pitch. It wasn't a thought, something I had to weigh. What I had been feeling all along simply bubbled to the surface. I couldn't leave Baby lying there in the form of all the slow and injured horses and now, in the form of all the horses who would be sent to their deaths because their trainers were going out of business. In truth, I never could. It would have gnawed at me terribly if the season had started without my saving horses. My conscience could never have come to terms with such a decision.

"I don't have the money to pay you," I blurted out, even though he had already told me it wouldn't cost me anything. Whatever extra money I had, I wanted to devote directly to buying horses slated for slaughter.

"I told you, don't worry about the money," he said. "This is my way of helping you help the horses. We will do it.

"What is the name of the organization? That will have to be on the Web site."

"It doesn't have a name," I replied. "It's just something I've been doing."

"Well, the first thing we have to do is think of a name," he answered.

Thus began my true entry into e-mailing. Not just Jeremy and I but also a woman named Jill Rauh, a librarian in eventing who lived on the other side of Michigan and knew about my work, began brainstorming online about a title for connecting people who wanted a horse with those who wanted to get rid of one. I said I wanted it to be an acronym so that whenever it was put into print, it would be in all capital letters—no periods between them—and have to jump off the page.

We worked in reverse, first thinking of an acronym and then trying to find words to fit the letters. At one point we came up with TROT and then filled it in with "Teaching Racehorses Other Talents," congratulating ourselves that we had come up with the perfect name. But after a fitful night's sleep, I came to terms with the fact that it wasn't going to work because Standardbred racehorses—those who pull sulkies—are called trotters. There'd be a disconnect between the name and the fact that we were saving Thoroughbreds.

Then one of us suggested CANTER, and the e-mails began flying as we worked over our virtual word puzzle. Finally, Jeremy wrote:

"How about this? Communication Alliance to

Network Thoroughbred Racehorses. I just can't think of anything for the 'E.'"

Immediately, I e-mailed back, "*Ex* Racehorses."

"Ta da," Jill typed, and we knew we had it. A little clumsy, but it would work, and Jeremy went on to create the Web site, buying the domain name and designing the pages.

Now, when the track opened, which coincided with Jeremy's going live with the Web site, I walked the shedrows doing more than just handing out "Horses Wanted" lists with their wish-list descriptions of horses that people in the sport disciplines hoped would materialize. "I can place a free ad for you," I'd say. "Do you have any horses you want to put on the site? You can get more money than the kill buyer would give."

Then I'd have to talk people into letting me take a picture of a horse they wanted to sell. It was not easy because a trainer would have to stop his work and lead a horse out of a stall so I could get a conformation shot—a photograph from the side so people would be able to see bone angles and other details of that nature. "The guy in the next row let me take a picture," I'd say in a teasingly nonchalant way when someone tried to refuse. "He's going to get a lot more calls than you."

Begrudgingly, the trainer would lead the horse out, and I would try to crinkle something to make it turn its head toward the camera. The animals look more fetching that way.

Then I had to bring the film cartridge to the drugstore and pay a premium for overnight development. There was no one-hour film development yet, and digital cameras were just coming into use for the general public. I was years from owning one.

Once I had the film developed, I'd label the photos and overnight them to Jeremy—I don't think I had even heard of the word "scanner"—and he'd get them up on the site.

Sometimes, I'd take five or six photos of a horse and have to go back and reshoot the next day because none of them was any good. It was always a race against time because the trainers could get a few hundred dollars from the kill buyer very quickly. Also, many had no idea what I was doing; they didn't even really know what the Internet *was*.

"Look, so-and-so in the next shedrow sold a horse in three days for fifteen hundred dollars," I'd tell someone itching to put a horse on the trailer. "If you could be a little patient, you could get many times more than you would otherwise." It was true. Now that people from outside the Detroit area would be "shopping" online for the racetrack's horses, prices would be driven up. More buyers meant more competition for Thorough-breds.

Still, I was looked on with no small amount of suspicion. Everyone always wanted to know,

"What's in it for you?" They couldn't believe I would do this just to save horses and not to turn a profit as a middleman.

I called CANTER an HBPA program to lend it legitimacy—the board trusted me enough to allow that and championed it as a win-win-win-win: one for the horses, one for those trying to make a last bit of profit off a horse before getting rid of it, one for those excited to buy a Thoroughbred for sport discipline purposes, and one for racing itself, which would benefit from the PR that the industry tried to find good homes for horses it wanted to retire.

Even so, CANTER was slow to take off—until Shane Spiess became involved. A well-respected trainer with a large stable, he sent horses to slaughter all the time. He was also savvy. After he made considerably more money than he could have gotten from a meat buyer by selling a couple of horses to people in the sport disciplines who had put their names and specifications for an animal on the "Horses Wanted" list, he started buying Thoroughbreds from other trainers. He'd snatch up different trainers' horses for $300, $400, $500, then turn around and sell them to eventers and others for $1,000 or more. "Shane to the stable gate," you'd hear over the loudspeaker, as nonracing people came to inspect a horse and needed to be signed in. I didn't care as long as the horses didn't go to slaughter.

After a couple of months, other trainers started to get wise to him. "Hey, I just *sold* you that horse," they'd say when they'd see a Thoroughbred going on a trailer to be taken away.

"Yeah, I just sold it, too," he'd answer.

That validated what I was doing in the eyes of the other trainers, making them much more willing to work with me. Now people were coming up to me and *asking* me to take a photo of a horse, asking, too, for my advice on how they should price a particular horse. Whereas at first there were fifteen to twenty horses on the Web site, most of them Shane's, the number began to grow from all the trainers wanting in.

They would even run up to prospective buyers who came to the backstretch with an appointment to see a particular horse, or ride up on bicycles. "Don't buy yet," they'd call out. "Take a look at mine first."

By the time summer was in full swing, CANTER was exploding with activity. People began coming from Ohio and Indiana. One woman drove from Virginia with her trailer in tow to take home a horse. Someone else bought a horse sight unseen and had it shipped to her in Florida. "Jo Anne to the stable gate," I kept hearing over the loudspeaker, as shoppers had to be accompanied by someone with a track license. Nowhere else in the country could someone in the sport horse world buy a Thoroughbred this way, with maybe 100 horses for sale to choose from at any one time. No other racetrack had a program anything like it; the track is normally a very isolated place. I knew it, and so did the horse world media. We were written up in *Horse Illustrated*, one of nonracing's highest-circulation magazines, along with a number of other horse-oriented publications. By August, I had saved more horses than I had the entire previous season. They didn't all go to people in sport disciplines. Some buyers just wanted a horse for trail riding, or perhaps for breeding, while others were willing to accept a pasture ornament, a horse whose injuries were so severe it could no longer be ridden but could still enjoy grazing and relaxing. My determination to make right on Baby's death was fully restored.

Horses still went to slaughter, sending my mood to the depths. One failure in particular hurt very bad. It was a two-year-old gelding, a gorgeous chestnut, with four tall white socks and a big white blaze between his eyes that went all the way from the top of his forehead down to his nose. He was so gentle and quiet, still looking like a baby without yet having developed his adult bone or musculature. He still had that childlike curiosity, the way he smelled my hand. The only reason he was being gotten rid of was that he had a leg that was toed in and wouldn't make it through training without breaking down.

His trainer was going to put him up for sale on the CANTER Web site, but he didn't have time; the horse had to go that day. I made some calls and, with no luck placing him, decided I would take him home myself. We were pretty full at our barn at home, but I figured I'd try to sell him to somebody later or just keep him. The trailer came sooner than expected, however, and by the time I came out of the HBPA office after I put down the phone, he was gone. It took all the strength I could summon not to cry right there on the backstretch, a reaction that I knew would only hurt my cause with all those long inured to the ways of the track.

Such occurrences were more the exception than the rule, though. And that shift in the balance offered me respite from the depression that I hadn't been able to see a way out of before. The herd at home sensed this and were happier for the change in my demeanor, which had been calm and gentle over the winter but still shadowed by sadness. I was glad that I was able to come to the barn in a good mood, happy that those at the track called the people who came to see about horses for sale "Jo Anne's tire kickers." Their zeal to sell their horses to people in the sport disciplines rather than for a low price to kill buyers looked comical at times. I'd see some of the top trainers jogging a horse up and down a shedrow for somebody, something they would have never done before, leaving such a chore to a groom. But they wanted to make sure they showed a horse for sale to the best advantage. And to their credit, not all were in it solely for the extra money. Some truly did prefer to be able to find a horse a home.

In the meantime, the suit began to take shape. My deposition was taken, as were those of many others. A number of them occurred out of state. Bill was doing a lot of traveling as well as having to go to court relatively often because the track kept filing motions to dismiss, just as I had been warned it would.

We had to have Baby appraised, and his value came in at only $25,000. He lost so many races with the first two trainers that his monetary worth had been brought down considerably. And the fact that he had injured a tendon signified that it could be reinjured. Furthermore, he died in a claiming race, Pam's strategy for a horse's first race of the year. He *had* been running in allowance races, losing by only a head, or a neck. Had that been the kind of race he was running when he suffered his fatal injury, his price might have been set above $50,000.

Still, I was pleased with Bill's efforts. I didn't care about the money. I just didn't want the track to get away with letting Baby die because it didn't want to spend the necessary amount to keep the surface smooth enough for a Thoroughbred to run safely at high speeds. And on that score, Bill was right there with me, never becoming frustrated with all the depositions and motions. He even appeared to relish the fight.

"I was having dinner at the Turf Club the other night," he said to me one day, "and had so much fun with Bill McClaughlin." The Turf Club was an exclusive, private dining club at the track that you had to pay a lot of money to join, and Bill McClaughlin was the track's new general manager. John and I never saw him at meals because we didn't belong. We always ate in the snack bar area, and on my own, I would pick up a bite in the track kitchen.

"Lots of chitchat, as always," Bill continued. "Then I mention your name. I like watching him when I do that. From his white collar it starts to get red on his neck, and it goes all the way to the top of his head. He just despises you!" Bill finished off with a hearty laugh.

It would have made me nervous had Bill not so obviously relished needling McClaughlin.

John was always interested in hearing about the suit. He was very much in favor of making the track admit its accountability, and I was glad there was a decision about how to handle Baby's death on which we agreed. And while he had never warmed to the idea of my continuing to go back to the track, he must have had something of a change of heart with my CANTER success because one Saturday afternoon in October, we were tailgating at a University of Michigan football game when he noticed that the Channel 7 news team from the local ABC affiliate had a canopy and a tailgating party only about ten car lengths away, and he encouraged me to go over.

"You know, that's Robbie Timmons over there," he said, pointing to the anchorwoman for the five o'clock news broadcast. "Why don't you tell her about the track closing and all those horses needing homes? Maybe if she did a story on it and it got on TV, you'd have more people interested."

I had been talking a lot to magazines and newspapers but hadn't thought of trying to make contact with television stations.

"My husband suggested I come over and talk to you," I said as I approached Robbie. "Are you aware that the Detroit Race Course is closing this year and that many horses there need homes or will go to slaughter? I know this is a bad time to talk about this," not giving her a chance to shoo me away. "But I could fax you information about the closing and how I am trying to—I have a rescue called CANTER, and I'm trying to find homes for these horses."

To my delight, she responded, "That sounds very interesting. Here's my fax number. Yes, why don't you fax me some information?"

Soon enough, I received a call that the station would like to come out to the backstretch to do a story. "I would need you to be there," Robbie told me. "You'd need to show me exactly what you're doing. We'd interview some of the trainers, too."

After receiving clearance from the track for access to the backstretch and permission to video-tape, which I had not been at all certain she'd be granted, she came with an entire news team, and they followed me around, videotaping how I took pictures of the horses outside their stalls, my clipboard in hand to record information. She also did interview various trainers, as she said she would, asking what they were going to do once the track closed. "I don't know," they'd answer. "I can't move out of state, and a lot of these horses are going to need homes." No one, including me, mentioned slaughter on air. The Racing Commission would have taken away our track licenses unceremoniously, Ladbroke would have barred me from the premises, and the HBPA would have asked me to resign from the board. If, damn it all, I *had* gone public with what is well known in the industry as "racing's dirty little secret" about horses going to slaughter, I would have been branded as a crazy lady. It would have been so easy for the track to say, "Her horse died, and she went nuts."

Although I struggled with withholding the truth, in the end the decision not to deviate from the script was the only one I could make. To refrain from saying the truth about what happened to discarded horses was the moral choice in this instance. It allowed me to continue saving horses, and that was the bottom line.

As luck would have it, a woman in one of the sport horse disciplines who happened to be on the backstretch picking out a horse during filming looked directly at the camera and said pointedly, "These horses are running for their lives." She was free to say what I could not.

After all the videotaping was complete, Robbie offered to put my name and phone number on the screen for people to contact me should they be interested in buying a horse. I jumped at the opportunity, but she insisted I weigh it. "Are you sure? Because you're going to get a lot of calls."

"Yes," I said. "I'm sure."

The piece ran two days later, the "running for their lives" comment not edited out, and the phone started ringing before the segment finished airing. "I just saw this thing on TV, and I want to know how I can get a horse. Could you tell—" "Beep beep beeeep." Call waiting was coming through.

"Can I put you on hold a minute?" I asked.

This back-and-forth between phone calls went on, without exaggeration, until midnight, without pause. The callers ran the gamut. There'd be some-one on one line who understood horses and had room to board one and someone on the other to whom I had to explain that "these are tall horses, not for children, they don't know the term 'whoa' because they're taught to run as fast and hard as they can." One person asked for a spotted horse, although no Thoroughbred racehorse is spotted, while a number of people were so moved by the story that, even though they didn't know anything about horses, they wanted to buy one and asked where they could board it, understanding that the Thoroughbreds needed to be saved.

A few hours in, a man called and said, "I was thinking the zoo should have one of these horses." A nut case, I thought. To my mind, the zoo kept wild animals. For all I knew, the zoo fed horsemeat to its animals.

"I don't think that would work," I said. I was so skeptical that I was almost rude.

"The zoo has a barnyard exhibit," the man persisted.

"Yes, I answered, "but it's really a petting zoo. I don't know about a horse for that."

"No," he said. "They really need a horse. Also, could you meet me at the track? I'm going to come with my trailer and my trainer. I want to pick out eight horses." It was getting weirder by the minute.

On and on the evening went, with calls ranging from heartening to bizarre, and would have continued past midnight if we didn't put on the answering machine: "Thank you for your call regarding the horses. Please leave your name and number, and we will get back to you."

In the days that followed, some people very

savvy about horses contacted me, a number of them willing to take, two, three, even four horses. A woman who ran a horse rescue even said she'd take *any* horse who had been injured. These knowledgeable horse people were critical to my moving so many horses off the track in a very short time, a particularly lucky break since it was very nearly the end of the season and a glut of horses would end up dumped if not sent to new homes.

As for the man who called about the zoo, a wealthy developer named Burt Farbman—he turned out to be legitimate. It so happened he was on the Detroit Zoo's board of directors. He had talked to the zoo director, Ron Kagan, who thought having a horse next to the barnyard exhibit was a wonderful idea, and he was willing to build a two-acre pasture to accommodate it.

Ron said the horse would have to be quiet and docile because the barnyard workers were not experienced in working with restless animals. Ron also wanted another animal in the pasture, if not a horse than perhaps a goat or a donkey. He knew that horses did not like to be alone.

I couldn't find a suitable horse at the track. But a vet north of Detroit who had seen the news segment called me about a Thoroughbred on whom he had just operated. The horse's racing injuries were so severe that he could never be ridden again. He was being kept at the owner's farm, unusual in itself because racehorse owners don't usually save broken down animals.

The zoo went to see him, a five-year-old gelding named Siberian Sun, and a more sweet and gentle creature you couldn't find. He lived comfortably at the Detroit Zoo, always with a pal such as a goat or pony, until dying peacefully more than ten years later. The sign by his pasture read in part, "Rescued Animal. Siberian Sun was particularly hard to place . . . he was in foster care for quite some time. . . . Unfortunately, many racehorses are not placed in retirement and are destroyed."

Ron, who has been described by Humane Society president Wayne Pacelle as a "rare zoo administrator" who keeps an eye out for animals in need, still serves as zoo director, and Burt did actually take to his farm more than a half dozen horses from the track.

The newspaper reported that when the horses were first let in the pasture to graze, Burt said they were touching to watch. "They had never been turned out and had never grazed," he was quoted as saying. "First they were afraid, then they started walking, then they ran and ran." Having been cooped up in stalls their whole lives, they had to learn how to be horses.

While good people like Ron and Burt were taking Thoroughbreds who would have otherwise been killed, many people who had seen the TV segment but knew they couldn't care for a horse sent money for Thoroughbreds to be purchased away from the track—ten dollars, twenty dollars, sometimes less, sometimes more. These were completely selfless acts, with not even a tax write-off to be gained because at that point CANTER was simply an HBPA program, not a nonprofit charity. These viewers so loved animals that they wanted to do something, anything, to help, and they trusted that I would spend their money in the horses' best interest. It was testament to people's humanity, and I felt like the warmth of these kindred spirits was so close, a great comfort to me as I worked to link the backstretch to the outside world and in that way change the horses' fate. Away from the economics of the track, I was heartened to learn, there was a world of like-minded people.

Robbie herself was one of them. Not long after the news segment aired, she took me to lunch and asked me if all the horses who needed saving had been taken care of, and I told her no, that while I was trying as hard as I could, I wasn't always successful. Right then and there she pushed a check for $2,500 across the table. "Use it to save more horses," she said. I was flabbergasted. Her heart was truly in this, right there alongside her professional instinct.

I used her money, as well as the money sent by others, to help buy horses that I fostered at my own farm until someone else could take them. I had two extra stalls plus a large run-in attached to the barn that could keep another six horses at least for a night or two. Sometimes horses needed someplace to stay short-term until their new owners could make it to the Detroit area. Because I lived so close to the track, I could take them from trainers who wanted to get rid of them as quickly as possible, not wanting to wait a day or two. Other times, I bought a horse outright without another buyer waiting in the wings, knowing I could figure a way to have it adopted once it was safe at my house.

Come November, with the season almost officially over and many horses having come from the track through my property and also to many other people's, the HBPA board decided to put on an auction of its own to help get rid of horses that nobody had bought through CANTER but that needed to be disposed of. Trainers and curiosity seekers would be there, as would kill buyers. I also knew that some of the people I had come in contact with as a result of the news segment would be present—people with room to spare in their barns and, we hoped, enough money to outbid those who wanted to buy horses for slaughter.

Not many days before the auction, during the last week or so of racing, I was walking down one of the backstretch roadways, still looking over possible horses to sell to people in sporting disciplines, when I could hear somebody calling out to me, running to catch up. "Thoroughbred Lady! Thoroughbred Lady!" It was a groom.

He was extremely anxious that a horse he had cared for over a long period and who had made $188,000 in races was injured but still at the track. "I know he can't win anymore," he said, "and I know that when this is over, his trainer won't let him go anywhere but in the auction. Would you please bid for him? His name is Don Pilafidis."

"Don't worry," I told him. "I'll be at the auction and make sure he goes to a safe place."

I knew it couldn't be me who did the bidding. With my reputation as a bleeding heart, some of the kill buyers would bid me up just to make it difficult for me to get the horse. It wouldn't be the first time my efforts would be thwarted. The culture at the track was such that I was mocked by many for trying to save horses, and sometimes, to taunt me, owners and trainers sold a horse to a meat buyer rather than to someone I found who was willing to pay just as much money for the very same horse. With that in mind, I asked one of the rescuers with whom I had become acquainted to make the bids, and she obliged. A number of us had pooled money, including some of the money sent to me by TV viewers, to save the horse from slaughter, so we were hopeful we'd be successful.

The poor horses that were led into the auction ring—their having no clue about what might happen to them made the sight all the more pitiful. They trusted the people around them, having done their bidding for years by running in rain, snow, and ninety-degree weather with fractured bones and torn tendons, injected with medications and standing submissively in ice buckets to reduce swelling. They had no idea they were now for sale and that few who took care of them cared about where they would end up.

The bidding for Don Pilafidis started at $200. My person nodded yes, and then a couple standing with one of the kill buyers and who I assumed were acting as a front for him upped the amount. I signaled our bidder to go higher, and it kept going back and forth, with the price rising higher and higher. We were already at $800, $900, now having exceeded the highest price the kill buyer would fetch for the horse as meat.

Shane Spiess could see I was trying to outbid the couple from the sidelines and came over. "Jo Anne, you don't have to worry," he said. "That couple really wants the horse. They've been following him. They'll keep it at a beautiful stable."

"Shane," I answered, "if we back off and what you're saying is not true, I don't even want to think about what I'm going to do to you."

"Trust me," he replied. "Let them take the horse."

I did, and the couple, young and well heeled, did

in fact board Don Pilafidis at a beautiful farm. They thought he had the look of eagles, of a class horse, and had no intention of putting him through anything rigorous.

Don Pilafidis *was* tall, with a regal bearing, yet so gentle in his stall. When he was turned out, however, he tore around. He rolled from one side to the other, got up, shook, and ran around some more. Freedom!

I never ceased to be amazed at what could happen at the track. While so many trainers blithely sent their horses to slaughter, and kill buyers couldn't have cared less about what happened to "used up" Thoroughbreds, here was Shane, who often made money off kill buyers, assuring me that Don Pilafidis would be okay and that I didn't have to spend any money to make sure of it. And there was that young couple fraternizing with a kill buyer himself. It didn't make sense, and yet it happened.

Larry Wales, the track vet, stepped up to the plate, too, stopping me one day to tell me he had a horse that broke down the previous evening and wasn't going to race again. "They're willing to give it away," he told me. "You don't have to buy it." Again, a trainer was putting his humanity above his wallet.

The horse, a filly named Shobonier, didn't load onto the trailer easily. The poor thing was terrified. But Larry sedated her, and off she went to the barn of one of my new contacts. She changed hands many times since then, having done dressage and low-level hunter-jumper competitions. Today, almost fifteen years later, she lives a comfortable life at the farm of one of the very first people I met as a result of the television segment.

Soon after the Shobonier save, ABC News ran a follow-up piece. It aired on Thanksgiving, and the viewers were told that all the horses found homes, giving the story a happy ending. But it was not true. A number of horses were forced to limp onto trailers either to race elsewhere or be transported to auction pens, after which they'd end their days on bloodied slaughterhouse floors.

Worse still, even with the track closing, the plight of the Thoroughbreds wasn't going to be over. News had broken on the backstretch that a new track was going to open somewhere else in the state. Where hadn't been decided yet.

Just as word of a new track was buzzing, the date for the annual awards dinner in eventing rolled around again. I knew Scarlett wasn't going to win in her category this year—the competition was going to be much stiffer at this level, and she was still relatively new to the sport—but I looked forward to the banquet nonetheless. It was a great way to socialize with people in eventing who, like me, loved their horses; a great way to see them without their "helmet hair." I brought Baby in my own way, too.

In Michigan, with the Eventing Association's permission, people in the sport are allowed to award trophies in a person or horse's honor. I decided to create the Reel Surprise Memorial Trophy, to be given to the ex-racehorse who achieved the most points that year.

"My family believes it was our privilege to have been loved by Reel Surprise and to have been at his side at the moment of his birth and until his last breath," I told the audience when making the presentation. "There was a song sung by Carly Simon that was popular soon after he was born. It contained the words:

From the moment I first saw you
The second that you were born
I knew that you were the love of my life
Quite simply, the love of my life.

"We heard that song so frequently in the barn when he was a baby," I went on, "that we started referring to it as Reel Surprise's song. If you read the engraving on the trophy, you will see that we have quoted from it, with a slight change to make the wording plural. It reads, 'Quite simply, the love of our lives.'"

I could barely get through the short speech, so hard was I crying, for the first time not trying to hide my emotions about Baby in public. I was thankful to see eyes glistening throughout the audience. It was a wonderful reprieve from my daily, incessant routine of trying to find horses homes, so often working against prevailing sentiment.

Back at the track, we were now between Thanksgiving and Christmas. The gate to the backstretch was going to be padlocked for good before a developer came in and razed the grandstand, the shedrows, and all else to make way for another industry on that spot. What, none of us knew. We had heard condos, restaurants, stores.

I took a look around where I had spent almost every single day for the better part of a decade and was about to leave for good when a security guard to whom I had given dozens of chocolate chip cookies over the years advised me to check every single stall. "It's possible some trainers will simply take off, leaving a horse behind," he said.

I took him up on his suggestion, spending hours looking deep into each of the 1,200 stalls. The entire backstretch, once busy with horses prancing to and from the racecourse, people walking, bicycling, or driving golf carts, the sounds of hundreds of whinnies blending with talking, shouting, music blaring, was deserted, a spooky horse ghost town. Alone, a spirit myself who now belonged somewhere else but with unfinished business here had not yet crossed to the next place, I made my way, silent, hollow, along the acres and acres.

It had by that point been two and a half years since Baby's death. In all that time, with all my cajoling trainers up and down the rows to sell their horses to nonracing people rather than to the kill buyers, I never was able to bring myself to walk down the road containing the block of shedrows where Baby and Scarlett spent their racing days. Now I knew I must.

I don't know how long I remained there. Time kind of went away. I just remember sitting on Baby's stall floor, sobbing, whispering his name between gasps and repeatedly begging forgiveness. "I'm sorry, Baby," I said to him. "I'm so sorry. I will find a way to make this up to you."

CHAPTER ELEVEN

It turned out the new track would be opening on the far west side of the state, in Muskegon, nearly three hours away. And it was going to open that very spring, not take a full year, as I had anticipated. The owners were going to use a vacated Standardbred track, which was still in excellent condition. The grandstand and restaurants were almost new, in fact. All that needed to be built were shedrows, since Standardbreds are shipped in for their races rather than kept in stalls on the grounds, like Thoroughbreds, and apartments for the grooms.

I was frantic. I had made a promise to myself, to Baby, even before Christmas that never again would I leave a horse behind. It was a vow, really. Whenever the new track opened, I would not lose another horse to slaughter, the way I lost that little chestnut with the big blaze, because I didn't have enough money to buy it right then and there or couldn't get hold of somebody to take it before the kill buyer did. Somehow, in each instance, I'd find a way.

I *had* to make that decision. I simply wasn't strong enough to come home to the barn and sob anymore. I could still see the fear on the face of every horse led into a trailer that would take it to its death. No more could I look into the eyes of a horse that needed help, touch its swollen leg or ankles, and walk away. No more could I say "No" to Baby, which was what I felt I was doing each time a horse destroyed by racing looked at me with trust and fright before going on to meet a brutal end. It was too painful to betray him like that.

Money wasn't going to be an issue. John said I could use all the pay from my court reporting work to do what I had to do, and I was still receiving donations from people who had watched one of the news broadcasts or read about CANTER in the paper. I had also written some personal letters over the winter in addition to sending out e-mails to people reminding them that CANTER would need funds to save spent racehorses when the new track did open.

I wasn't going to let space be an issue, either. I'd keep horses in my garage if I had to.

But I couldn't do this by myself from the eastern end of the state, just north of Ohio, when the new track was going to open a couple of hours north of Indiana.

I had no time to lose. I had spent the winter quietly, enjoying my own horses in the barn once more and also getting Scarlett situated with a new eventing trainer. I had never become comfortable with the fact that at her old facility, while her trainer was a terrific rider and knew horses well, there was no grass to munch on during turnout. In her natural state, a horse will graze 60 percent of the day. Also, I had concerns about the fencing— metal piping with sharp edges on which she could hurt herself.

Scarlett's new training site, ten minutes closer to my house than the other, had grass pastures instead of dirt paddocks, and trees here and there, which would provide some shade in the summer heat and protection from flies. And the stalls were bright and clean, always, with no odor of urine. Better still, the people who ran the place paid attention to which horses got on with which, and they made sure to turn out "friends" at the same time.

I was thrilled with the trainer, too. Jennifer Merrick-Brooks, a well-known eventing profes- sional, was respected on a national level both in the U.S. and Canada for her activities in the Pony Club—an organization for serious equestrians in which she had achieved the highest level of learning about horses. She also loved working with ex-racehorses. What could be better?

Scarlett took to her new trainer and new surroundings without hesitation, letting down and acting comfortable right away. Horses tend not to do that, remaining a little on edge for a while when they're new to a setting. But her pleasure in this facility was almost like a sigh. "I really like this place. I think I'd like to hang out here a while.

And Mom comes many times a week to complete the picture."

I did enjoy coming often that winter and watching her buddy up with horses she really liked. I enjoyed watching her run toward me when I clapped my hands, put her head over the gate so we could breathe into each other's noses, then wait for her treat of carrots. And I loved that there was an airy indoor arena and indoor shower with warm water so she could clean off comfortably after working out in the winter cold.

But now I had to make up for the months I lost taking pleasure in her new comfort as well as tending to Beauty, Pumpkin, Pat, and Sissy back home. E-mailing Jeremy, I asked if he could put on the home page of the Web site a call for CANTER volunteers at the new track, which was going to be called Great Lakes Downs. I needed people to take pictures of horses at the track, volunteers to trailer horses away from the backstretch, homes for fostering horses with no immediate buyers, and so on. The only way I was going to be able to make good on my promise to Baby was to enlist the help of others.

Within minutes of the posting, e-mails started coming in. The first was from a woman named Judy Gutierrez, who lived fewer than five miles from the new track, closer than I lived to the Detroit Race Course. We spoke on the phone, and I could tell immediately that she was horse savvy.

Not only did she own her own horses, she also had an indoor arena and knew everything about basic injury. She knew about Thoroughbred racing and horse slaughter, too.

From that first phone call I felt confident that everything would be okay, that I'd be able to line up a team of volunteers and be more successful saving horses than I had been the previous year, even though I lived on the other side of the state.

I was right. Within just a couple of weeks, I had a bevy of volunteers willing to do everything from take pictures of horses for sale to transport horses who needed a "safe house" between being saved from the kill buyer and getting chosen for adoption. One of the new volunteers even had a digital camera, which would really speed up getting photos to Jeremy, not to mention save money on film development and overnight deliveries.

Along with showing CANTER's new volunteers the ropes, I needed to retrain the trainers trying to unload their horses. While 20 percent of them were new to me, coming up from Indiana and Illinois, both on Michigan's western side, 80 percent of them knew me from the Detroit Race Course, and they were used to getting hold of me whenever they wanted. But no longer could I come every single day. It was close to six hours round trip. I made it clear that CANTER would be at the new track during Saturday morning training only and that if they had a horse they wanted to list, they needed to leave their name at the stable gate. That didn't relieve me of having to walk up and down the shedrows for hours looking for more horses to save, but it at least insured that those who knew ahead of time that they wanted to unload a horse wouldn't be overlooked.

I also became savvier myself about how to go about saving horses for the least amount of money possible, horses that would be going on the truck if I didn't take them right away. I'd go to the bank and withdraw cash in all different small denominations—fives, tens, twenties. Then I'd put varying amounts of money in my four jeans pockets—$200 in one, $300 in another, and so on. When someone said he wanted $400 for a horse, I'd go into my $300 pocket and count out the bills very carefully, as if I were spending my last dollar.

"Well, I've got three hundred dollars," I'd say. "I'm going to have to have the horse transported. And I can see he has an ankle," track lingo for "fractured ankle" or "swollen ankle," the implication being that it would cost money to fix it. Sometimes it would work, affording CANTER $100 to spend saving another horse.

The season started out slow—most trainers weren't ready to get rid of their horses in April, May, and June because they still believed all of their charges might prove winners—but even so, I fostered a horse during that period. He had run his last race the previous season and ended up in Ohio, closer to me on the eastern side of the state than to the new volunteers. His experience at my house had a powerful impact, making me realize close up just how much horses missed when their lives were relegated to racing.

Named River Wolf, he was a beautiful chestnut, meaning reddish in color, with what I recall as a small star on his forehead that had a strip coming down, a four-inch comma that looked like it was applied with the side of a paint brush that had been dabbed in bright white.

River Wolf was twelve, old for a Thoroughbred to still be racing. In fact, he had run for a total of eleven years in a punishing total of 170 races, having won his various trainers and owners more than $200,000. His relatively early and middle years had been his best. He even set a new track record at Philadelphia Park. By the time he was slated for the slaughterhouse, however, he had earned only a little more than $3,000 for the whole previous season, whereas in earlier years he made anywhere from $15,000 to almost $50,000.

As they always did whenever a new horse came to our house, Beauty, Pat, Pumpkin, and Sissy whinnied at the sight of the trailer. They were out in the pasture, jockeying to see who would exchange breaths with the horse before any of the others, although it was a foregone conclusion as

Beauty, boss mare over the others, always had first dibs.

When River Wolf stepped off the trailer, I let him stop and look around, smell the air, and whinny back. Horses are always in fight-or-flight mode when they first approach a new herd, not knowing what to expect, and you have to pretty much leave it to them to decide how quickly they want to exhale into the nostrils of the horses already there. They tend to stand frozen at first, some longer than others as they need more time to assess the situation.

While River Wolf was getting his footing, Sissy was trying to come out in front of Beauty and Pat. She always did. Though skittish around people, she was starved for the friendship of another young horse who would be willing to play with her and remained forever hopeful about new companions. It was her aim to be the Greeting Committee.

But Beauty would have none of it, and neither would Pat. As Sissy's mother, Pat needed to make sure the new horse was suitable for her child.

With River Wolf, as with most of the other horses we eventually fostered, Beauty put her ears back and kind of flattened her head outward like a snake's head as she went nostril to nostril. "You don't want to mess with me," her body language was saying. "I'm in charge. Don't get any ideas." Sissy, impatient, tried to push her way in, but

Beauty had only to turn her snake head toward her. "I'm not *done* yet."

Pat's reaction was typically anxious, although friendly. She put her ears back but did not make any aggressive movements. After a short initial wariness at first breath, she was ready to get along.

Poor Pumpkin, so retiring, never really would have a chance to say hello. She hung back, probably thinking, "It's the three of them and the new horse. I'm not about to get in the middle of that." She also by that point had Cushing's disease, an endocrine disorder, and was unsteady on her feet, having lost a lot of muscle control in her hind quarters. That allowed Sissy to finally succeed in shoving herself forward, ears pricked and ready to be "new best friends."

Once I let the herd smell River Wolf over the fence (you never know if horses new to each other will start biting and kicking), I led him into the barn and gave him the end stall so he could look outside whenever he wanted. He liked me, as well as other people, very much. Even though I was a complete stranger, I could go into his stall without his backing away or running into a corner. He enjoyed smelling my arm and letting me scratch his neck.

But he was terrified to leave the stall. I could leave the stall door open and walk away, and he still wouldn't come out. He had spent his entire life alone in stalls, never in pastures with other horses, and he was scared to death. It took days for him just to walk out of the barn to graze in the lush grass, and then only after he had made sure that none of the other horses were out there. It was the equivalent of a child's being afraid to dig into a big bowl of his favorite flavor of ice cream in the company of other children.

After about a week, I decided to lead Sissy to the pasture when River Wolf was already grazing. She tended to be the one who got put out with a new horse first because of her eager friendliness. Also, huge as she was, she still clacked submissively, opening and closing her mouth repeatedly while her teeth clicked together, a don't-hurt-me habit most horses outgrow when they're still weanlings. There was no way another horse could misinterpret her intentions. Still, River Wolf froze when he saw her. You'd have thought she was a mountain lion ready to attack.

Sissy was oblivious. She walked briskly over to him to "say" hi and find out if he wanted to play. At racing speed, as though Sissy were going to kill him, River Wolf ran to the farthest corner of the pasture. Sissy, still completely unaware of his terror, walked gamely toward him again, almost running the last few steps, the way a person might who hadn't seen somebody they cared about in a long time, sprinting toward their friend as they came closer in order to give a big hug.

Again, River Wolf ran to the farthest corner.

"Oh, is *that* the game?" I could see Sissy wondering, as she chased him in that direction, too. This went on and on until finally, giving up, she put her head down in the middle of the pasture and began to graze.

River Wolf stared at her for five minutes straight, not budging, every muscle in his body tensed. Then, gingerly, and still keeping his eye on her, he began grazing in the corner himself.

For two days, he kept as far from Sissy as he could get. On the third day, however, the two ate side by side, walking and grazing, walking and grazing. It broke my heart. I could see so plainly in River Wolf's behavior what an unnatural thing racing was for horses. Cooped up in stalls and run ragged his whole life, he literally had no idea what it was to *be* a horse, utterly unable to read the body language of another one, and had to learn by degrees.

But he did. It wasn't long before Sissy and River Wolf were playing halter tag, the way Baby and Scarlett had, and nipping lightly at each other's legs, then kicking up their heels and running off, finally grooming each other like tired puppies. Although twelve, River Wolf was actually playing like a weanling, enjoying the childhood he had missed.

Sissy hated to see him go about a month later, when he was adopted by someone who wanted to do Western trail riding, which would allow him to lead a much better life than at the track. So did I. It was always wondrous to see a herd shaping and reshaping. Horses, like people, have their favorites, their friends that they like instantly, and those that they can get along with but for whom they don't feel an immediate affinity. Even Beauty, once in a great while, would take right away to a new horse, pricking her ears in friendship, and the two of them would choose each other as grazing/grooming partners.

Things were proceeding as smoothly at the new track as they had for River Wolf. I even enjoyed my Saturday drives out there. It was a straight shot on I-96 from the Detroit suburbs on the east to Lake Michigan on the west, which was just a few miles from the new track. Starting out before the sun rose at 5:15 on a weekend morning after spending about forty-five minutes taking care of my horses down at the barn, I could go for the longest time and not see another car. Except for the loop around Lansing, trees surrounded the flat highway on both sides, and, the car in cruise control, I relished my private time.

I had by that point quit the HBPA board. There was nothing acrimonious in it; the new board president was disappointed to see me resign, in fact. But knowing that I would never race a horse again, I realized that I didn't have a right to vote on issues that would affect the livelihoods of those still involved.

I had also by that time been voted vice president of the Michigan Eventing Association. Life was to some degree spinning in a different direction.

One thing I was glad to finally put behind me was the lawsuit. Back in the previous December, it had gone to mediation, with a suggestion handed down that both sides settle for $12,500, splitting the difference between Baby's $25,000 valuation and no money whatsoever, which was what the track wanted to pay.

We had accepted that recommendation—by that point the cost of going further would have been prohibitive—but Ladbroke had not, insisting that we go to trial and dragging out the case till the end of June, when, after wasting more of our lawyer's time in motions for summary judgment and hours and hours of preparation for debating the case in front of a jury, they accepted the mediation terms and sent me a $12,500 check.

Ladbroke insisted on a confidentiality clause for a period of twenty-nine months, until the statute of limitations ran out, I assumed. Their aim, I believed, was to muzzle me so no one else would sue for the death of their own horse out on the track. That bothered me on principle, but Baby by that point had been gone for three years. If anyone else was going to sue, I realized, they would have already come forward.

I was glad not to have to keep revisiting Baby's death by way of the suit, going over witnesses' statements and looking at other documents having to do with his life being cut short. It always churned it all up to the surface. But I did want the settlement to have some kind of meaning. My family had been so hurt by Baby's tragedy. We all still loved him, still thought of him all the time.

I told the girls I was going to put the money in a separate savings account, and that whenever the time came for them to marry, Baby would buy them their wedding gowns and throw them their bridal showers. That way, as our family member, he would be with each of them on their wedding day and forever after that. No woman throws away her wedding gown. It's the most important day in her life, after the days on which her children are born.

I couldn't bring Baby back other than symbolically, of course, but I was able to take comfort in the fact that I was doing so well at saving Thoroughbreds at Great Lakes Downs that by midsummer, the major kill buyers had stopped coming around. There simply weren't enough horses for them to pick up because CANTER had either been placing them or taking them outright. I had gone from acting solely as a conduit for trainers and buyers in the sport disciplines to a full-fledged rescue, not only arranging transfers off the track but also intaking horses trackside in CANTER's name that could be brought to area farms to be fostered until someone could be found to adopt them permanently.

No other horse rescue organization in the country was taking horses from the racetrack, literally. Our being on-site made all the difference. While other rescues were placing on the order of perhaps fifteen horses a year, we were now placing as many as fifteen a week.

Horses did still go to slaughter. There were trainers who continued to refuse to deal with me. But I never had to turn down a horse that a trainer was willing to unload on CANTER.

Part of what spurred the action were posters I would bring to the track entitled "Racing's Graduates." They contained photos of ex-racehorses in their new disciplines. I got the idea to bring in the posters after I received a call from one of the trainers one night. "We're at the bar," he said, "and are trying to figure out how you make money with CANTER."

I couldn't believe that I was now in my third season of getting racehorses off the track, yet there was still suspicion that somehow I was on the take. "Louie," I said to the man on the other end, "I have told you. I've told everyone. I don't *make* any money from this."

"We don't get it. Why do you do it, then?"

"I do it because it's the right thing to do. Why should a horse go to slaughter?"

"Okay, alright," he answered, half laughing, half

defensively. "Everybody was kind of sitting around here trying to figure it out. And I just said, 'Well, I'm going to call her and ask her.'"

It was then that I decided to bring in the posters, hoping they would ease skepticism. One Saturday, as soon as I arrived, I left one inside the HBPA office and proceeded to go about my business. When I stopped back hours later, trainers were crowded around it.

"Wow, this is really neat," I heard one of them say. "Look, there's so-and-so."

Others were laughing. "No wonder your horse couldn't win a race," one ribbed a buddy standing nearby. "It's not a Thoroughbred. You got yourself a cowboy horse."

"Look at my horse jump," another called out. "*Look* at that!"

"It's been like this since you put that here," the HBPA secretary said from behind her half doorway. "There's been a crowd all day."

Each time I'd get a poster board's worth of pictures, I'd bring in a new board. "Would you make sure my horse gets on the next one?" trainers started asking me. That simple step of showing them their horses in their next life went a long way toward reducing their cynical view of my intentions—and keeping my horse-saving efforts successful, so successful that I realized CANTER was no longer simply a little program that had the blessing of the local HBPA. It was time to become a rescue in the formal sense, a full-fledged, tax-exempt charity.

I knew that if people could write off their donations, more money would come our way to save horses. Moreover, I'd be able to convince some trainers to *donate* their horses in exchange for a tax donation receipt rather than demand the same price as the meat buyer.

Having worked as a legal secretary early in my career, I filed the papers to make CANTER a 501(c)(3) myself, putting down my name as the incorporator. But the IRS sent me notice that I had to have three incorporators, and none of them could be a spouse. Fortunately, Judy, my first volunteer, agreed to be named, as did Robbie Timmons. I knew she had a soft spot for the horses and was glad that she let me use her name to dot the i's and cross the t's.

Happy as I was about CANTER's humming along by that point, I knew the time had come to lose one of my own. My vet had actually made the recommendation months earlier. One of the complications of Cushing's disease that Pumpkin had was the inability to shed her thick winter coat, twice as heavy as the coat that grew in the spring. In hot weather, a horse with such a coat can die of heat stroke. We had body clipped Pumpkin in April to get her down to her normal length of hair, but still she was uncomfortable. Worse still, she was becoming weaker and weaker, to the point that just standing in the pasture and grazing, she seemed ready to fall over. Once a horse falls, she can't stay down long. It compresses her lungs and doesn't allow her to breathe. Even a horse who chooses to lie down for a while will keep shifting her body weight. What if Pumpkin fell one day when I wasn't home, flies swarming around her, unable to rise? I had promised Pumpkin when we took her home fifteen years earlier that she would never have to suffer anymore, and I needed to make good on that promise, putting her needs above the emptiness and aching for her that I knew I would feel.

Rebecca took the decision harder than Jessica had. Just ten when we brought Pumpkin home on Christmas Eve 1984, she had grown up with her. Not only that, Rebecca also seemed to have inherited my horse gene. Jessica always loved horses and all other animals and still does, but by the time she reached adolescence, if I'd say, "Come on down to the barn, I want to show you something about one of the horses," she'd answer, "I just washed my hair, and I'll have to shower and wash it again because I'll smell like horse." But Rebecca never reached that point. If I had told her on her wedding day that there was something in the barn I wanted her to see, she would have run down there in her wedding gown. Whatever boyfriend she had, she'd drag him to the barn and make him get on a horse. And she was the one with whom I did the most riding, the one who "took over" Pumpkin by herself once Jessica went off to college.

I had a hard time with the decision myself. It wasn't like with Baby, which was a tragedy in the true sense of the word—no time to prepare myself for the loss of a five-year-old horse with whom I had fallen completely in love and who I expected to be able to see gallivanting in the pasture behind the house to this day. But it was sad, so awfully sad. Pumpkin and Beauty were truly the horses of my dreams, the ones I finally got to have after a lifetime of wanting horses of my own so badly; the first ones I could see grazing together in the pasture when I looked out the window while working on my court transcripts; the ones who turned a good life into a perfect one. Even though Pumpkin was thirty-three, much older than horses usually live, I hated to say good-bye to her, to a wonderful, innocent part of my life before I knew the way in which people could treat horses they no longer wanted.

Once Pumpkin was gone, I scattered some of her ashes in the pasture and put some more in a plastic bag that I placed next to Baby's ashes in the stein. The rest I gave to Rebecca.

I took comfort in the fact that I wasn't running into any situation in which there was a horse at the track that needed my help but to whom I couldn't give it. If no one wanted to buy a horse, there was always a foster home to which to take it. But people *were* buying horses to repurpose them for various other disciplines. Transfers from trainers to people in the sport disciplines were brisk, in fact. Being on the western side of the state, hours away from the site of the Detroit Race Course, I had a whole new local market to tap into. People who wouldn't have come to the old track were willing to come to Great Lakes Downs, and along with the Web site, the "Horses Wanted" list was more active than ever, sometimes reaching to twenty-five pages. Again, I'd go into the men's bathroom and Scotch tape copies all along the wall; into the racing secretary's office, where the trainers went at eleven each morning to enter various horses into races, taking down the previous week's list and putting up the new one.

Still, as fall approached, things were going to become more difficult. More and more trainers would want to dump horses that weren't going to earn them any more money, and more of those horses would have serious injuries, making them unsuitable for other kinds of competitions. I called it Fall Rush. The Detroit track's closing for good the previous year certainly brought a special frenzy to the end-of-season dumping, but every October and November saw trainers trying to unload "useless" horses with increased intensity. Even uninjured, the Thoroughbreds who were good enough for our cheap claiming races in

Michigan would never have been able to compete in Florida, where many of the trainers raced in the winter months.

That so many more horses were coming into CANTER with serious injuries made our work much more expensive. Even checking for soundness could be complicated. A horse who had had multiple cortisone injections might still be able to run without pain—the shots would take down inflammation in soft tissue—but any bone at the injection site would be deteriorating, and that might not be readily apparent. *People* are given cortisone injections sparingly. Cortisone destroys bone, so you can't keep administering it. But in racehorses, there's no limit. They're forced to run on a bad knee or ankle until the repeated cortisone shots given to mask their pain wear away their bone to the point that running becomes impossible. The bone actually collapses, and the horse can't even walk without a severe limp.

X-rays become necessary to assess the extent of the damage. Often, an operation is called for. A joint may have a dozen bone chips floating around in it, and every time the horse moves, the chips' sharp edges dig into cartilage like tiny razors, tearing up the joint and other soft tissue. The bone chips have to be removed in an arthroscopic surgery for the horse to have a chance. That can easily cost $1,500. With so many horses needing evaluation and, often, expensive procedures to fix the cause of their lameness, CANTER would be at a financial loss. The money simply wasn't there to take care of all their medical needs. Even chemically euthanizing a horse for whom there was no hope of a pain-free life—a much more peaceful, dignified end than slaughter, accompanied as it was by soft words and a kind touch from people who cared—cost in the neighborhood of $300, more than I often had to pay to keep a horse from the kill buyer.

I hadn't run into this problem before because in the previous years, CANTER wasn't a formal rescue. The very damaged horses not bought by people in the sport disciplines went to the kill buyers. Now, I was intaking those horses personally as the head of the organization and sending them to foster homes. In fact, by the end of the season, the work was almost purely in the realm of rescue—taking horses off the track ourselves to keep them from the slaughterhouse. There were fewer and fewer sound horses left for sale that anyone in eventing or any other sport discipline would have wanted.

With no options at hand, I decided to go begging, propelled by the fact that the daughter of the HBPA president, a trainer herself, had given to me at no charge a horse that she had already had x-rayed and was found to have a bone chip in her knee. She wasn't sure if the horse, a beautiful filly named Lookalike with the look of eagles, had sustained the injury during training or during a race.

I called the veterinary teaching hospital at Michigan State University in East Lansing, a little less than two hours away from the track. I had already had some good luck there, if you can call it that, when I had to put down a horse named Fabled Wolf earlier in the season. His last race had been July 4th—a Sunday that year—and when I came upon him the Saturday after, he had an ankle in such bad condition he was head-bobbing lame. Just seven years old, he had already raced in five different states and been claimed ten different times, which did not include all the times he changed hands privately rather than via claiming races—an anathema for horses, who crave routine and familiarity and need time to become used to new people, new surroundings. During those five years, stabled in barns from Delaware to Florida until finally taken to our end-of-the-road track in Michigan, he had won his various owners more than $80,000 in allowance races.

But he had run out of soundness. I had him trailered to Michigan State to be evaluated, and it turned out that *both* ankles were fractured beyond repair. There was no way to save that absolutely gorgeous animal, a great big grey, not only beautiful but also so very sweet and trusting.

We had already spent a good deal of money to have him checked out. I needed to hold onto as much money as I could to save other horses. Fortunately, one of the veterinarians there, Hillary Clayton, whom I had met previously at a horse expo in Lansing, told me she would take care of euthanizing Fabled Wolf as well as disposing of his body. Her program would pay for it.

With that in mind, I thought maybe Michigan State would be willing to donate surgeries. Perhaps the students could perform the operations with the oversight of their professors, not only affording the school a way to train its pupils but also giving it a way to look good.

I didn't know who to ask for and kept getting transferred to different departments. Finally, a voice came on and, instead of announcing a department name, said simply, "John Stick."

I started explaining the situation and could tell pretty quickly that I wasn't going to get transferred again. He didn't interrupt me to say I had reached the wrong person. I talked for so long, explaining about how I started the program two years earlier and, in my nervous desperation, going into so many particulars, that at one point I wondered whether he was still on the line. He hadn't so much as said "Mmm-hmm," or even grunted.

Finally, after quite some time, he said, "Hold it. Can you wait for a minute?"

I was ready to burst into tears. I hadn't honed my point strongly enough, hadn't rehearsed what

I was going to say, and now was going to get shot down before I had a chance to make all the important arguments for operating on the horses, having taken up the man's time with extraneous details.

"Do you know how many times a year I am asked to donate surgery?" he asked rhetorically, "and not just to individuals but to rescues? I am asked so many times that my secretary has a form letter explaining why we can't do it—"

It was over. This was Baby I had been pleading for. These were the horses that needed me most, not the Scarletts who were going out and doing wonderful things, and I had failed them.

"—but I would have to be crazy not to get behind this."

Then *he* talked. "I owe my career to Thoroughbred horses," he told me. "You happened to call one of the first universities in the country that perfected arthroscopic surgery on horses' legs. We do this on a fairly common basis. Thoroughbred racehorses have built my career, giving me everything in life I enjoy today. And I have always felt I needed to give back to them. But I never found the right vehicle to do it. This is that vehicle."

It turned out I was talking to the chief of staff for the entire equine hospital, a nationally renowned orthopedic surgeon, and he told me that what I was asking for would be ideal not only for him but also for the university. "If you would allow the students to do the surgery," he said, "and I'd always be in the operating room directing them—they'd be directly under my supervision—I think we could have a deal here. Let's try it with six horses and see where it goes."

The word "elation" couldn't begin to get at what I was feeling.

"But you know," he then added, "I have people over me. This is a public university. It has to be clear that the university is not using tax dollars to pay for these horses' care. I do have graduates of the vet school who turn around and donate money for me to use as I see fit. Right now I have an equine veterinarian who is retired and used to be a racing breeder, trainer, and owner. He donated twenty thousand dollars to the Large Animal Hospital for me to use at my discretion. I will call him and ask him what he thinks of my using it for this program. Then we'll see about hooking up with our development department. Maybe between you, me, and them, we can keep a fund for these surgeries.

"I'll give you one little hint," he added. "I still have to justify this, justify this use of our facilities, to the people at the university. And I will tell you that universities love good publicity. If you could get an article in the paper about our doing this, and I could show it to the dean, it would help solidify that this is a good thing to do. Just a little tip for you on your end."

Instead of calling the local paper, I tried a Lansing TV station, keeping in mind how well we had done with TV the previous year, and reached the program director. As luck would have it, she was a horse owner herself. We spent the first twenty minutes just talking to each other about our horses, and when I finally was able to get around to why I was calling, she thought it would make a wonderful story.

Dr. Stick was delighted, even allowing the news team into the operating room to watch the surgery on Lookalike, Michigan State's first CANTER arthroscopy patient. He had also cleared using the $20,000 donation with the contributor, a Dr. Lyle Hartrick, who, it turned out, knew me and the CANTER program from the Detroit Race Course.

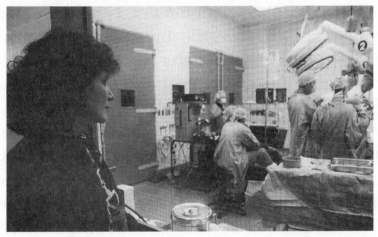

I watched nervously during Lookalike's arthroscopic surgery to remove a bone chip in her knee. It was the first surgery donated to CANTER at Michigan State University.

The piece ran a week or so before Thanksgiving, at noon, five o'clock, and eleven o'clock, and it even ran for more than one day, far beyond anything I had hoped for and certainly far beyond anything Dr. Stick expected. Our relationship was off to a solid start. And Lookalike—she came through her surgery great, ending up as a family horse used for Western trail riding. She was the first of five CANTER horses to be operated on successfully that year.

The season was soon over, and I'd have a few months before needing to go out again to Muskegon every Saturday. I missed Pumpkin. We were now into December, and I was constantly reminded of her, as I had taken her in just before Christmas so many years earlier. But I was finally at peace, to some degree, because of our ability to keep the kill buyers from the new track and to rehabilitate those horses who were so injured they had no chance whatsoever of moving to a new life without surgery.

It was during that period of letting down, of coming to realize that I could finally take a breath, with the tree already in the house and the girls soon coming home for the holiday, that John started shouting.

"Jo Anne, Jo Anne, get in here!" It was a Saturday afternoon, and he had been flipping channels to watch different football games, when there, on *CNN Headline News*, was the segment that had run in Lansing.

I was so frustrated that we didn't have a tape in the television. "Sometimes they repeat," John said. "Let's put one in just in case."

Sure enough, around it came again, right after a story about the Pope and then another segment on pandas at the San Diego Zoo, just like the previous time. It kept coming, in fact, every single hour. After about the third or fourth time, John said, "they're probably going to change stories now," and it seemed they had. The Pope and the pandas were bumped. But the CANTER piece ran yet again, and kept running!

Checks started coming in from as far away as Washington State. Magazines with wider circulations than any who had already covered us began calling for interviews.

CANTER was now on the national stage. More racehorses than ever were going to be saved.

CHAPTER TWELVE

The CNN segment did prove to be the kindling that allowed CANTER to transition from a precarious flicker to a steadily intensifying glow. In 1999, our budget was $15,000 and change. By 2002, it was $107,000, and by 2004, $220,000. We were written up in publications ranging from *The New York Times* to the *Chicago Tribune*. A single article's worth of coverage in The Associated Press garnered us placement in more newspapers than I can count.

Feature articles about CANTER, some with huge spreads and lots of color photos, also appeared in magazines that for non-racing equine enthusiasts are the equivalent of *Sports Illustrated* for guys who love pro ball: *Equus*, *Chronicle of the Horse*, *Practical Horseman*, *Horse Illustrated*, and a number of others. We were even written about in the *USCTA News* and *USDF Connection*, the official publications of the United States Eventing Association and the U.S. Dressage Federation, thereby reaching people all over the country who might want to repurpose a Thoroughbred who was no longer going to race.

Dr. Stick was thrilled about all the publicity, as Michigan State's involvement was frequently mentioned. That made it easier for the development department at the university to go after new funding to support CANTER's surgery program there.

For me, "thrilled" was an understatement regarding how I felt about CANTER's growth. The more money we took in, and the more people who knew about us, the less likely it became for us to lose a Michigan Thoroughbred to slaughter. Better still, people from other states were contacting me about starting CANTER affiliates at racetracks in their own locales. By the end of 2000, there was a CANTER Illinois and a CANTER West Virginia, with plans in the works for CANTERs at racetracks in Ohio, Pennsylvania, New England, and Texas. Unfortunately, we had to rescind the Texas franchise early in the process. Its director refused to display anti-slaughter information on the Web site's opening page. There were at that time two active slaughterhouses in the state, and she did not want to risk offending anyone. But CANTER's entire raison d'etre was to save horses from slaughter. To attempt to remain neutral on that score ran counter to the heart of the mission.

While my administrative responsibilities kept growing, much of the day-to-day work continued to revolve around the rescued Thoroughbreds themselves, with so many cases proving particularly charged emotionally.

At one point I received a call from a woman who said she had a former racehorse who never performed well at the track and couldn't do anything else. She needed to get rid of it because there was something wrong with its legs, and she couldn't afford the veterinary bills.

It was Simply Darling, whom I had met some ten years earlier during my very first season at the Detroit Race Course, when her trainer overfed her on grain and risked colic rather than split her rations in half and pay to have someone feed her the rest later in the day.

The beautiful, gentle mare, with so many years of questionable care since I last saw her, let me stroke her neck as soon as she came off the trailer, happy for me to breathe from my nostril into hers. I learned that in sixty-six lifetime races, she made only $11,000. Why anyone would put a horse through sixty-six races for so little money I will never understand.

Simply Darling's temperament was true to her name, and a veterinarian from Michigan State University adopted her immediately. But she had a serious case of cellulitis in her legs, a bacterial infection that proves very painful, causing swelling. In severe cases, like hers, the skin cracks and oozes yellow fluid and is very difficult to treat. The vet, who adored her, tried everything. But her condition eventually led to her having to be euthanized. I rued that she had to live such an awful life but was glad that at least in the end, she knew the best in veterinary care, not to mention kindness, sweet words, sufficient feed, and water.

Then there was Twoey, or Two Links Back, as he was known officially. A black bay who was never going to be able to enter a sport discipline because his knee was already too compromised, he was sold to CANTER for $600, with his trainer advising me to also take the goat who lived in Twoey's stall.

Twoey was so attached to his goat that he shared not only hay with him, but also grain. Mares won't even share grain with their foals, but that's how strongly Twoey felt about his friend.

Goats on the backstretch were not uncommon. Horses are such herd animals that they need companionship, and goats can live well in horses' stalls, going in and out to say "hello" to different horses at will by slipping under the gates. But Twoey's goat belonged only to him. They were so bonded that Twoey could not even be taken out to the race track without the goat accompanying him.

He was a wreck if the goat so much as walked down the aisle a little bit, away from his stall, to get some water.

I did take the goat along with Twoey—I would never have been able to load him into the trailer otherwise—after finally finding a foster farm that would have them. Goats can be destructive, and many people want nothing to do with them. From the foster farm, I eventually managed to get Twoey adopted by a sister rescue organization called the Thoroughbred Retirement Foundation. The foundation took the goat, too, named Captain Kidd by the owner of the farm that fostered the duo, and the two lived, with no exaggeration, happily ever after at a wonderful facility in Missouri.

If only it always went that way. One day I received an e-mail both ominous and anonymous: "CANTER horse, Make It Happen, has been sold for slaughter."

I remembered Happy—Make It Happen's barn name—immediately. It fit him perfectly; he had such a sweet disposition. When I had gone to meet him in his shedrow, he was gentle and curious, wanting only to smell my face, and very people oriented, just like Pat. He liked for me to touch him, to stroke him. He had a beautiful, fine-boned head, too, which he hung out of his stall on a tilt with a "Don't you want to take me home?" look, like a puppy in a store window.

I had to buy him for $700 from his racing

trainer. But I wasn't worried about the price. With his good looks and agreeable character, I knew I could adopt him out through the CANTER Web site for $1,000 and use the extra money to steer another horse away from the kill buyers. I was right. Within hours of posting his photograph, I heard from a woman who wanted to take him. It turned out she was on the board of directors of an organization in Southwestern Michigan that needed horses for its summer camp.

It wasn't going to work. I explained to her all the reasons that a horse coming directly off the track is not a good choice for children. It doesn't know "whoa." And pulling back on the reins, which to most horses means stop, means "go faster" to a racehorse. Furthermore, I told her, Thoroughbreds are thin skinned for leg pressure. They're not used to legs dangling around their sides; the jockeys ride tucked up. If someone rides with a heavy leg, the horse might bolt. Finally, I said, racehorses go left very well because they run around the track counter-clockwise. But it's hard to get them to turn right. They haven't been taught "right."

The woman, friendly, smart, and articulate, countered that the camp wouldn't be opening until the summer and that in the meantime, her husband, a Grand Prix dressage trainer and rider, would retrain Happy at their farm. I said I still didn't think it would work because being trained alone at a farm is different from being out on a trail with a group of other horses and that children were not professional riders, like her husband. I was concerned, too, because I knew by that point that there were rescues designed specifically to save camp horses from slaughter each fall, when a lot of summer camps gave them up because they didn't want to pay to take care of the horses over the winter. Come spring, the camps went to classified ads offering horses on the cheap and picked up new ones all over again. I even told the woman that I didn't adopt horses to children's camps unless the camps kept their horses through the winter, to which she replied that her particular camp did.

She also said that some of the children at the camp did have experience riding horses and wanted to do more than just walk/trot. *That* resonated with me. And so, after being worn down by her smarts and her persistence, I agreed to adopt Happy out to her.

That's why, when I read the e-mail, my stomach plummeted. If this anonymous tip-off was correct, I had made a ghastly error, the worst possible kind of error I could make. That horse had had CANTER's name on its papers. *I* okayed this camp. How was I going to be able to live with myself?

"Would you please come forward?" I implored the e-mailer. "I need more information."

In the meantime, I called the camp woman, who

denied in no uncertain terms that Happy had been sent to slaughter. I reminded her of the terms of a CANTER adoption—that she could not transfer the horse without our being aware and without our approval, or she would be flouting the terms of the contract.

"Is the horse even at your farm being trained by your husband before camp season, like you told me?" I asked.

"No," she responded. They had decided to let it settle in from racing with the other horses housed at the camp through the winter and would train the horse come spring. She was insulted by my even questioning her.

But my anonymous e-mailer told another story. In a subsequent e-mail communication, she said that the camp owed a construction company money and gave Happy to the company in exchange for the funds due. The construction company, in turn, traded Happy for a pony that a kill buyer had on his trailer.

I called the camp woman back and repeated to her what I had been told.

Irate, she said she'd call the camp to make sure the horse was safe there and would call me right back. When she did call back, she said that she had spoken to the camp manager and that the horse was on the camp grounds. "I don't know what your problem is," she said, "but leave us alone."

Back at my computer, I once more e-mailed the anonymous informant, saying, "You must come forward. I'm hours away from this place. You apparently are near there. I need to talk to you on the phone. I need to pursue this."

Come forward she did, giving me her name—Peg Yordy—and phone number. The reason she had been hesitant was that the woman in the construction company who traded Happy for a pony with the kill buyer was a friend. By coming forward on Happy's behalf, Peg ended up ruining that friendship—a courageous and ethical act.

Unfortunately, the transfer of Happy to the meat buyer had occurred eleven days earlier. The chances that he had already been slaughtered were high. I managed to get the phone number of the kill buyer, but when I called him and started to talk about "this horse that I think you took in," he interrupted by saying, "I don't know anything about any such horse," and hung up.

Crying, I called Shane Spiess. I never cried in front of trainers; it only hardened them against my cause, but I couldn't help it. Besides, Shane was different. And he knew Happy, having trained him before the trainer from whom I bought him. "Shane," I said, "I will pay a one-thousand-dollar bounty to anyone who will return that horse to me. I don't know where to start, though. The kill buyer hung up on me."

"When did this happen?" he asked.

When I told him, he said, "I'm going to make some calls. It's a small circle. We all know each other. I don't know this particular guy, but someone will. I want to prepare you, though. Eleven days doesn't sound good. I don't think we're going to have any luck. I think he's gone."

Still crying, I asked, "Would you please try, though?"

"Yes," Shane said.

Horrible images of Happy in the slaughterhouse were running through my head. Making his way in a single-file line, he'd see his fate by watching the horse ahead of him, finally reaching the metal box himself, perhaps slipping on blood and urine. Then he'd heave after being slammed in the head by a four-inch bolt shot from a gun, meant to render him unconscious but not necessarily succeeding. The gun operator would shoot again and again, slamming the bolt until Happy dropped to the blood-soaked floor.

Many of the horses, I knew, were still conscious when they were finally hoisted into the air by a chain tied around a single hind leg. It was while those horses were upside down and frequently fully aware that their throats were slit and blood spilled from their necks. I couldn't bear it. I felt strangled from inside.

Shane called me back within the hour, telling me that the kill buyer had already taken Happy to a meat auction in Kentucky, where he was sold for

$390 to the Bel Tex Slaughterhouse. "Try the auction and see if Bel Tex has picked up its horses from that day of bidding yet," he advised me.

"Okay," I responded, "but would you keep putting out the word to anyone you know in the business that I will pay a one-thousand-dollar bounty for this horse?" I was becoming more frantic by the minute.

"I already told the guy who took him to Kentucky," he answered. "He said, 'For a thousand bucks, *I'll* drive down to Kentucky again and try to find this horse.' "

When I called the auction, they verified that Happy had been bought by Bel Tex and that he was still in the holding pen waiting for the slaughterhouse to pick him up. They didn't know for sure when the truck was coming. A bit of relief.

I immediately called Shane back to let him know Happy was still there. Could he please get back in touch with the guy who said that for $1,000, he'd go back down to Kentucky and get him?

The meat buyer told Shane he'd get the horse from Kentucky and take him as far as the Shipshewana Auction in Indiana, where he was going with some other horses, anyway. By dint of incredible luck and good will, Peg told me she'd pick up Happy from there, which was a great relief to me since I lived more than three hours from Shipshewana, and she lived much closer.

On the designated day, she called me from the Shipshewana Auction parking lot. "Jo Anne, the parking lot is full of emptied trailers. We went up and down looking in them. But I did find one trailer that had a horse inside instead of being taken out to the auction. He looks really bad, like he's ready to go down any time. How do I know if it's him?"

I gave her the tattoo number. Every single Thoroughbred registered with the Jockey Club has a number tattooed on the inside of his lip before his first race.

She flipped his lip, called me back, and said, "It's him." Then, never having met me, not knowing me at all other than through our few e-mails and couple of phone calls, Peg found the kill buyer and gave him a $1,000 check, trusting that I would reimburse her.

She also kept him at her own farm for a couple of months until he was strong enough to make the trip to my house on the other side of the state. His several days in the kill buyer's hands and then in the holding pen both before the auction and after he was sold, waiting for the slaughterhouse to pick him up, had taken its toll, as it invariably does. Once he was sold for meat, he probably was not given any food or water. Instead, he was confined for days to a space overcrowded with other horses slated for removal to slaughter. Insane with hunger and thirst, they no doubt aggressively bit and kicked at each other in desperation, with the weaker of them, often already in horrific pain from bone fractures that stopped them from running, sustaining gashes and sometimes even gouged-out eyes.

That was Happy's fate. By the time Peg got him, thirteen days after his ordeal began, he had been bitten up and had gouges across his entire body, with a large, festering, pus-oozing wound on his head, just above his right eye. Peg said both his eyes were expressionless, lifeless. He stood with his legs splayed, like he was ready to collapse at any time. He was extremely dehydrated.

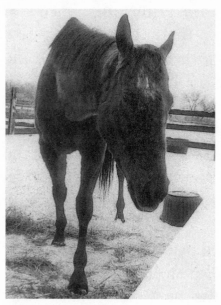

Happy when he was first rescued. You can see the wound above his eye.

But gradually, he came back to himself, strong enough to finish recuperating at my farm. By the time he got to me, he was no longer the horse at death's door that Peg had picked up. I was so grateful that my mistake in allowing him to be adopted by the wrong person hadn't ended in the worst way possible. I was so glad he now had green grass to munch on and somebody to say his name every time she saw him. "*Hap*-py!" I would call out, and up would come his head in response, not with a whinny but with a nicker, a quieter response—content rather than exuberant. He had already seen too much.

Sissy adored him, and he enjoyed her company as well. He didn't have that fear of being turned out with another horse that River Wolf had had. He was at home in the pasture, where he stayed until midsummer, when he was adopted by a woman named Mary Hejna who treated him wonderfully and went on to successfully compete with him in eventing competitions from Michigan to Florida, Kentucky, throughout the Midwest,

Happy with Mary Hejna in his new life, after recuperation.

and even into Canada. Not only did he get to become a pet, life once he was saved became rewarding, illustrious even.

I had been lucky with Peg in Happy's case, and also with the meat buyer. A lot of people in racing wouldn't hand over a horse even for money. At auctions, the auctioneers often wouldn't acknowledge our bids, even if they were higher than the kill buyers'. We were taunted in the shedrows, too.

But it was not unusual to find CANTER adopters themselves who, like Peg, tried in various ways to help the cause. Early in 2001, a woman from Grand Rapids named Cheryl Johnson who had taken a horse that would have otherwise gone to slaughter called me to say that she made her living as a nonprofit consultant and wanted to offer her services to me *pro bono*. "I can help you build your program," she told me, "and my husband is a university professor who knows how to write grant proposals."

One of Cheryl's most helpful suggestions was to broaden our board of directors. At that point, our board consisted of six people, all women, all of whom, except for Robbie (who was invaluable for getting us TV coverage), were hands-on, either buying up horses at the track, trailering them away, or fostering them on their farms.

One of the board members was Judy, my very first volunteer, who with her model-worthy good looks, tall stature, and long reddish hair, proved a real asset in getting the attention of trainers on the backstretch. Their eyes would light up when they saw her. When she was with me, in fact, I had no difficulty getting them to stop what they were doing and talk CANTER. More than that, she gave CANTER her all. Living just five miles from Great Lakes Downs and within a mile of the track's annex barn, she had trainers dropping off unwanted horses at all hours, showing up in her driveway at ten o'clock at night without any notice. Even with three small children, two of them not yet in school, she'd take in the horses and sweet talk the men, letting them know that CANTER was good for the money.

Another member of the board was Joy Aten, who was with me the day I bought Twoey. An oncology nurse about my age, she dealt with suffering and death on the job, which toughened her to the goings-on at the track. She also had owned horses herself for many years and understood that sometimes the kindest thing you can do for a horse is euthanize it rather than make it continue on in pain.

Like Judy, Joy was very pretty and had a good rapport with the trainers, always smiling and, when negotiating over a pitiful horse that might be standing right next to her in horrific pain, not acting accusatory or demanding but, instead simply using all of the skills she must have learned in dealing with death as part of her work. She was very deft at saying the right thing to the right person to get things to go her way, and this made her invaluable at extracting spent horses from trainers' hands. She was able to make a lot of time for CANTER as well. As a night nurse who was divorced with four grown children, she could pretty much decide her own hours. I admired her strength, her ability to raise two boys and two girls by herself, picking up and doing what she had to do to make life work.

Joy and I also mirrored each other in certain ways. She, too, had lost horses in a tragic accident. Three of hers managed to escape through the gate one day from one of the pastures at her ex-husband's place, where she was boarding them. All were hit by a car on the highway, dying on the spot. Like me, she knew about being driven by guilt, about taking that extra ten minutes, that extra hour, that fourteenth phone call—whatever it took—to never give up in order to save a horse. And like me, while she could act nonchalant on the backstretch, pretending to take it all in stride and hold it together, she'd start crying in her pickup and weep all the way home, sometimes with a horse in tow that she knew nothing could be done to help. She'd call me on the cell phone, and I could hear her voice, at first cracking, then breaking into sobs. It made me feel less alone, made me wonder less what was wrong with me.

With time, that closeness naturally spilled over into other areas. To this day, Joy and I talk at least three times a week on the phone and hardly ever pass a day without texting or e-mailing each other. She has even flown halfway across the country with me to squeeze my hand before I went up to the podium to give an important speech in Washington, to be there for me when I felt wobbly.

Invaluable as Joy and Judy and the other women on the board were, however, Cheryl told me it was very unusual to have a board whose great majority of members were boots-on-the-ground. Most nonprofits, she explained, especially when they reach the point at which their budgets are into the six figures, are made up mostly of people *not* in the trenches, people who bring renown to the organization and with it, more funds.

The reality, she said, is that if, say, a foundation is considering where to donate money, its managers are going to look at a non-profit's board and ask themselves, "Do we really want to give six women thousands of dollars? Are they going to go shopping with it?" None of us even had letters after our name, she added. In addition to people working directly with the horses, we needed to have a variety of professionals, men included.

It was then that I invited to join the board a couple of veterinarians, a CPA, and Cheryl's husband. Later on, I brought on an insurance broker and an attorney. All of them were men. These additions paid off, as Cheryl said they would. Broadening our inner circle translated into a broadening of our outer circle—more people who knew about us, entry into various echelons of society other than horse lovers, more publicity, and more checks. That was critical. As exponentially as our budget grew every year, we were always in need of more funding. The money Michigan State's development department managed to garner for us for surgeries was never enough. We were now the university's largest equine client at its hospital for large animals, and when its CANTER funds ran dry, we had to kick in the shortfall. It sometimes took a while; the university would let us get thousands of dollars into the hole. But we were always good for it. Adding to our expenses was that trainers became less and less inhibited about giving us broken horses whose medical needs meant skyrocketing veterinary bills. Thank goodness for all of our volunteers, none of whom ever took a cent.

Between expanding our board of directors, getting horses off the track, taking care of them at home, and doing what I could to raise funds, I hardly had any time for my own horses.

I paid a high emotional price for my neglect when, in the winter of 2001, something happened to one of my own that couldn't be put on hold. Pat, the mother of Baby and Scarlett, my children, began having vision problems. It had actually started the year before. She wouldn't notice me approaching and would jump, spooked, when she realized I was near her. She would also act a little lost when she wanted to come into the barn. She'd pause before making her way into the run-in. At first I thought it was because the barn, including the run-in, was often crowded with CANTER horses, but she wasn't bothered by the other horses. She, Beauty, and Sissy always enjoyed the hullabaloo of horses coming and going, in fact, never failing to whinny as yet another horse-bearing trailer drove up. No, it was that she was having difficulty finding the doorway.

I had had my farm vet out, and he told me that Pat had cataracts, and that they would get worse. He also told me that there's cataract surgery for horses, but that it cost thousands of dollars. I needed to be realistic, however. Pat was twenty. Her bad knee was now restricting her freedom of movement considerably more than in her younger years.

The vet assured me that there were many horses that did very well even totally blind, usually by hooking up with a companion horse, who I knew could be Sissy, if need be. If Pat went blind gradually, the vet said, she had a particularly good chance of being okay. "Don't change her stall," he advised. "Don't go moving the water trough.

Don't rotate her from one pasture to another; keep her routine the same."

I followed his advice to the letter, but after that first year in which I noticed the problem, Pat's sight seemed to slip particularly quickly. She was never a dominant sort, but she would become frantic to get out of the way if she heard another horse approaching, not knowing where she was in relation to the other animal. She didn't even know when it was Sissy, her own daughter, coming near. And if she got in Beauty's way by accident, Beauty would snake her head forward and snap at her. Twice, when Pat hurried to avoid Beauty's bite or some other threat, she smacked her nose into the edge of the barn doorway so hard that she cut it. Another time, missing the doorway for its framing, she incurred a large cut right on the side of her eye. That made her even more tense. She didn't know where to stand, and she was afraid to make a move. Walking forward, she'd stop dead if she heard even a faint sound.

I could no longer soothe her by talking to her, by breathing into her nose, putting my hand on her neck. Nothing I did could relax her. One incident proved especially frightening.

We have an area of land near the back of our acreage that's a little wetter than the rest of the pasture. And in the middle of February, we had a thaw/freeze. Snow had melted, but then freezing temperatures set in, and the low wet area where the melted snow had not seeped into the frozen ground became a sheet of ice. When I went down to the barn late one afternoon to give all the horses some hay, I saw Pat standing in the middle of that ice, stark still.

"It's alright, Pat," I called out to her. "Mommy's coming." By the time I grabbed a lead line and reached her, she was trembling, very aware that she was on unsafe footing. Footing is extremely important to horses. They do not want to go down accidentally. It's why they don't like to go from grass to asphalt, from asphalt to dirt, from dirt onto a ramp that will lead them into a trailer. It's why I had spent so much time teaching Baby and Scarlett how to walk across planks of wood and up the patio steps and other unusual surfaces. I wanted them to build confidence in their ability to step from one material onto another.

I made my way onto the ice with my rubber muck boots and was slipping and sliding every which way. Finally, I was able to attach the line to Pat and lead her—slowly, very slowly—off the large ice patch.

I locked that pasture shut after that, but it was clear that Pat, now twenty-one, had become a danger to herself and wasn't going to be able to handle being blind. So a few weeks later, after deliberating over and over, I said my final good-bye, and she went peacefully, as Pumpkin had, via injection, with me regretting that I was so busy I barely spent any time with the beloved, gentle mother of Baby in her last days. Making it feel all the sadder was that euthanization was no longer novel. I had to euthanize so many track horses that Dr. Stick, after careful evaluation, would tell me were unsalvageable and could not be helped with surgery.

After Pat was cremated, I spread some of her ashes in the pasture and put some more in the stein with Baby's and Pumpkin's. More of my herd was now in a vessel in our great room than cavorting behind our house.

Only Beauty and Sissy were left. Scarlett was traveling the country, winning more and more eventing awards at ever higher levels of competition. Many times she competed at the beautiful Kentucky Horse Park in Lexington, and she also went to strut her stuff at competitions as far away as Florida and North Carolina. To this day, her trainer, Jennifer, recalls Scarlett as the horse with whom she received her best eventing dressage scores ever—a 27 in the Kentucky Classic and a 29 at the Long Leaf Competition in North Carolina. The numbers don't mean anything if you're not an eventer, but they are proof of amazing feats.

Year after year, the rhythm of the racing season would repeat itself, with things kind of slow in the spring, when trainers still believed all of their horses had big wins in them, and then picking up in the summer and becoming extremely busy in

Scarlett eventing with her trainer,
Jennifer Merrick-Brooks.

the fall, when they wanted to unload all their failed charges as quickly as possible as they moved on to race tracks in warmer climates for the winter. Often, come October, I had to play musical chairs with trailer space. A trainer or jockey's agent or groom or even the track vet would come up to me and ask whether I had such-and-such a horse on the trailer because it broke down and needed help right away. Such horses, the most unsound of all, took precedence. They were a financial liability to everyone who stood to earn money at the track and needed to be vacated so a horse able to race and be wagered on could take its place. If they weren't removed as quickly as possible by me, they'd go to the slaughterhouse to free up lucrative space in a shedrow. Often, they were in terrible pain, another more pressing reason that they needed to be examined and tended to without delay.

In such cases, if a trailer was already full, I unloaded the soundest horse and brought it back to its trainer, having explained that I had another horse who couldn't wait. "I know you," I'd say. "I can trust you to hold onto the horse for me," never having a clue whether that was actually the case. But as luck would have it, each trainer always complied, having my assurances that I'd send another trailer for his horse within a week.

Once the season ended, I had a little time, as always, to catch my breath. But after the 2001 season, my efforts to stop the atrocities of racing were about to ramp up. In February of 2002, right around my birthday, I received a letter from a newly formed organization called Blue Horse Charities. It had been founded by John Hettinger, a very well-known name in the racing industry. John was at that point the owner of one of the largest auction houses in Lexington, Fasig-Tipton, where sheiks and others with unfathomable amounts of money come to buy the fastest, most well-bred horses in the world. I was told Fasig-Tipton was second only to Keeneland, the premier auction for top Thoroughbreds.

John was proracing but decidedly antislaughter, in favor of the welfare of a horse above all else. When a Thoroughbred was done performing at its best, he wanted to see it not drop into lower-level claiming races where it would be run to death, literally, but move on to a new career.

His charity was new, the letter said, but he was writing because he felt CANTER would qualify to receive funding from it since so much of what we did was find Thoroughbreds new disciplines at which to excel when their racing days were behind them. The letter instructed me to fill out the forms enclosed, and for every horse I had adopted out the previous year, Blue Horse Charities would send CANTER a check. The money came from his persuading sellers of horses to donate a percentage of their profits, with his matching the amount in every single case from his own coffers.

I couldn't believe our good fortune. Even with our budget increasing by leaps and bounds every single year, we were always barely squeaking by, and that was with everyone on the board who could afford to putting in some of their own personal money and all the volunteers fostering horses, feeding them at their farms, trailering them, walking the shedrows, for free.

I shot off a letter that I couldn't have received a better birthday gift, and he must have liked what I said because he quoted from it in Blue Horse Charities' national brochure. It leant CANTER a great deal of credibility to be recognized by someone so well respected in racing himself. The very first year, Blue Horse Charities sent us a check for $11,000.

Although John loved racing, he so put the horses' welfare first that I even convinced him to send money to euthanize horses who were too broken down and in too much irreversible pain to go on living, let alone switch to a new discipline. It was a wonderful understanding between us, that a euthanized horse, too, is a saved horse because it gets to die a peaceful death rather than be sent to an awful slaughter.

It meant so much to me because the horses who needed to be put down, more than any others, were Baby. Had I not been an involved owner, Baby would have been forced to limp onto a trailer and withstand a trip of many hours, his head bent low on a double-decker trailer meant for cows and pigs, to meet a scary, painful end with a bolt gun and a knife. And that would likely have been *after* an auction and time in a holding pen, probably without food or water but with aggressive horses to take him down.

For all it meant to me that John Hettinger understood my point of view, however, the most felicitous aspect of my coming to know him was that he brought me into a circle of people with whom I otherwise never would have had entrée. Through John, I met Staci Hancock, the wife of Arthur Hancock, who co-owned two Kentucky Derby winners and was also very antislaughter. In addition, I met Kentucky Congressman Ed Whitfield, antislaughter as well. I became part of a select group of people who would meet to strategize about a bill of Whitfield's called the American Horse Slaughter Prevention Act. If the bill went into law, it would ban slaughter in the U.S. and prohibit the transport of horses to slaughterhouses in Canada or Mexico. At that time, the majority of the 100,000 or so horses put to death every year went to slaughterhouses operating in Texas and Illinois, but there were still thousands going to Canada and Mexico every year. About one in five of them were Thoroughbreds.

As much as I had to learn about the inner workings of government from these luminaries, they had questions for me. Removed in their daily lives from the goings-on at lower-level tracks like Great Lakes Downs, they wanted to know how things worked. "What happens when a horse comes in? How does it end up going to slaughter? How does it get taken from the track? Had I actually *seen* horses removed by kill buyers?" They literally didn't know how the backstretch of a cheap track operated. Why would they?

I was glad for the progress I was making in talking with people who were in a position to choke the slaughter pipeline at its root, rather than at its end, as I was working to do in a manner that was much less efficient. But I was also reaching my breaking point. I had been working for twenty-four years at a high-stress job as a court reporter, taking down everything verbatim, never missing a single word, and continuously meeting strict deadlines. Concurrently, at any one time, I had thirty to forty horses boarded at farms all over the state, visiting them to check their injuries, to meet with veterinarians that CANTER would pay to take X-rays and examine them before it was decided whether they should be sent to Michigan State for further evaluation. Often, at Michigan State, I spent time signing euthanization paperwork for horses beyond help, a particularly draining task. During the season, I was running out to Great Lakes Downs virtually every Saturday.

My own barn was a revolving infirmary, with up to six or seven visitors at a time, some having to stay in the barn aisle because I had run out of stalls. Most horses came there *after* surgery, so I'd take care of them through weeks or months of stall rest, hand-walking them in larger and larger areas as they healed, giving them medications when necessary, hosing off injuries to keep down swelling. The only other person who took post-surgery horses in volume was a volunteer named Martha Denver, who lived northeast of me in what is known as Michigan's thumb; the state is shaped like a mitten. Not only did she have a larger facility than I did, she also had experience treating equine injuries. Between the two of us, we were kept extremely busy helping horses recuperate.

Through all of this, I had to keep placating the

racing industry by continually telling the media only good, happy-ending stories. I had to answer the phone at 1 A.M. and remain pleasant when a prospective adopter from California would call without regard for time zones because she couldn't tell from the picture on the Web site whether a horse's tail was very bushy and exactly how many inches from the ground it was. I had to continually write new grant proposals and meet with Michigan State's people to brainstorm about new ways to drum up money. I felt so squeezed I developed painful stomach ulcers. I had more trouble sleeping than ever.

Things came to a head during the fall rush of 2002. One Saturday morning I expected to have as many as six horses to remove from the track. Joy was there with her trailer, as were a couple of others with theirs, but I also arranged for a large rig. Nearby foster homes were nearly full, so I knew I needed to be prepared to have some horses hauled across the state to the more populous eastern side, where I had more foster families who could take on any overflow.

The day turned out much more hectic than I ever could have anticipated. Trainers were chasing me down the shedrows, paging me over the loud-speaker system. At the end of the afternoon, we had not six but twelve horses that needed quick removal. It took me more than a half hour with a pen and notebook just to organize the logistics of an exodus of twelve horses on four trailers to twelve different foster homes. Each horse needed to be matched with each foster home's requirement for accepting a horse. One farm might take stallions, while another had to have a quiet horse, and yet another still might not take an injured horse.

When I left the track following the large rig with six of the twelve horses, I still didn't know where they'd all be going. I just told the driver to head east and got on the cell phone, frantically calling people and asking them to take a horse for at least a few days. "I'm driving toward your house now," I'd say to each. "Can you do this?"

The last of the twelve was delivered a few minutes before midnight, with the final farm even farther east than my own. I had left my house at five that morning, having woken well before that to feed Beauty and Sissy and take care of all the foster horses in my care. I was happy—none of the horses had been sold to a kill buyer—but spent, and the stress and exhaustion played themselves out on my body, not just that day but every day.

My ulcers were acting up with such ferocity that I would become nauseated within thirty minutes of eating. I'd go without food in order not to feel sick. When I did finally eat, toward evening, I'd go into abdominal spasms.

Finally, John put his foot down. "You're quitting

your job," he said. It was on a day that I had to drive an hour and twenty minutes to Michigan State in order to bring in a horse for surgery. I barely had enough time to get there as it was, but he insisted I stay put for a discussion.

"How can I quit work?" I asked him. "Some of the money goes to CANTER." The gas alone crisscrossing the state cost a lot.

"I'll take care of the CANTER part," he told me. But he reminded me that most of the money I earned went to Scarlett—boarding her and paying her trainer for a total of almost $1,000 a month, entering her in events, which could cost hundreds of dollars a pop, flying to different states to see her compete and having to get hotel rooms and meals on the road. I'd have to retire her, John said. *That* we'd no longer be able to afford. She'd have to come home.

I felt truly awful. One reason was that at eventing competitions, when I looked through the programs, I'd sometimes see the names of horses who had been taken off the track by CANTER. Sometimes I even saw their names in eventing programs at Lexington's Kentucky Horse Park. Horses that would have gone to slaughter instead ended up at one of the most prestigious eventing venues in the country. It was living proof that the operation was working, giving Thoroughbreds new lives.

At one particular competition, upon reading the

program I had shed a flood of tears. A horse named Fuel Efficient was listed. I knew him as far back as the days that Baby raced and followed him with fear for more than two years after Baby's death. He was raced an unconscionable ninety-nine times, risking his life in cheap claiming races nearly every time, often on the dangerous track surface at the Detroit Race Course. When I was preparing for the lawsuit, I was always afraid to see the letters DNF, for Did Not Finish, next to his name on racing programs. But there he was, eventing with a loving owner, sound enough not only to do dressage but also to jump. The woman must have bought him on the backstretch without having gone through CANTER, which happened rather frequently. Someone would come to look at a horse they had seen on the Web site, but other trainers would entice them to come see *their* horses, even if they weren't listed. That was fine with me—anything to take a horse off the track.

I was going to miss moments like those—seeing a horse I had worried about over the years finally safe and, literally, sound.

I was also going to miss watching Scarlett compete. She loved jumping and was so good at it—winning blue ribbon after blue ribbon. One eventer even offered me $40,000 for her, although there was no amount of money that could ever separate me from one of my own horses. She was family. But now she would never again have her name in a program, be presented with a ribbon, do a victory gallop. I arranged for her to come home in November, right after the end of the eventing season.

Soon after she arrived, completely unfazed by all the convalescent horses I was taking care of, the two of us had a "talk" in the barn one night. I "explained" to her that she had to give up the glory of her eventing career for her brother and that I was sorry to be asking her to make the sacrifice. It was during my last check of the horses for the day, around 10 P.M., and I was scratching her neck under her mane.

She responded by turning her head and grooming me in return, running her teeth along my back to give me a feel-good scratch. She had never done that before, and strictly speaking, it could have been dangerous because sometimes when horses groom, they bite. But Scarlett didn't. "Don't cry," I imagined her saying as she offered me that gesture of affection. "It's alright. I love you, and I'm glad to be home."

Truth be told, Scarlett seemed no worse for having been pulled from her glory days, graciously accepting that from then on she would be the Secretariat snow globe in my backyard that an innocent lifetime earlier was all I had intended. But I had a hard time pulling *myself* out of the game. To my discredit, I even thought about *racing* Scarlett, along with Sissy. The track, like a busy airport, has a buzz of excitement, of things about to happen, and I struggled against my impulse to get in on that. Like crack cocaine, racing called to me, working to wear down my resolve with promises of an intoxicating ecstasy and in an instant throw away everything I stood for and had worked so hard to accomplish.

Scarlett and Sissy were both mature, I rationalized to myself, not just two or three years old. Then, too, it was known that the fillies sired by Baby's father did even better on the track than the colts. Maybe Sissy could do what her brother never was able to, I thought, telling myself that I wouldn't make the same mistake with picking a trainer as I did with Baby's first two. I'd be able to go straight to Pam.

With my competitive nature itching to be unleashed, I started to make excuses: Sissy could prove that Baby would have been 100 times better than he was had he not gotten off to a rough start those first couple of years; the new track was owned by a man who had his own stable of racehorses rather than by a corporation, like the previous track, so he'd make sure the surface remained safe. Both Sissy and Scarlett would *like* some adventure.

It was a long ride to and from the new track, and I had a lot of time to think.

But I would catch myself, shake it off. Baby's stall was empty. His honk was gone. Sissy could be gone; Scarlett, too. I was neglecting my husband, my daughters, as it was. And the track was the same as ever, with horsemen of every stripe all too willing to let horses go to their deaths if that would improve their bottom line. Going back to racing was clearly and irrevocably out of the question, a fleeting aberration in my thinking in which the very drive that had proved Baby's undoing managed to tempt, but too weakly to prove a real risk. Like a drug addict or problem drinker who has licked her vice, I was able to call up the strength to squelch the impulse.

I put my focus on settling in for the winter, not having to go out to the track between racing seasons and, for the first time, not having to run into Detroit for court reporting. I still had CANTER work—helping horses heal after surgery, finding adopters, writing grant applications—but I actually had time to let down a bit and enjoy my own horses again.

It didn't last. One February morning, when the sun had not yet climbed over the tree line at the back of our property, I was walking down to the barn to feed everyone when I saw Beauty splayed out on her side in the middle of the pasture. A horse would never choose to sleep there at night, especially not in winter. She'd want to sleep away from the wind.

I ran over, and she picked up her head a bit as if looking to her stomach, her eyes glazed and her breathing labored. She was colicking and had been for who knew how many hours. She had been absolutely fine the night before, eating and relieving herself as necessary.

I ran back to the house and grabbed my cell phone so I could be right by her once I phoned the vet. Before making the call, I pressed my finger to the gums above her teeth to see if her blood flow upon my letting go was okay. It was not. Her gums remained white too long before turning pink again, meaning her capillary refill time was slow.

Beauty, more than any of my other horses, had borne the brunt of my neglect.

Normally, she couldn't wait for me to come home from my court reporting work and go for a ride. But I never had any time to take her out anymore. As soon as I arrived at the house, I'd either be responding to phone calls and e-mails or driving an hour or more away to one of CANTER's many foster farms to see a horse and assess its injuries, determine whether it needed to be referred for possible surgery. I was torn— Beauty would see me step toward the car after spending a little while in the house and look at me as if to say, "Aren't you coming over? Are we going out now?" Invariably, I had had to disappoint her. Sometimes, I wasn't going anywhere but had the barn full with horses who had already undergone surgery. They needed their bandages changed; they needed to be checked for infections. They needed to be hand-walked rather than let out into the field by themselves so they wouldn't tear their stitches, a procedure that took much more time than wrapping their wounds, at which I had become a pro. And that left no time for riding, let alone grooming, Beauty.

Holding in my emotions in order not to upset her, I talked soothingly, going down on my knees by her head and breathing into her nose. "It's okay, Beauty. I'm here."

I reached the vet's answering service and had to wait for a call back. As soon as the phone rang and I heard the vet's voice, I lost it. "Beauty's dying, Beauty's dying!" I screamed. "Please come as soon as you can. She's down. I can't get her up. She's cold."

The vet knew who I was and said she was on her way. In the meantime, I was begging Beauty, pulling on her lead line, trying to get her up and out of the cold, but she would not respond. I even tried pushing her, although it is impossible to push 1,000 pounds into a standing position.

Beauty was twenty-seven years old—and I knew that the older the horse, the higher the risk that a colic surgery would not be successful.

Twenty minutes later, when the vet arrived, she injected Beauty with pain medication. She wanted to walk her into the barn—it was warmer in there, and it's always better for a colicking horse to be standing rather than prone—but still, we couldn't get her up. "We've really got to make this happen," the vet insisted. "I don't want to go to my car and get the cattle prod. It'll hurt."

So we tried some more, and Beauty finally did rise and stagger inside. I put her in the large double stall where Baby had been born, and then Scarlett and Sissy, and she went down on her side immediately. But in her new position, the vet was able to listen to her gut sounds and her heart rate, which was exceedingly high, and gave her some more pain medication. She said she had two more emergencies but that she'd be back in a couple of hours and that I should continue to try to get Beauty standing, if I could.

I couldn't budge her. Beauty was breathing heavily, not responding to my urging at all. I wondered how many hours during the night she had been suffering, and didn't want to put her through a few more while the vet made her rounds. So I called another vet, who arrived very quickly and who also tested capillary refill rate, heart rate, gut sounds.

"Jo Anne," she said, "we need to think about letting her go."

I started crying. "That's why I called you," I said. "I couldn't bear to have her wait any longer."

"I wouldn't do that," she responded. "Her heart rate is so high, even with all the pain medication she has been given. We need to do this." Then, as a vet will invariably do, she backed away to give me some time with my horse. I was shuddering hard as I cried, right by Beauty's head. Her age was clearly showing. We had had almost twenty years together, and now she had a lot of white hairs on her face. She had been so young and vibrant when I first brought her home.

The woman who sold her to me had said she would only let Beauty go to someone for whom she'd be their first horse. She didn't want her to be somebody's fifth horse.

When I finally left Beauty's side, I saw that the vet, too, was crying, for which she apologized, saying her behavior was unprofessional. "Please don't apologize," I told her. "That only makes me appreciate you more."

When I was ready, the vet injected the solution, and Beauty slipped quietly away. I was allowed to remain right by her head since she was already down and couldn't fall on me.

The vet then told me that to be able to get Beauty out of the stall, it would be easier if we positioned her more tucked. Otherwise, once the rigor mortis set in, removing her would be a problem. John came down to the barn and took off the two bottom rows of wooden planks on the wall surrounding the door that faced the barn aisle, so it would be easier to slide her out. The doorway itself wouldn't be wide enough. We curled up Beauty's legs while it was still possible and turned in her head and neck as much as we could.

Before cremating her, I had her necropsied because I wanted to know what, exactly, had gone wrong. Her diet hadn't been changed at all, and she was drinking at last check the evening before she died.

It turned out she had multiple fatty lipomas inside her abdomen that, like stalactites, grew in from above, at the top of the abdominal wall. The lipomas wrapped all the way around her intestine, strangling it in a number of areas. Their growth had finally hit a tipping point. The equine pathologist said they were the most common cause of death in a horse over the age of twelve. I was relieved I hadn't done anything wrong and that there was nothing I could have done to save her. But I felt terrible that Beauty spent most of her last days disheartened at my not having time to ride her while I was making up for what I had done to Baby.

It was not a good start to 2003 and to my new freedom from my work as a court reporter. It made me think not just about the time I took from Beauty but from my entire family. We used to travel frequently, taking long weekends to places like Niagara Falls, going white-water rafting on the Colorado River in the Grand Canyon, visiting Yellowstone. We had even been to Russia, where Rebecca performed in the International Dance Festival, both in Moscow and Minsk. All of that had pretty much come to a halt once CANTER got off the ground, yet I still didn't feel fulfilled.

It's not that I wasn't happy about having saved so many hundreds of horses. But that could never bring Baby back. And no matter how much I accomplished, all around me were horses who were horribly injured, in great pain, surrounded by people with the most blasé attitude toward them. I was plagued by constant anguish and sadness.

Making matters more upsetting still was that there were now rumblings among some of the newer board members who never came to the back of the track that by taking in so many unsound horses who couldn't be rehabilitated for other disciplines, we were cutting into CANTER's profitability. CANTER was just a dumping ground for maimed horses, they argued, and we should be saving only sound horses that we could adopt out for more than we paid the trainers, insuring the organization's financial viability and keeping us from the constant struggle for more donations, more grants.

This unnerved me considerably. The whole reason I started CANTER was to save maimed horses, to save all the Babies out there. What was a rescue if not a dumping ground?

Most of the original board members were all horse lovers. They were there at the track, touching the horses, looking into their eyes, seeing the horses look trustingly back at them as these volunteers haggled for their lives. They could never have put a price on the value of saving a Thoroughbred at risk. But the nonhorse people, while very impressive in terms of their credentials and their ability to attract funds and the attention of important people in other spheres, hadn't had the same experiences. They might have appreciated animals but not with the same passion as those who dragged themselves to the track week after week to do the difficult, time-consuming work of saving horses from the brink. They hadn't lived their lives longing for a horse. They never soaked a hoof with abscesses or cleaned and bandaged a laceration. In strengthening our board, I had diluted its singularity of purpose. Some of our board members would have let Baby hobble onto a double-decker trailer headed for the slaughterhouse rather than provide him with humane euthanasia.

With time to think after quitting my job, I had wanted to create some balance in my life, put my family back into the center of the picture. Rebecca had become engaged a few months earlier, and I wanted to devote time to helping plan the wedding. I was looking forward to it, ready to scale back a bit on my CANTER activities. But worried by the attitude of some of the board members, and driven not to let happen to any other horse what could have happened to Baby, I was right back in the thick of things come the start of the 2003 season.

We were dealt a blow early that year, in May,

when Judy forwarded to me by e-mail an ad from a Web site called dreamhorse.com, where people could advertise horses for sale. The ad was for a horse named That's R Groovy, listing him for $3,500 and declaring that he was capable of jumping. We were both frantic and furious.

That's R Groovy had come into our program three years earlier with fractures in both knees. He was never going to jump, even after surgery. We had paid $600 for him.

After his operation to remove all the bone fragments, he came to my barn to recuperate for four months, and I fell in love with him from the start. He was more than flashy-looking, not simply red but bright orange, with a huge white blaze that ran from under his forelock to his upper lip. He also had one white sock—and, standing at 16.3 hands, was the largest horse I had ever had at my house, and even one of the largest ever at the track. Even his hooves were huge.

His size intimidated me a bit at first. In came this gigantic horse with his front legs all bandaged from surgery, and I knew he had a lot of pent-up energy in him from having been laid up a couple of months prior to the operation. This was because he had had to wait for cortisone to clear from his body, as the drug greatly raises the risk for infection. How was I going to keep him content on stall rest and just a little bit of hand walking every day?

I took him down to the barn with a lot of pre-caution, expecting him to be fractious, prancing around, and hard to handle. Yet he was none of those things. He wasn't even bothered by the other horses in the pasture running around and whinnying at his arrival. He took it all in stride, never tensing his muscles or freezing and staring intently, let alone trying to bolt. Instead, I was able to lead him into the barn like a puppy dog, which right then and there endeared him to me. I loved his trust and the sense that I got from him that he felt he was "home." I loved that he took an instant liking to me, as I did to him. It was like having just met someone yet feeling like you've known the person your whole life. There was an understanding between us, an immediate comfort level.

If Groovy had an itch on the side of his face, he'd blithely use me as a scratching post, rubbing his head up and down my body the way Scarlett liked to, knowing instinctively that I wouldn't reprimand him, even as I had to brace myself so I wouldn't topple over while he relieved his itch. He liked to nudge everything, too, which I also loved. Five years old, just at the turning point between childhood and adulthood, he still showed an inquisitive nature. I could see the wheels turning."Water pail," he'd think, putting his nose up against it. "Boring. Feed pail! Anything in there? Nope. What's down here? Ah, pockets."

Then he'd go sniffing, smelling my jacket pockets to see what I might have on hand, but not in a pushy, aggressive way, simply a curious one.

As sweetly playful as he was, however, he made taking care of him so easy. Many horses, when you change the bandages on their knees, continually readjust their legs so you keep having to start all over. They can't stop fidgeting. But not Groovy. He knew I was trying to help him and that bandage changing was serious business. He'd stand perfectly still.

I was definitely his favorite horse at the barn. He got along well with the others, but he enjoyed my company the best. And although I may not have put it together at the time, that especially endeared him to me because it's how Baby was. He loved his herd mates, but I was always his first pick.

"Slow down, you move too fast," I'd croon as I cleaned around his stall while he was in there, the buoyant lines from the Simon & Garfunkel song "Feelin' Groovy" matching our mood. And in his high-jinx way, he'd follow me, making sure I didn't miss any spots, whereas another horse might have stood off to the side. "Oh, one of the manure balls fell off the fork." He'd let me know by nudging me with his chin on my shoulder, or even grabbing the fork handle with his mouth. *"Life, I love you, all is Groo—vy!"*

I was horrified to learn that the original, CANTER-approved adopter who bought him from us for $700 sold him to a student of hers as a trail horse in violation of our restricted lifetime bill of sale, which stipulated that a horse couldn't be sold, leased, or undergo a change in oversight without our explicit approval through notification by certified mail and that we'd take a horse back if such approval were withheld. It was the student who then listed him for $3,500, hoping to exploit him further and make a tidy profit by lying about his ability to compete in jumping.

That scared me terribly. Thoroughbreds are known for their heart. They'll go out and do what you ask of them until they die trying. Groovy, in particular, was that kind of horse.

The original adopter insisted she was ignorant of the dreamhorse ad, and also refused to give us information on the whereabouts of the student to whom she had sold Groovy. The woman's name was not listed on the site. We noticed that the ad was quickly removed, however, and then received an e-mail from the first adopter that her student was going to keep the horse for life. Of course, she was still in violation of the contract. More to the point, we didn't believe her. We suspected that the sale of Groovy, sound only for trail riding or for grazing in the pasture, proceeded underground.

I wanted to sue for breach of contract and retake possession of Groovy. But I needed an attorney near the woman, and she was hours away, in

Northern Michigan on the western side of the state. And no lawyer I knew in Detroit or Ann Arbor would take the case *pro bono*.

I had hit a wall, and I was inconsolable. I now went to sleep at night worrying about Groovy, worried that he would do whatever was demanded of him, even if it destroyed him. "Where *are* you, Groovy?" I'd think to myself while waiting to drop off to sleep, as if he could tell me by telepathy. He, more than any horse I couldn't ultimately save, haunted me.

Rebecca's bridal shower followed not long after the incident, bringing with it a lot of opportunity for retrospection. I remember, while writing out the invitations, pausing at the line that says "Given by." I wrote "Family" but wanted to put down "Baby," because that was the truth.

The shower itself was particularly joyous and festive because only a week earlier, Jessica, too, had become engaged. The venue for the get-together, a meeting room at a golf course, had a beautiful view of the fairway. I was glad for my daughters, but for a few moments, while looking out over the links, I let myself be transported out of the moment I was in, away from everyone in the room and back to another time. There was Baby, alive, and I was happy.

Rebecca's wedding itself came at the worst possible time—October, right in the middle of fall rush. I was in Las Vegas for ten days, where the wedding was held. Rebecca had moved there after college. She had already danced in the Lexington Ballet, but when the doctor told her that an injured ankle would never heal enough to dance *en pointe* again, she dejectedly left the world of dance and received a degree in anthropology at the University of Michigan. As she was graduating four years later, an old dancing friend of hers suggested she come out to Las Vegas and audition for one of the major shows.

Rebecca was thrilled to have the opportunity to dance—any kind of dance, even if it couldn't be ballet—and was quickly accepted into Jubilee, one of the most prestigious and well-paying revues on the Strip. Like a CANTER horse, she had repurposed herself into a different kind of discipline after an injury and had made her peace with it, excelling in her new activity. I remember visiting her soon after she moved out there, when she had me try on one of the heavy, Bob Mackie–designed headdresses she wore as part of one of her costumes. In *I Love Lucy* fashion, I staggered about. But Rebecca, she carried it off like a swan.

She met her husband in Vegas, too, and they were going to be making their home there, which is why the wedding took place out west. Some sixty of us flew out from Michigan for the event, not just John, I, and Jessica and her fiancé but also aunts and uncles and cousins and lots of friends. It was almost like a destination wedding. Yet as much as I tried to enjoy myself and be happy for my daughter, half of me was back home, worrying what was going on with all the intakes. Were the volunteers taking the extra time to go back through the shedrows at the end of the day in case someone decided at the last minute that he had a horse to list? Was every tactic being tried to wrest an unsound horse from his trainer? Joy and Martha Denver were in charge and were very driven, like me, so I no doubt worried needlessly. But saving the horses had become an obsession, probably not even a healthy one any longer, and I couldn't help it. This simply was going to continue to be who I was. I kept phoning Joy, calling Martha, double-checking things.

It turned out the ten days I was gone were among the busiest CANTER ever experienced, with one of the highest intakes of horses in such a short period of time. But the two of them handled it all beautifully, as did all the other volunteers.

Whatever we did could never be enough, though. After I came back to Michigan, a few horses ended up in the wrong hands, as they always did, no matter how hard I tried to keep that from happening. One failure would loom over 100 successes.

After the season ended, the year ended on a frightening note *away* from the track. Around four or five o'clock on December 31st, before things became crazy on the roads, I went over to see my parents and wish them a Happy New Year.

"Your Dad's been sick for about four or five days," my mother said when she came to the door. "He even went to the pharmacist and asked what he could take to stop throwing up, and they gave him Pepto-Bismol. But he's still vomiting."

I immediately suspected that my father had not felt well since before Christmas but hadn't wanted to ruin the holiday for the family. He was that way.

"Dad, Mom says you've been sick," I told him. He was reclining in the La-Z-Boy, ashen, but rushed to put the seat upright and act normal when he saw me.

"Yeah, I don't know," he answered. "I don't feel good, and I can't stop throwing up. But it's getting better."

"You need to be checked," I said. I called Jessica, by then an emergency room doctor at a major hospital, and she came over immediately. "He's going right to the hospital," she said when she examined him. "It's his gallbladder."

She was right. It turned out my father's gallbladder, his whole intestinal area, was gangrenous. Surgery was performed right away to remove the corroded tissue, and when my father was wheeled out of the operating room, he put his thumbs up as he went by. Then the surgeon came over.

"It doesn't look good," he said. The gallbladder had already ruptured. "We flushed and flushed the entire abdomen as much as we could," the doctor went on, "but the idea that we could get all of it out and that it wouldn't come back—it usually doesn't happen."

I felt sick. My father, who was eighty-nine, was very tall and to that day retained his military bearing, always standing ramrod straight. He had been an MP in World War II, specially selected for extra schooling and special training in hand-to-hand combat, and subsequently chosen as one of General Eisenhower's guards.

When I was a little girl I used to badger him relentlessly. "But *why* can't I have a horse?" We lived in a subdivision eight miles from the Detroit line. Each two-bedroom house was attached to a tiny backyard.

My father, always my go-to parent, had indulged me as best he could. When he came home from a long day at work, he would sit at the kitchen table and read the paper while waiting for dinner. I would go and get a towel and put it over his knee—that was my saddle. Then I would bring out one of his belts and slide it behind the back of his knee and fasten it. That was my bridle, my reins. Finally, I'd climb up on my horse—my father was not just tall but also broad—and say, "Giddy-up. Come on, horsey." My dad, a carpenter, would move his heel up and down to simulate the feel of a horse going along, all the while reading the paper, never complaining that he was tired after his day on the job.

It took him a month to die. He would have turned ninety at the end of March. He had already booked a hall and an accordion player for the party, so excited was he at the prospect of reaching his tenth decade. But at two-something in the morning on February 1st, a Sunday, he passed.

I went to the hospital every single day through January. I still had to write the annual Blue Horse Charities grant application, answer e-mails, and deal with some phone calls, but I was able to handle a lot of that from his bedside. Poor Jessica, there she was trying to plan her wedding yet checking in on her grandfather as often as she could.

With my father gone and the hall picked— Jessica was going to get married over Thanksgiving weekend later that year—I headed into the 2004 racing season, continuing to grieve but knowing that I had to continue on.

One Saturday in May, when things were still slow for CANTER at the track, I was going to drive out to Great Lakes Downs for the morning and then meet Jessica at a bridal salon to help her pick out her wedding gown late that afternoon. That would give me enough time to get home, take care of my own horses, and shower. I was looking forward to it. Because Rebecca lived in

Las Vegas, she had picked out her wedding dress on her own, trying to describe over the phone the choices to which she had narrowed it down. Now, I'd be able to enjoy that motherly rite of passage with Jessica, not to mention have another "moment" with Baby, who was paying for the dress. I needed the respite from my work. It would be a chance to create some of the family balance to which I had given such short shrift.

The day at the track proved uneventful, as I had expected it would. Just before I was getting ready to leave the backstretch and head back to the Detroit area, however, the track vet came up to me and asked if I had been to a particular trainer's set of stalls.

I responded that I had walked down that shedrow but hadn't seen him.

"Well, you need to go talk to him," the track vet said. "He has a horse there that he won't do anything with. It's been colicking for over a week. See if he will give you the horse and let you put it down." The track vet, Hal Davidson, had no problem injecting horses with ever more cortisone and other painkillers, as that was his bread and butter, but he also looked after them, whether to assuage a guilty conscience I don't know. He even took thousands of dollars' worth of X-rays of CANTER horses for free over the years and traveled to Judy's farm a couple of times to treat horses for free.

I found the horse Hal was talking about. Named Naseer Spirit, he had already raced three times for his trainer the previous year but earned only $171, just enough to pay his jockey fee.

Naseer Spirit was down on his side. Unlike a dog or cat, horses cannot vocalize their pain. They suffer in silence, and the utter lack of any whimpering makes their physical distress all the more pitiful. If there was one thing I could change about horses—and I know it's sacrilegious to talk about wanting to change something in beings so magnificent—it would be to give them voice when they're in pain, allow them to moan. The lack of noise reinforces to people the notion that horses are not feeling pain when they are.

I spent at least an hour with Naseer Spirit's trainer, trying to talk him into giving me the horse. Finally, after much haggling, he agreed.

"I can bring him to emergency at Michigan State right away," I said, "but we have to find a trailer."

"I have a trailer," the trainer responded eagerly.

"Great," I answered. "Let's load him right now and get him over to the hospital."

"That's so far for me to drive," he then said. "Can someone else do it?"

"I do not have a trailer volunteer here today," I told him. "This is your horse. I'm going to take care of all the veterinary expenses. He suffered for a week. You need to drive to the university hospital in Lansing with me." The horse should have been euthanized right then and there. But the trainer wouldn't have let me. He had an idea in his head that the horse would be okay. I was lucky enough to get him to donate the horse and let me see about a colic surgery.

Finally, I convinced the trainer to make the drive, and I followed him out of the race track. On the way to Lansing, a drive of an hour and forty-five minutes, he needed to stop for gas and wanted me to pay for it—even though if the horse could have benefited from a $5,000 colic surgery, CANTER would have footed the bill.

I had had it. "There comes a point," I told him testily, "where *you* have to take some responsibility for your horse, and it's going to happen at this gas pump." The man did end up paying for the gas, and when we finally got the horse to Michigan State, it was just as I had suspected. The trainer had waited too long, and the horse needed to be put down.

I signed the euthanization papers at the front counter, tearfully, as always.

I was still crying as I drove home, thinking about the horse and all he had needlessly gone through, about my father, about how nothing made any sense, when the cell phone rang. It was Jessica. It was already close to an hour past the time I was supposed to meet her at the bridal salon.

CHAPTER THIRTEEN

A couple of months before Jessica's wedding, John started needing to take breaks after walking just short distances. "Wait a minute," he'd say if we were going down the hallway of the mall or a long grocery store aisle.

"Are you out of breath?" I'd ask. So many times over the years he had given up smoking, and so many times he had gone back to it.

"No," he answered. "My leg's just cramping." John never complained about his health, and he also never went for a physical. In our thirty-six years of marriage, I couldn't remember him once ever going for a checkup.

Concerned that something significant might be wrong, both Jessica and I got on him to go for a checkup, and he said he would, but not till after the wedding. I think he figured I'd forget to keep nagging him, but I didn't. I couldn't. After just a half block of walking, he'd have to stop because the cramping pain was so intense.

The doctor immediately referred him to a cardiologist; his blood pressure was high, as was his cholesterol. Thus began a battery of tests that took place over the course of several months— ultrasounds of various arteries, CT scans, contrast dyes sent through the blood vessels in and around his heart to see whether an artery there was blocked, and so on.

While the doctors were trying to figure out why John was cramping—we were now just a couple of weeks into January of 2005—I received a call that my mother, who turned eighty-nine just before Christmas, collapsed and had to be rushed to the hospital. She lingered only two weeks, dying a year after my father, almost to the day.

Soon after, it was confirmed that John had peripheral artery disease. His femoral arteries—the ones that branch off at the pelvis, one going through each leg all the way down to the feet—were 100 percent blocked.

We were referred to a vascular surgeon. Both the right and left leg were going to need a femoral artery bypass—a fem-pop, they call it, with a new blood vessel to replace the blocked artery extending all the way from the abdomen to the ankle. The surgeon would start with the better leg, the left, so John could see how uncomplicated the procedure was. His concern had been that he'd miss an entire summer of golf, but the surgeon said he'd operate in May, schedule a second operation for the right leg in June when the left one healed, and that John would be golfing again before the summer was over.

We dodged a bullet, we felt. There was no significant blockage in the heart itself, and once both legs underwent the procedure, John would be out of pain.

In the meantime, CANTER work went on as usual—there were always horses to protect, horses to look after once they were out of danger—but this year, the board also started talking about taking our rescue's work to another level. We discussed at meetings the idea of having our own farm rather than boarding horses at foster farms all over the state. It would be a state-of-the-art facility near the university so that horses who needed surgery wouldn't have to travel far and would receive the best of care after their operations. We entertained as well the notion of having at the farm an education center and an event space for holding fundraisers. Horse rescues that took in just fifteen horses a year had their own farms. Here we were intaking more than 100 horses annually yet still boarding them at far-flung locales that required many miles of driving in order to visit convalescent Thoroughbreds. A CANTER "center" would not only make our work more efficient, it would also bring us more renown, which in turn would bring in more funds to save and care for more horses.

I was glad for this forward thinking, but things were about to take a headier turn still. In June, as new ideas were swirling and John's recuperation was progressing without a hitch, I received an e-mail from a woman who lived in Montreal. It was one of close to 500 that were waiting for me, as we had just returned from a four-day visit to Rebecca, and on a typical day, more than 100 CANTER e-mails poured in. At first it seemed business as usual.

"I have a horse that I think was yours," this one said, "and I can't keep it anymore."

"Can you tell me the name of the horse?" I wrote back, also asking for a little more information.

"Groovy," she responded. I could literally feel my heart racing. It had now been four years since he had left my farm and a year since I lost track of him when he was, presumably, sold underground. "I will take him," I responded. "How is he doing?"

The woman, pregnant, explained that she didn't have time to ride him or take care of him anymore and that he had a problem with his coffin bone, the main bone in the foot that supports a horse's weight. She wanted me to come get him as soon as possible.

Not since the moments before Baby broke down on the track had I felt so elated. How much sleep I had lost over Groovy, even through Jessica's wedding and John's ordeal with his legs. How I longed to see him, to stroke him, to make sure he was safe and happy, as he had been at my farm.

As luck would have it, an adopter of CANTER horses who lived on Northern Vermont's Canadian border, only an hour from Montreal, said she would retrieve Groovy for me and bring him out to the Midwest. I knew the woman, Brenda Lamb, wouldn't let me down. She had once retrieved a horse from the farm of a trainer in Michigan and stayed an extra night to clean the stalls there because the man had crippling arthritis that made it hard for him to take care of things.

It was going to be a few months before Groovy arrived back at my own farm. He was underweight and had two abscesses, one on his shoulder that was really festering, along with some benign skin tumors and various welts, scrapes, and cuts, and Brenda didn't want me to see him in that condition. He was in good hands in the meantime.

"Groovy was born to be a Lhasa Apso," Brenda e-mailed me. "He's *so* darling. . . . During a stiff neck moment, he just put his nose in my hand and leaned on me with one little blinking eye, saying 'Fix this.'" I couldn't wait to see him.

Unfortunately, only days later, my joy was alloyed when John developed his first post-operative complication: pain in the leg on which the surgeon had operated. Testing showed that the bypass, now only a little more than a month old, had already occluded, becoming filled with plaque, just like his femoral artery. They said it would take only about an hour to reopen it, but hours and hours went by before the vascular surgeon came out to tell me it was all over. It had gone very slowly because the plaque had already solidified.

Two weeks later, on July first, we were back in the emergency room once again. The bypass reoccluded and the pain, quite severe, had returned a second time. The surgery on John's right leg was going to be delayed until the surgeon felt sure that the left would remain stable.

Later that same month, I was spun in yet another direction when I was notified that I had won the Dogwood Stable Dominion Award. It was an incredible honor, a prestigious award given once a year to an "unsung hero of the racing industry." Among those sitting on the panel of judges was Secretariat owner Penny Chenery.

For CANTER, the timing couldn't have been better. The award would be presented, as always, at the Saratoga Race Track in New York at the beginning of August. Everybody who was anybody in racing would be there—the biggest names with the deepest pockets—and we felt that was our "in" for generating donations to make our idea of a farm a reality. Even after I was nominated but before I won, a number of racing publications interviewed me, bringing more attention to our cause.

The farm in our minds now became the CANTER Thoroughbred Midwest Rehabilitation Center. All CANTER affiliates in the Midwest would be able to send their horses there, not just horses in Michigan. From there, we'd establish rehabilitation centers in New England, in the Mid-Atlantic, and in the Gulf area. We already had affiliates, or would soon have them, in all of those regions.

In a ten-minute speech I would be allowed to make following the presentation of the award, I'd be able to drive home my point that the Thoroughbreds needed help. Those in the highest echelons of racing—not people at our crummy track trying to eke out a living but the most distinguished breeders, trainers, and owners in the country—would hear my plea.

I rehearsed the speech during my hours in the car driving back and forth to Great Lakes Downs, taking a stopwatch with me and saying the lines I had written over and over to put the emphasis on the right words while making sure that I didn't go over my allotted ten minutes. I even pulled off the highway when necessary to scratch something off or make changes, perfecting the speech until the last minute.

John was able to come with me to Saratoga—the pain had not returned by the first week in August—as were my daughters and several members of the CANTER board, including Joy. The track there was unlike anything I had ever seen in Michigan. Instead of an asphalt parking lot crammed with cars and flanked by a grandstand with flaking paint, it was a pastoral scene with a large picnic ground. The tableau reflected the money and pedigree of the Social Register set who flocked to Saratoga each summer for a month of parties. They also watched races filled with horses who, in the prime of their careers, had not yet had the life run out of them. All was pageantry and tradition, as if the previous 100 years hadn't gone by.

While I was taken with the setting, the irony of it was not lost on me. Horses who raced at elite tracks such as Saratoga were sold over and over when they no longer performed well enough to compete at the country's few top courses and finally ended up broken and limping at tracks like ours in Michigan. As much as I was awed to suddenly glimpse people I'd seen on television over the years—owners of Kentucky Derby winners, nationally famous trainers like D. Wayne Lucas and Todd Pletcher—I was fully aware that they prospered at the horses' expense. The custom-designed hats women wore at tracks like Saratoga and Churchill Downs cost more than the couple hundred dollars I regularly haggled over on the backside, trying to keep a Thoroughbred from going to slaughter.

My award was presented at an exclusive luncheon given in my honor by Cothran "Cot" and Anne Campbell, in honor of their beloved horse Dominion, who died in old age. Under a tent on the grounds of a private club with a five-piece band and waiters in uniform, I received an introduction as someone who through CANTER had saved more than 4,000 horses. Normally, Cot and Anne do the honors, but John Hettinger requested that he present me with the award—a $5,000 check and a sculpture of Dominion—and the Campbells obliged him. I was so touched by that gesture. John, a champion of Thoroughbreds as much as he loved racing, was suffering from a brain tumor at that point and could barely make his way forward with a cane.

I was so moved that John Hettinger wanted to present me with the Dominion Award even though he was quite sick by that point.

I made my speech as gracious as possible. I truly was thankful that my work was being recognized, but beyond that, I was mindful of my aim to make a good impression so that when we went asking for money for our rehabilitation center, those with the means to help us would be well disposed toward us. Still, I did connect the dots for those present, suggesting in as pleasantly couched terms as possible that they bore at least some of the responsibility for what happened to their racehorses once they dropped down in the ranks and away from beautiful tracks like the one at Saratoga. In a talk filled with effusive thank-yous and vague references to the Thoroughbred industry's "unwavering concern" for racing's Thoroughbreds, I pointed out that only within the last few weeks, I had to sign a euthanization order for a horse at Great Lakes Downs who had won a race at Saratoga just three years earlier. During the same time frame, another former Saratoga winner was admitted to Michigan State for surgery after breaking down on our track.

I knew this with certainty because while I was preparing my speech at the end of July, it seemed like we were euthanizing or hospitalizing an awful lot of maimed horses, more than usual, and I wondered whether it was true or whether things just seemed worse than they generally were because of what John was going through and my mother's death earlier in the year. So I reviewed the Excel spreadsheets I always kept on our intakes and found that from the beginning of the year till July 29th, 56 percent of those who came into the CANTER program crossed the finish line only to find death. Many of them had started their racing careers at high-level tracks, including Saratoga. It was as it had always been. Horses who ran at our cheap little track just a couple of hours from a slaughterhouse, pumped with drugs to mask injuries, had often changed hands after illustrious starts in California, in Kentucky, in New York, and in other states with reputations for television-worthy racing.

I wasn't sure how my allusion to the deaths of former Saratoga Thoroughbreds would go over, but Joy told me afterward that people were not offended, that she even saw tears well up in people's eyes. And I could see that those present were acting warmly toward me; I hadn't ticked anyone off.

The choice not to come off accusatory had not been easy. I wasn't talking about wetlands being built on. This was pain and suffering and death in the worst way possible, year after year, horse after horse, and sacrificing the expression of my real feelings, as I did every week at the track when I asked trainers if they had "anything" they "wanted to get rid of," took its toll emotionally. But what choice did I have? If I wanted to save horses, to raise money to save even more, I had to take the ingratiating route, even though I was speaking to people at the source of the trickle-down effect that allowed horses to reach Michigan lame and often unfixable. Pointing a finger wasn't going to get me anywhere.

After the speech, John Hettinger suggested to me that I should use the national attention from the award to advance the cause of saving horses from slaughter. I told him right then about our plans for a Midwest rehabilitation center and asked if he would consider becoming the honorary chairperson of an advisory board CANTER wanted to create with people at the top tier of racing in order to shine a spotlight on the plan. He agreed immediately, and also suggested that I approach Cot and Anne, a very well known trainer named Nick Zito, and a couple of others at Saratoga that day, all of whom said yes.

I spent the rest of my few days at Saratoga participating in events I would never have chosen to attend on my own. For instance, included in the honor of receiving the Dominion award was watching a race named for me, so in special box seats with Cot and Anne, I politely sat looking down or to the side as the horses ran by, the way a child might play with the peas on his plate to make it look like he had actually eaten some. I had not watched a race since Baby died, and I didn't want to see one now. To have done so would have been a direct betrayal of him, a violation of his memory.

Still, I did not leave feeling angry. I felt positive, buoyed by John Hettinger's enthusiasm and ready to make new inroads. I even was offered help by a woman named Annette Bacola, one of my guests at the award luncheon. I had known her for a few years by then as she had spent some time as Michigan's state racing commissioner, and I liked her because unlike so many other racing commissioners, she truly did care about the horses. Also, she, too, had lost a horse to racing, a grey she still thought of, and that deepened our bond.

Annette took Joy and me to lunch the day after the award ceremony, and while the three of us chatted about our love of horses, I asked her to join the newly created advisory board to help us get the rehabilitation center off the ground. Not only did she say yes, she also invited me to her home in Lexington to strategize. Flying back to Detroit, I knew we were on our way.

I drove down to Lexington the last weekend of August to meet with Annette, who put me up in her guesthouse, a beautiful brick edifice filled with antiques, mahogany furniture, and spacious rooms, including a library, with doors that spilled onto a large portico. While the surroundings, replete with bronze horse sculptures and other equine touches, were intimidating, Annette was not. Classy but warm and sweet—a beautiful person inside and out—she suggested that she and her husband host a fundraiser at her home, offering to cover all the costs. I was overwhelmed by her largesse.

It wouldn't be a major fundraiser, Annette said, rather more of a getting-people-interested kind of thing. The thinking was that it might bring in somewhere on the order of $25,000. True, that wasn't enough to build a rehabilitation center, which would cost millions. But for one night's work, I thought such a number would be terrific.

When I arrived home from Lexington, I called Congressman Whitfield and asked if he and his wife would join our advisory board along with Annette, John Hettinger, and the others. He said yes, and when I questioned whether he knew anyone else who might be interested, he gave me the phone number of Bo Derek, who had been very active in antislaughter legislation, even making a trip to Washington and visiting with a number of congressmen to raise support for the American Horse Slaughter Prevention Act.

I felt nervous calling her, but after the first few words, once two people know they're both about horses, all the differences between them fall away. Also, she created no wall or feeling of distance. She was without airs, just very soft spoken and both passionate and compassionate about horses.

The conversation lasted only a few minutes, but Bo did agree to be on the advisory board and said that if she could make the fundraiser in Kentucky—we hadn't decided on a date yet— she would. My mind was racing. If Bo Derek committed to being present, we'd be beating people away from the door.

The date for the fundraising soiree was soon set

for the end of November, and I made three more trips to Lexington that fall, a five-and-a-half-hour drive each way, to meet with Annette in preparation. I knew even without her telling me what the event would be like. She would have someone playing music on the grand piano, valet parking, a man who took coats at the front door, butlers carrying trays of appetizers. Annette was a society woman. I even made the Society Pages myself because of her back in Michigan one year when I attended her annual Michigan Horse of the Year Ball.

We sent out 250 invitations. Beige with brown lettering, they looked like wedding invitations, down to the little reply cards. They went to all the important racing people in Lexington and a few others we knew of in other areas. Some had been at Saratoga.

RSVPs only trickled in during the first weeks, with a good number of responses saying "will not attend." But we weren't too concerned. Dr. Stick had already said he'd be coming—a big coup, because he was well known and well respected by those in the upper echelons of racing.

In the middle of this excitement, and with the urgency that always went with more and more horses taken in by CANTER during fall rush, Groovy came back to me. From the bottom of the driveway, I could hear him bellowing full-body whinnies from inside the trailer—not distress calls, which are more like odd snorts of warning, but sounds springing from deep within his chest. He knew where he was. "Open the door, open the door!" he was calling. I could hear his feet going up and down on the trailer.

He shot out of the back like a bullet once the driver unhitched the doors but didn't try to go running around. Instead, he breathed into my nose, then pulled immediately to the fence to see Sissy and Scarlett. I believe with all my heart that he knew, as I did, that he was home, that he would never be leaving again. He was the only CANTER horse out of thousands that I ever kept for myself.

*Got my
Groove back!*

"Is this the same?" he wanted to know about everything he passed, sniffing a pail he came across, a piece of equipment. "The trough is still here. Good. Let's go out into the pasture."

Sissy and Scarlett didn't need any reintro-ductions. Scarlett sniffed into his nose, then, the next second, pulled her ears back, as was her way. "You remember, I'm the boss, don't you?" her body language warned him. Then she went right back to acting friendly.

Sissy, for her part, was delirious with joy. She and Groovy would graze together as if they were joined at the shoulder, not an inch between them as they walked.

But I was still his favorite horse in the herd. "How can I make your life easier?" he seemed to ask as he stood still while I picked up his feet to clean them, or while he let me spritz him with fly spray. That eagerness to please was why I had been even more afraid for him than other horses. He would have jumped for someone no matter how much it hurt him and no matter how much it would have destroyed his body.

Not that he didn't still enjoy his high jinx. He'd go into my pockets, pull off my hat to make me laugh. He'd play with latches, trying to figure out how to open gates on his own. "How does this work? Hmmm, more horses over there. Maybe I'll go visiting."

He also loved to be scratched under his chin, and on his trunk if he had a fly bite he couldn't reach. "You want me to get it for you?" I'd ask.

"Oh, yes," he'd respond by moving into position so I could reach it more easily. A pasture ornament who couldn't be ridden because of multiple problems—significant arthritis in both knees as a result of fractures, arthritis in both hocks in his back legs—Groovy slept every night in Baby's stall, the one he stayed in when he first came to my house years earlier.

My bond with him was different than with the others. Your children you love because they're your children, which is how it was with Sissy and Scarlett. I was there when they were born. I saw them take their first steps. But Groovy and I were bonded by circumstance. If you've ever met someone you had to have in your life—that's how we felt about each other. Being together took some of the pain away. It made everything right again. It was a feeling I hadn't had for a long time.

Groovy's homecoming made the upcoming fundraising event in Lexington all the more wonderful to prepare for.

By the middle of November, however, worry was setting in. Not only were we not receiving a lot of responses that people would be coming, we pretty much stopped getting RSVPs either way. Bo Derek was a definite "no."

Annette's house was cavernous. A sparse showing would look disastrous.

In the end, only about twenty-five people showed up, some of them friends of Staci Hancock that she managed to corral at the last minute, whether or not they had been on the invitation list.

Our total take for the evening: $2,900. It seemed painfully apparent that eyes filling up during a speech about saving horses' lives was one thing—racing's wealthiest participants were happy to have CANTER protect the Thoroughbreds they threw away. But participating in the rescue—writing a check for the amount of a designer hat to be worn once in the grandstand—that was quite another.

CHAPTER FOURTEEN

It was time for a break. It wasn't just the disappointment of the small turnout at Annette's house. In fact, it was easy enough to rationalize that away. The event had been held the Tuesday after Thanksgiving, a difficult time of year to gather people. Also, a lot of those on Lexington's Who's Who list had already left Kentucky by then for their winter residences.

Staci Hancock steadied my spirits further by suggesting that her newly founded Kentucky Equine Humane Center and CANTER put on a combination fundraiser on a much larger scale come the 2006 Kentucky Derby. The social scene around the time of the Derby was especially bustling, drawing people from both Lexington and Louisville for balls and other galas, and it so happened that a coveted date was open because a big event scheduled for that time had just been canceled. Even Bo Derek would attend. She promised me she would definitely come to CANTER's next fundraiser if I could give her more notice.

But from August through November alone, I had made eight out-of-state trips on CANTER's behalf. I was exhausted. And my husband, who still could hardly walk and was waiting for the other shoe to drop, so to speak, by expecting that his new artery would reocclude, needed me.

We were ready for a vacation—a true vacation not punctuated by phone calls about horses having broken down and calls in the middle of the night from potential adopters in different time zones and constant visits to foster farms all over the state and at least 100 e-mails a day.

John and I rented a condo in New Smyrna Beach, Florida, for the month of January '06. It was right on the water, not only so John and I could enjoy the view at all times but also because he wasn't capable of taking walks on the sand. He was using a cane by that point, and couldn't get far.

I left detailed instructions with both volunteers and board members on how to deal with evaluation of new intakes, transporting surgery horses, and working with veterinarians, with farriers. I also left guidelines for handling fundraising, answering e-mails, and overseeing CANTER affiliates in other states. This would be my first time away from the organization since starting CANTER almost ten years earlier, and I was determined not to be contacted. I had spent so much time away from John, taking him for granted while placing the needs of the horses above his own. We were now going to enjoy our first real vacation by ourselves since the girls were born.

It didn't work. From the time we reached Florida, the cell phone never stopped ringing—which, in turn, led to my buying a month of cable service so I could retrieve e-mails. So many of the phone calls were about e-mails sent but left unanswered. "I wrote CANTER an e-mail but didn't hear from anyone," the person would say. "Someone needs to return a horse she adopted, and they want to bring it to my farm tomorrow, but I don't have any room."

One of the e-mails waiting for me was an angry diatribe from a fellow board member. I had not approved a potential adopter—a friend of a friend of his who had already adopted and returned two CANTER horses and now wanted to try a third—and the board member was furious, to the point that he threatened to resign.

While I had thought that along with giving John my undivided attention, I would be able to heal, or at least soothe, my psyche on this Florida trip, it quickly became clear that neither was going to happen.

"Can't someone who lives closer handle that?" John would ask at first, or "How much sleep did you get last night?" knowing that soon after he went to bed I dialed up the Internet on the slow connection I had rented to tend to business. But it wasn't long before he stopped asking questions and, each time the phone rang, just rolled his eyes. Knowing how well he knew me, I'm sure he had wanted to trust that this time away would be about the two of us but probably suspected, correctly, that I wouldn't be able to abandon the horses, not even for a month.

The phone would ring at any time, including when we managed to snag seats in a favorite eatery we found with little areas that jutted right out over the water. Not living near the ocean, it had particular meaning to us to be there, but at that restaurant, or on our lanai looking at the sunrise over the water, I was as often as not on the phone discussing where a horse should be transported, how swollen its leg was, whether someone had or hadn't followed through on a particular detail.

At the first CANTER board meeting in February, after we returned home, I gave notice that I would be resigning as of March first. There wasn't going to be any turning back. I didn't know how I was going to handle not taking care of the horses at risk, how I would square that decision with what I let happen to Baby. But it became clear, even to me, that I had gone around the bend, my life completely ceasing to have any balance or even moments not dedicated to the rescue.

John Stick asked me to stay on as advisor and consultant, arguing that I was the only person who had the institutional memory that would be necessary to keep the operation running as well as possible, and I agreed. But I knew the fundraiser with Staci Hancock would not take place, and also that we'd never raise the money or maintain the vision for a Midwest rehabilitation center. CANTER had a wonderful reputation and even national recognition, but the opportunity to make the leap to the next level, to mature it into the kind of organization that could earn a half million dollars in a night of fundraising, would be lost. This was to say nothing of the fact that a number of people on the board continued to feel it was a waste of money to save horses too injured to repurpose into one of the sport disciplines, cutting into the very heart of the reason I founded CANTER in the first place.

I felt overwhelmingly sad, like I was abandoning my "foal" for someone else to nourish, to raise. But there wasn't much time to ponder my decision. Only four days after my resignation went into effect, just before midnight on March fifth, John awoke screaming. I had been in such a deep, sound sleep that I didn't realize at first what was going on, but when I opened my eyes, he was holding his left leg, and I realized he was shouting out in excruciating pain, much worse than anything he had experienced with the previous occlusions.

John has a very high pain threshold, so I knew this had to be particularly bad. Trying to control my panic, I called Jessica, who said to get to the hospital and that she'd meet us there with a vascular surgeon.

Unfortunately, the ambulance insisted on taking us to the nearest hospital rather than the one where Jessica was—those were the rules—and we lost hours while they triaged him and poked and prodded him until they determined that they couldn't handle his condition and would have him sent by helicopter to the hospital where Jessica had wanted him sent from the beginning.

It took almost an hour for the helicopter to arrive, and the EMTs then did *their* triage—taking John's blood pressure, checking his pulse, and so on. I actually beat the helicopter to the second hospital in my own car, without any lights or sirens.

By the time John reached the next emergency room, the sun was almost up. The doctor said they would try to save his leg, but he warned that a limb can go just so long without blood, and many hours had already gone by.

John was then admitted for observation, then finally taken to the operating room. The left leg had to come off. In a grim, cosmic irony, it was the same limb that Baby had shattered the day he'd died.

"We managed to stay below the knee," the doctor said afterward, explaining that the ability to ambulate is much greater if an amputee still has his knee, allowing him to walk with a normal gait, to golf, to move about much as he had before. He said, too, that he hoped the leg would heal successfully with the cut where it was, as the leg was extremely compromised and there might not be sufficient blood flow for the stump to stabilize. There was a possibility that John would require a "revision," meaning the removal of more of the limb.

It was then that I began to cry. Before, I needed to be strong for John—and for myself. Now, the gruesome procedure was over.

John had to stay in the intensive care unit for a week after the operation. He ended up in critical condition, his life hanging in the balance, not because of the amputation but because his heart-beat coming out of the anesthesia was wildly erratic, along with his experiencing other cardiac issues, and the medical staff was having a hard time normalizing his rhythm and the other aspects of his cardiac functioning. Machines would start beeping, and the nurses would come running in. We called Rebecca home.

Some of the medications John was taking caused hallucinations, which he recalled vividly. In one, it was his turn to give a speech at the Master's Golf Tournament, but he couldn't get down. There weren't enough beds at the hospital, and one of the nurses had taken him home and had him hanging up by a meat hook. In another, he was in charge of all the football equipment for the University of Michigan. The team was going to an away game, and he had lost all of it—uniforms, pads, cleats, helmets, everything. The team coach from 1969 to 1989, Bo Schembechler, was yelling at him.

My husband, my rock, my capable, athletic, confident doer, was reimagining himself immobile, incompetent. He had been my first crush. I knew him since the age of ten, when I was in the fifth grade and he was in the seventh. My heart was broken when he gave me up for a while to date someone else before coming back to me.

I did not go home while John was in the hospital. The first few nights, I slept in his room. Then, once Rebecca arrived and she, Jessica, and I rotated, I would sometimes go to Carol and Dave Rhodes's house at two in the morning and sleep until five or six, then head back. Carol and Dave, our best friends since high school, lived much closer to the hospital than we did. I had had a key to their house for many years.

Various other friends took care of Scarlett, Sissy, and Groovy, the only horses in the barn at that point as there were no more CANTER rescues. There was no question that I would stay close to John rather than go home and take care of them, but tending to the animals in the barn had always brought normalcy, routine, comfort. Like a temple, the barn was a place of release, of letting go of stress and tension, and now I didn't have that, that rhythm of the day around which my life revolved.

The doctors did eventually bring John's heart problems under control, but the whole time he was in the hospital, he didn't want to take the covers off. He wouldn't look. It did prove extremely distressing to see nothing there. You can understand the word "amputation" intellectually, but when you look for a part of you, of your life mate, and it's gone, it hits you.

Even after John was finally discharged, he couldn't bear to look. He would stay perfectly still for me as I unfurled the rolls of gauze and tape and other special material that covered the stump in order to cleanse and rebandage it. But he kept his eyes closed.

For me, it wasn't so much looking at the wound and stitches of the stump (how I hated the word "stump," yet even the doctors had no euphemism for it) as knowing that it wasn't completely healed and that if it didn't heal sufficiently, he was going to have to go through this procedure again and have even more bone and leg taken off. The fact of it was there all the time. While we sat and watched TV, while I went and got John something to eat, there was no leg, and the prospect of even worse to come. The loss of a limb—it's not something that you become used to in a month or two months or six months or a year. It's something you *never* really get used to.

Then worse did come. Within days of John's homecoming, the stump began showing signs of what looked like bruising with deep discoloration, after which patches here and there started to turn black, first a very small spot, then another and another until the whole bottom of the stump looked as though someone had taken a blow torch to it and charred it black as black can be. The tissue there had died from lack of sufficient blood.

Back to the hospital we went for more leg to come off, just five weeks after the first operation, and more life-threatening heart rhythm complications immediately following the surgery. John was returned to the intensive care unit, critical once again. The good news, for lack of a better term, was that the vascular surgeon was still able to retain the area below the knee. It was a tough judgment call—the last thing anyone wanted was to go in a third time, especially with John's poor reaction to anesthesia—and we were all hoping for the best.

The doctors told John that he should also have a bypass on the artery in his other leg, but he refused. He knew that would eventually make him a bilateral amputee, but he didn't want to risk becoming one sooner than necessary.

A week later, he was home once again, healing extremely slowly, like someone with diabetes, because blood circulation to his leg was so poor. He couldn't be fitted for an artificial leg at that point because the doctors didn't want him wearing a tight prosthesis over an area that was still coming back to itself; he wasn't healed yet. They also didn't want him using crutches because he was on a high dose of the blood thinner Coumadin. Were he to fall, he might break his other leg and also suffer internal bleeding. So all he could do was transfer from an easy chair to a wheelchair. Theoretically, he could also use a walker, but he'd have to hop on his remaining leg. And because the blood supply to that one was also blocked, he didn't have the strength in that limb for that. So for five months, until he was fully healed and could be fitted for a prosthesis, he was pretty much stuck in the great room, hopping to the car only for doctor's appointments. There was not even any coming upstairs.

In the meantime, having to lift his forty-three-pound wheelchair, get it into the trunk, and then back out at the doctor's office, I developed numbness in my right arm that wouldn't abate. A visit to a neurologist showed that I had a compressed disk in my cervical spine near my shoulder and had to be in traction three days a week at a rehab center. A device around my head and under my chin and neck pulled me in one direction to decompress the pinched disk. I was used to hauling and throwing thirty-pound bales of hay, but not getting an unwieldy piece of metal that would keep unfolding into the tight spot of a trunk while trying to make sure the body of the car didn't get dinged.

Worse than the compressed disk was the loneliness, which descended with crushing silence. Just months earlier and for years before that, I had been so very busy. The phone never stopped ringing with someone concerned about a horse or some CANTER detail. Now it never did. Inquiries about John fell off, too. People, even many who are close friends, stop calling once a health crisis has passed and a compromised life looms ahead in an indefinite stretch.

The one place I didn't feel lonely was down at the barn, with my other family members. I could talk freely there, not worrying about expressing my fears. At first I did a lot of crying, wishing life could be the way it was. But the way it was when? Before John lost his leg? Before CANTER? Before Baby died? Before we got into racing?

There, among the horses, I also faced my very real fear of not knowing where this was going. Would we have to give up the farm? If we stayed, could I handle everything on my own? John had always done a lot of work fixing broken gates, adjusting heavy stall mats, and such.

If we did stay, I'd definitely keep Scarlett, Sissy, and Groovy; I couldn't fathom doing anything else.

Groovy—even in the midst of everything that was happening, he made me laugh. The comic of the barn, he'd purposely do something that he knew would end in my shaking my finger at him in a mock reprimand, like take something from me or purposely nudge the water pail I was carrying so that water splashed all over the both of us.

Groovy liked his hay in a tight flake; he'd bury his nose in it. Scarlett and Sissy—they liked their hay broken up for them. That wasn't as easy as just tossing a flake into each of their stalls, but none of it was ever about ease.

For what I gave them, I received ten times as much in return. While Groovy offered me his stand-up routine, his goofy antics, Scarlett, the most mature, the worldly one who had been all over and seen so much, lent me her assuredness. She also allowed me an eye on the past, when things were better. Looking at her, I could think about all of her competitions, all of our travels together. I'd fly to my hotel and go immediately to where she was stabled, checking in with her and making sure her accommodations were suitable. Also, she was my tie to Baby, even though she was only his half sister while Sissy was his full sibling. She had been Baby's best friend, the one who had gone through everything with him, the one who was at the track the day he died.

Sissy, she was my homebody, the one who never would have been happy to go off to kindergarten. I loved her cautiousness—she would hang back while Scarlett and Groovy inspected a box or piece of paper that had blown into the pasture— and I loved her friendly, welcoming disposition toward other horses. I loved, too, how she and both of the other horses, like all horses, lived in the moment, accepting whatever was going on right then. I needed their example at that time, worried as I was about all the "what ifs" going forward.

I had started to ride Sissy in an effort to make up for some of the short shrift I had given her in her early years, when her presence only reminded me of my grief over Baby. But when you ride a horse, it's not *if* you fall off, but *when*—it's simply going to happen at some point—and now that couldn't be an option. I couldn't afford a broken wrist or ankle because I was going to have to do everything, not just in the barn but for the household.

So I had to let Sissy go back to being a pasture ornament, content to seek safety in her herd mates' shadows. That was okay. She was happy to play the role of baby sister.

About half a year after I started going back down to the barn on a regular basis rather than relying on friends, John received his first artificial limb. Your first prosthesis is like a trial leg that you use for six months before you're fitted for your final one. The stump is still recontouring, but the new leg provides an opportunity to learn how to balance again, to go for physical therapy in order to get ready to move about without a walker.

Over the next few months, John went from

hopping to balancing without leaning on something. He was gaining a lot more control, to the point that he would be able to learn to walk eventually with a cane, then without one. The process, after a year and a half of hardly being able to walk and then undergoing an amputation, was uplifting, providing something positive, finally, to look forward to.

By the time Christmas came, we actually felt grateful. After all, he could have had a massive stroke or heart attack and died, or been utterly incapacitated, unable to communicate. Instead, he was here, he was himself, he could joke around and talk to his children—and they to him. Both Jessica and Rebecca were expecting. John would get to see and hold his grandchildren rather than miss that joy, miss looking forward to it.

The two pregnancies ended in two healthy grandsons born just a few months apart. Unfortunately, however, the final prosthesis did not afford John the freedom of movement we expected. We had joined an amputee's club at the hospital, in which either a husband or wife lost a leg. And we had been heartened because all of them were walking normally. One man had even gone back to work as a firefighter. That kept our hopes for John's mobility very high. He'd be golfing again by the next summer, we believed. We even spent extra money on a high-end leg that would allow his movements more flexibility, a closer approximation to the ambulation of someone with his own leg.

But when you're sixty and have a multitude of cardiac issues on top of an amputation, life is not going to be the same as for a fit fireman in his thirties. John tried golfing once and never attempted it again. Using the prosthesis proved far harder than the success stories in the amputee club had led us to believe. The artificial limb is heavy, and your other leg has to be strong. But both of John's thighs received very little blood supply, and the main artery in his other leg remained 100 percent blocked. He just could not, and never would be able to, move around like somebody without extremely poor circulation in his lower limbs.

It was a surprising life change, not the kind of premature retirement we had envisioned. We had seen the final-fit prosthesis as the light at the end of the tunnel, but the light went out before we ever reached the other side. What we had been through, we realized, wasn't a temporary setback; life was never going to go back to the way it had been. I was sorry we had gone to those amputee meetings, because it made facing the limitation that much harder.

Not long after the aborted golf attempt, John was hospitalized again for one of many cardiac emergencies that would occur over the years. On the way home from visiting him one day, I needed to stop for groceries and household odds and ends. If I waited until I reached my own semirural area, I'd have to shop in several different stores, which would take time I didn't have between tending to John and tending to the horses. But just off the expressway on the way home from the hospital, at exit 176, there was a Meijer's—a huge Michigan supermarket chain store that also had aisle upon aisle of sundry items.

I had not been to that branch since it opened several years earlier, as part of the shopping center that was built on the site of the Detroit Race Course. I couldn't bear to go, even though every single time I passed exit 176, a part of me was still ready to get off the highway. Once I even exited by mistake, having to take the service road in order to get back on.

That day, however, I was so rushed and so exhausted from the stress of running back and forth to the hospital that I needed to consider stopping there.

I tried, as I walked from the parking lot to the store, to be right where I was—in the middle of a large shopping complex with a Costco, a Home Depot, a Marshall's, a Michael's. But I couldn't. Crying as I moved toward Meijer's, I could see the security guard's shack, the track kitchen, the grandstand. I was making my way past all of it.

Inside the store, well oriented to how things had once been laid out because the entrance road to the shopping center was the same as the road leading to the race course, with the railroad tracks on the south end, I knew I was in Baby's shedrow right where the baby items were displayed—bibs, onesies, diapers, car seats. Around me, with people casually looking over their shopping lists, picking supplies off store shelves, their toddlers scampering about, I could see his stall, could just about make out his head sticking over the door to look out; it was more than ten years earlier, and he was still alive.

While I was clearly able to look at everyone around me, inconsequential details to the scene though they were, they couldn't see me. I was a leftover, an unperceived remnant of something that should have been long gone but lingered still. I hurried away.

It wasn't long after that day that I started tooling around on the Internet. John's condition kept me from going out much, but going online provided access to the outside world. And with time on my hands that I never had when I was down in the trenches, I began to take a wider lens to some of the issues in racing. Who, exactly, was in charge? Who made the rules and oversaw them? I knew how things worked in Michigan and, to some degree, in the states where we had affiliates, but not as a whole.

What I learned was that no one was in charge. Whereas sports like baseball and football had a commissioner to oversee operations and keep things fair, racing had thirty-eight separate jurisdictions overseeing more than 100 tracks around the country, most of them little non-televised tracks like ours, and they all made their own rules, then decided whether or not they were going to follow them. It was like a small western town where the sheriff was also the judge.

There was an Association of Racing Commissioners International that *recommended* rules for all the separate state racing commissions, I found out, but adopting those rules was not mandatory. Each track was free to do as it liked.

The problems, I discovered, had a long history, going at least as far back as 1973, when a Congressional committee convened to investigate racing practices focused on doping and the lack of state enforcement. There was even a bill ten years later, in the early 1980s, that would have banned doping in horse racing, ending the practice of masking a horse's injuries with drugs so that it could race until its bone was chewed away so severely it would be forced to limp off the track. But powerful racing lobbyists in Washington must have talked the government out of passing the bill, saying that racing would step up and do a better job of policing itself. In the meantime, things continued as they always had, with some horses drugged and some not, the public never knowing the difference and betting on races that were, for all intents and purposes, fixed. When some horses take drugs to improve their performance and others don't and no one in the stands knows which is which, it becomes a rigged game.

None of this went on anywhere else in the world. In Europe, in Asia, drugs on race day were banned, with spot testing of Thoroughbreds in training and stiff penalties handed out to those caught committing infractions rather than just slaps on the wrist. Horses ran purely on hay, oats, and water, which kept lame horses on other continents safe from having to run.

Nor did other countries allow excessive use of the whip or the American practice of heel nerving—severing a nerve in the foot to prevent a racehorse from feeling pain that should keep it from running. They also didn't allow toe grabs, traction devices put on horses' shoes to propel them forward faster. While permitted in the U.S., they are illegal in other countries because they cause catastrophic injuries by virtue of impeding the slide phase of a horse's stride and thereby interfering with the mechanics of what nature intends.

Perhaps worst of all that I came across in my research was information on breeding practices that included an entire nurse mare industry, practices that took place in wealthy racing states producing Thoroughbreds worth six figures and more. Often, I learned, when a high-priced

Thoroughbred mare gives birth, she is sent off within ten days to be bred again. But it's too much of a risk to transport her valuable newborn along with her, so it's left behind with a wet nurse not worth much. The wet nurse's own foal, born solely so she can provide milk to a prized Thoroughbred infant, is considered a byproduct, often left to die or sent to slaughter. Seeing photos of discarded foals, I wanted to retch.

I was given a chance to have some of my concerns aired in 2008, when a filly named Eight Belles crossed the finish line in second place at the Kentucky Derby and, in front of fifteen million television spectators, collapsed, her nose slamming into the dirt. She struggled unsuccessfully to rise before a canvas screen was brought out to hide her from view as she was euthanized. The incident led to a hearing in Congress six weeks later, for which I was asked to produce exhibits detailing the injuries and untimely deaths of racehorses, showing that what occurred at the Derby was only the tip of the iceberg.

Again, the racing industry talked the government out of taking matters into its own hands, promising to police itself. But again, it was all business as usual.

In the meantime, I began working on behalf of Senator Tom Udall of New Mexico, providing both him and Representative Whitfield with research and data to support their bills to ban race-day drugs. A law against drugs would cut down dramatically on the number of horses that go limping off the track. In addition, I continued my work with Representative Whitfield on his anti-slaughter bill.

As time has worn on, I have even managed to venture from our farm now and then when asked to give antislaughter speeches at conferences put on by such organizations as the Equine Welfare Alliance, the Animal Law Coalition, and Equine Advocates, and have provided information on abuses in racing to the Equine Protection division of the Humane Society of the United States.

For as much as I have tried to remain involved, racing has been experiencing its own slow decline apart from my or anybody else's efforts.

In the 1960s, when horseracing was the only form of legal gambling, attendance at Michigan racetracks was three million yearly; it was the number one spectator sport in the country. Into the 1970s, in fact, racing remained a very popular venue for betting. But as its fan base aged and lotteries became legal in more and more states, as did casino gambling, people turned to scratch tickets for wagering and then Powerball in convenience stores, as well as to slot machines, particularly machines with slick casino video gadgetry. There's not even a Thoroughbred track in Michigan anymore. Great Lakes Downs closed at the end of the 2007 season, and while another track opened for a couple of seasons back on the Detroit side of the state, it could not pay for itself, either.

Still, racing is not going away. At the very least, people continue to enjoy watching the glam Thoroughbred races on television, like the Kentucky Derby. Bettors or not, they unknowingly cheer on animals who may very well someday be sent to a low-level track and be sold right from there to a kill buyer for roughly thirty cents a pound, ending up as food on someone's plate. And advertisers remain willing to support the industry because of the large viewership.

Furthermore, tens of thousands of horses each year continue to be forced to run lame on smaller tracks, confined and abused their entire lives until ending up in the slaughterhouse. The number of Thoroughbreds put to death each year is, in fact, equal to 60 to 70 percent of the annual number born. The fight to save them continues, with those trying to shield horses up against those who work to stonewall Congress at every turn in order to protect, even beyond its glory days, what is still a $40 billion industry.

It has been a long haul, and continues to be one. When Baby was born, I was a forty-three-year-old mother with two teenagers. Today, my daughters have long ago worn their wedding dresses and together have given John and me four grand-children.

I look out my kitchen window at Scarlett, Secretariat's amazing granddaughter, ambling over to the water trough after grazing peacefully. Although still beautiful and in wonderful shape, time has crept up on her, too. She is already twenty-one years old. Sissy, somewhere nearby, has turned seventeen. Groovy, my beautiful barn clown whose very presence righted so many wrongs, had to be put down in 2011 because his arthritis in all four legs became so debilitating he couldn't make his way out to the pasture to graze.

Most horses gently bend their heads to the trough, then put their lower lip under the surface and lightly draw in the water. But Scarlett is dunking in her whole head, up to her eyes. She learned it from Pat.

When Pat had been at our house only a day or so, almost full-term with Baby, I heard a ton of splashing, water sloshing all over. "What in the world is going on?" I thought. I ran over to the trough and saw her nose dipped all the way in. She twirled it very fast, the way someone would mix batter. Then she heard me behind her, lifted her head, dripping with water even near her eyes, and looked at me nonchalantly, as if to say, "Oh, it's just you." Then she went right back to what she was doing.

Her children, Baby, Scarlett, and Sissy, were taught by her to drink in exactly the same way. If Baby were here, in fact, he would run over and brush alongside Scarlett to dunk his own head, even if he were not thirsty. He loved being "in." But Baby's not going to come. There's no honk, no exuberant, stocky pet who I took from his mother's body and who loves to gallop toward me for a brisk scratch when I clap my hands. I'm still waiting for him, waiting as always. But except for the sound of the water in the trough, all remains still.

Scarlett and Sissy (foreground) grazing under the apple tree behind the house.

BE PART OF THIS STORY

The memoir may have come to an end, but the story has not.

And you are part of it by virtue of having bought this book. A portion of the proceeds go directly to Saving Baby Equine Charity, established in 2011 to save not just Thoroughbreds but all equine breeds from the brink. You can learn about horses you've helped save by going to www.savingbaby.org. There's more, however.

There is a bill in Congress that, if passed, would prevent the reintroduction of horse slaughter operations in the United States, end the current export of American horses for slaughter abroad, and protect the public from consuming toxic meat dangerous to human health. There is also a bill that would provide for oversight of the racing industry and ban drugs that allow injured Thoroughbreds to keep racing and endure further pain. To learn more about these initiatives and how you can help get them signed into law, visit www.equinewelfarealliance.org and www.water hayoatsalliance.com.

All three organizations named here can be found on Facebook. There's a Facebook page for the book as well.

ACKNOWLEDGMENTS

Both Jo Anne Normile and Larry Lindner thank:
our enthusiastic and supportive St. Martin's
Press editor, Brenda Copeland, and our savvy
and nimble agent, Michelle Tessler. Both "got it"
when many other gatekeepers didn't—and got
that the reading public wants the truth over a
formula.

We also thank esteemed colleague and friend
Nicholas Dodman, BVMS, the world-renowned
veterinarian who introduced us to each other.
Director of the Animal Behavior Clinic at the
Cummings School of Veterinary Medicine at Tufts
University and author or editor of more best-
selling books on the care of animals than you can
count on one hand, Nick is also a cofounder of
Veterinarians for Equine Welfare (www.vetsfor
equinewelfare.org), an organization that believes
"treatment decisions should not be made based on
matters of convenience or financial gain, but on
the welfare of the horse."

We thank, too, Elaine Rogers, entertainment
lawyer, for her ongoing encouragement. When the
chips were down, we took comfort in her steadfast
belief that this is a story that needed to be told.

To Susan Richards, we give gratitude not only
for her beautiful introduction but also for her

willingness to lend the considerable heft of her name in order to help draw attention.

Much appreciation goes to David Provolo of Manos Design (www.manosdesign.com), who provided invaluable help in the book's early stages. Dave is a consummate design professional (and happens to be a great guy, too).

Thanks as well to photographer Mary Vogt (http://maryr vogt.com). The horse on the back cover, save for the fact that Baby's eyes were larger and the length of his head shorter, is a Baby lookalike. Mary, without reservation, let us use her photograph for our purposes.

Finally, we give thanks to Karen Drayne, friend and copy editor extraordinaire. Her painstaking work saved us from syntactical tangles, typos, and more. Any inconsistencies you may have run across in the reading are ours and ours alone.

Jo Anne Normile thanks: More people than I could possibly list, as that would require a second book; my life could never have unfolded in the manner it did without the help of an untold number of individuals involved at various times from the moment of Baby's birth to this very day. Still, I must name at least some of them, first and foremost Joy Aten, my friend and soul mate to the very core. Joy lives by the credo, "I am only one, but I am still one. I cannot do everything, but I can still do something. I will not refuse to do the something I can do." Thousands of horses have benefited as a result. How fortunate are all animals that Joy shares this world with them, and how lucky I am that life has allowed me to cross paths with her.

I thank, too, Don Shouse for allowing his broodmare Pat to foal at my farm and thus bring Baby into our lives; for allowing me to free lease Pat so I could have my Secretariat granddaughter, Scarlett, and then Sissy; and for actually giving Pat to me rather than break my heart by taking her back.

I am so grateful to Phillip and Christa Winfrey and Gwen and the late John Park for their financial participation, without which I would never have become privy to all I learned.

Much gratitude to those in racing who accepted my efforts to protect my horses, and ultimately their own, even if they did not understand.

I am appreciative, too, to Pam Thibodeau, our last racing trainer, honest and true, who understood my deep love for Baby and Scarlett and who, with that in mind, always cared for them as pets.

Many thank-yous to Annette Bacola, Michigan's former Racing Commissioner for too short a time, who always believed in the welfare of *all* racehorses. Only while under her leadership was the Racing Commission active in raising funds for the rescue of Thoroughbreds. On her own,

Annette has provided foster care for rescued horses at her farm, contributed generously, and even hosted a fundraising event at her Lexington home. She will always be counted a friend of mine and a friend of horses.

I am so honored to have known the late John Hettinger, founder of Blue Horse Charities, and to have had the opportunity to work with him on trying to end horse slaughter not just in the racing industry, but also in general through our efforts to help pass the American Horse Slaughter Prevention Act. Sadly he left us before he could see his mission become reality. In a similar vein, I am thankful and honored to know and have worked with Staci and Arthur Hancock, Gretchen and Roy Jackson, George Strawbridge, U.S. Representative Ed Whitfield, his aide, James Robertson, his wife, Connie Whitfield, U.S. Senator Tom Udall, and his aide, Kevin Cummins. All have been engaged in outspoken, unending efforts to protect horses' welfare.

Bows of gratitude and appreciation to Cot and Anne Campbell, Penny Chenery, and Jerry Bailey, who, in selecting me as the recipient of the 2005 Dogwood Stable Dominion Award, gave me yet a greater platform to decry the mistreatment of Thoroughbred racehorses.

Thanks and more to my tenacious and savvy attorney, William (Bill) Mitchell III.

What fun to look back fondly on the enormous

help given to me by Jill Rauh and Jeremy Bricker, without whom the word CANTER, literally, would not have become synonymous at one time with the rescue of Thoroughbred racehorses. Jeremy also suggested, designed, and maintained the first CANTER Web site for many years without any compensation, making possible all that ensued. Linda Long of Long2 Consulting eventually took over as webmaster, driven by her compassion for all animals. She has also donated her professional expertise to design the Web site for Saving Baby Equine Charity. I am thrilled to count Jill, Jeremy, and Linda among my friends.

These amazing people are not the only ones who donated their time and know-how without ever looking for anything in return. Teddy Roosevelt once said that "credit belongs to the man who is actually in the arena, whose face is marred by dust and sweat and blood, who strives valiantly . . . who spends himself in a worthy cause; who . . . knows, in the end, the triumph of high achievement." I am quite sure he was talking decades in advance about the dozens of boots-on-the-ground CANTER volunteers, who stoically dealt on a constant basis with horses suffering from neglect, injuries, and damage from the administration of both legal and illegal drugs. These people walked the shedrows, talking to trainers while the trainers' slow and injured horses stared at them with hope, or worse, resignation. They trailered horses away from the track, gave them foster care and surgical aftercare, and, when possible, retrained them for other pursuits. They also arranged for euthanasia when necessary, giving horses with no hope of a pain-free life a last stroke along the neck, a last kind word.

Among these saviors was Judy Gutierrez, the first to volunteer to work alongside me. Her enthusiasm for saving horses knew no bounds. Peg Yordy galloped in to save Happy from slaughter. Brenda Lamb picked up Groovy from Quebec and lovingly cared for him for months before arranging transport of him back to me. And Leah Minc and family fostered innumerable rescue horses, including Twoey. It was Leah who officially named Twoey's goat companion Captain Kidd. A shout of whinnies from saved horses, and from me, go as well to Kristie Buckley Fillips, Kim Nietzka, Rebecca Baucus, Martha Denver, Heidi Rice, who lost the tip of a finger trailering rescued horses, Nancy Suttles, Keri Dutkiewicz, Jennifer Merrick-Brooks, Cathy Henderson, Sherry Hansen, Tiny Luick, Annika Kramer, Lenora Blood, Ginger and Larry Sissom and their daughter, Halley (Ginger began encouraging me to write the story of Baby nearly fifteen years ago), Karen Hunchberger, Barbara Moss, Eilene Sinelli, Cheryl and Jerry Johnson, and the students of Michigan State University, to name just a few. More whinnies and nickers for the equine veterinarians across the state of Michigan who provided services at a discount.

Of course, none of these people could have done their humane work without the good will of financial donors from around the country. Rescue cannot be possible without them, and it is humbling to know that so many trust someone they have never met to do the right thing with their contribution.

Others who must be thanked include the tenacious and tireless Victoria McCullough, who single-handedly has done so much in the effort to help stop horse slaughter; Ann Marini; Pat Mendiola; Laura Allen, founder of the Animal Law Coalition (www.animallawcoalition.org); and Joyce Moore, founder of Animal Advocates of Michigan (www.animaladvocatesmi.org). I am especially grateful to Susan Wagner, founder of Equine Advocates (www.equineadvocates.org) and a dear friend with a kindred heart who has helped out in critical ways. Gratitude also goes to John Holland and Vicki Tobin of the Equine Welfare Alliance (www.equinewelfare alliance.org). Ditto to Keith Dane, Director of Equine Protection for the Humane Society of the United States (www.humanesociety.org), and Humane Society equine protection specialist Valerie Pringle.

For accepting me as I am, always with hay in my hair or smelling like a horse, and also for their unending encouragement and good humor, I thank my sister and brother-in-law, Dianne (Dee) and Ron Winfrey. Little did Dee know when her annoying baby sister used to dominate the dinner conversation with horse talk that one day she and her husband would be of tremendous help in reading the initial drafts of this book. Thanks and love, too, to my and my husband's best friends, Dave and Carol Rhodes, who have put up with me for fifty years. When we go to a restaurant and the hostess tells us it's a forty-five-minute wait, Dave is fond of saying, "No problem. We can fill in the time. Jo Anne, how are the horses?"

Finally, I thank my coauthor, Larry Lindner. I did not understand when we first met that what lay ahead were uncountable hours over the course of years relaying my memories, many of them filled with tears as I relived almost hypnotically the most awful of moments. At those difficult times, Larry was tender and sympathetic and cried with me. It was also his job to rein me in when I rambled on, and rein me in he did! "Jo Anne, I am not listening anymore, and if you say another word off topic, I'm hanging up." But indeed he was listening. From someone who did not know a pony from a foal or hocks from withers, he could now recognize and treat a colicking horse and, most importantly, understands these peaceful, sentient, magnificent creatures who rely on us— who consider us their herd mates—to save them from pain and suffering. Ours is a relationship that started as collaborators and continues as loving friends, not just with each other but also with each other's supportive spouses and children. Without you, Larry, *Saving Baby* would remain solely in my heart and mind, and I thank you from the depths of my soul.

Larry Lindner thanks: Jo Anne, who has changed my life. I've always had a great love for dogs, each with his or her own attributes, but I never knew that horses were people, too. I resisted working on this book, in fact. I grew up in New York City—what did I know from horses? But because of Jo Anne, I will never again look at horses—or any other animal, for that matter—the same way. She has proven a magnificent, transforming friend to me, and has made me a better friend to animals.

I thank, too, my son, John, fellow animal lover who, through this work, understands our responsibility toward a species that has become an iconic figure in American lore and history.

Finally, I give my heart and my thanks and all I hold dear to my wife, Constance, who goaded me on when I feared no one would listen by insisting I follow the instinct that has always guided her: once you are aware, you may not turn away.

ABOUT THE AUTHORS

Jo Anne Normile, principal of Normile Racehorse Protection Consulting, advises senators, congressmen, filmmakers, legal firms, rescues, and humane organizations on all aspects of racing pertaining to the welfare of the Thoroughbred racehorse and the integrity of the industry.

In addition to her consulting work, Normile founded two successful horse rescue organizations: CANTER, the first organization to take Thoroughbreds right from the track to safe havens; and Saving Baby Equine Charity (www.savingbaby.org), for which she currently serves as president. She is also on the board of directors and secretary of Animal Advocates of Michigan and is a member of the Equine Welfare Alliance as well as an active advisory board member for the documentary film, *Saving America's Horses: A Nation Betrayed*.

Normile has received the Catalyst of the Year Award from the Michigan Horse Council for her "significant contribution to the Michigan horse industry" and the prestigious national Dogwood Stable Dominion Award as an "unsung hero of the racing industry." She was described in *The Thoroughbred Times* as having "rescued more horses than any other organization in the equine industry." Normile has been written up in *The New York Times*, the *Chicago Tribune*, and *The St. Louis Dispatch* as well as in *The Blood-Horse*, the *Daily Racing Form*, *Equus*, *Horse Illustrated*, *ASPCA Animal Watch*, and numerous other publications. In addition, she has appeared on CNN and many local television broadcasts.

Normile's dedication to horses includes research on equine self-mutilation syndrome and compulsive behavior in formerly feral horses, which resulted in her coauthoring studies that appeared in the prestigious *Journal of the American Veterinary Medical Association* and the *Journal of Applied Research in Veterinary Medicine*. She was also cited for her contributions to a research paper published in *Food and Chemical Toxicology* about the public health risk of selling horsemeat laced with phenylbutazone, or "bute," routinely given to Thoroughbred racers.

Normile has provided exhibits for a watershed Congressional hearing on the use of drugs in racehorses and has been an invited speaker at equine safety meetings around the country, including the International Horse Welfare Conference and the American Equine Summit.

She lives in Plymouth, Michigan, with her husband, John; Scarlett, age twenty-two; a new barn friend, Cash; and two burros adopted by Saving Baby Equine Charity from the Bureau of Land Management, Marci and Winnie.

Lawrence Lindner is a *New York Times* best-selling coauthor and collaborating writer on a wide variety of books ranging from memoirs to animal care to health topics. He also penned a nationally syndicated biweekly column in the *Washington Post* for several years and wrote a monthly column for *The Boston Globe*. His freelance work has appeared in publications ranging from the *Los Angeles Times* to *Condé Nast Traveler*; the *International Herald Tribune*; *Reader's Digest*; and *O, The Oprah Magazine*. Currently, Lindner serves as executive editor of *Your Dog*, a monthly publication of the Cummings School of Veterinary Medicine at Tufts University, and as secretary of Saving Baby Equine Charity. In addition, he is the Literary Cultural District coordinator for the City of Boston, working under the auspices of the writers group GrubStreet.

He lives in Hingham, Massachusetts, with his wife, Constance, and his son, John.

ADDITIONAL CREDITS

Center Point Large Print
600 Brooks Road / PO Box 1
Thorndike, ME 04986-0001 USA

(207) 568-3717

US & Canada:
1 800 929-9108
www.centerpointlargeprint.com